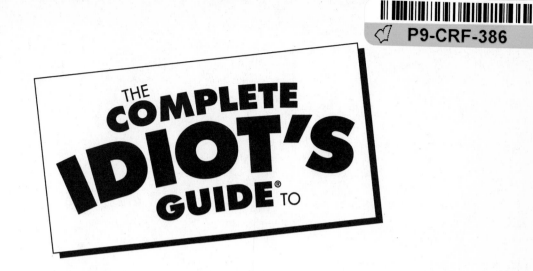

THE COMPLETE IDIOT'S GUIDE® TO

Hypnosis

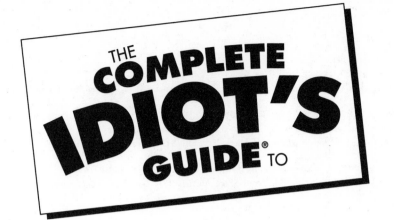

THE COMPLETE IDIOT'S GUIDE® TO

Hypnosis

Second Edition

by Roberta Temes, Ph.D.

ALPHA

A member of Penguin Group (USA) Inc.

ALPHA BOOKS

Published by the Penguin Group

Penguin Group (USA) Inc., 375 Hudson Street, New York, New York 10014, USA

Penguin Group (Canada), 90 Eglinton Avenue East, Suite 700, Toronto, Ontario M4P 2Y3, Canada (a division of Pearson Penguin Canada Inc.)

Penguin Books Ltd., 80 Strand, London WC2R 0RL, England

Penguin Ireland, 25 St. Stephen's Green, Dublin 2, Ireland (a division of Penguin Books Ltd.)

Penguin Group (Australia), 250 Camberwell Road, Camberwell, Victoria 3124, Australia (a division of Pearson Australia Group Pty. Ltd.)

Penguin Books India Pvt. Ltd., 11 Community Centre, Panchsheel Park, New Delhi—110 017, India

Penguin Group (NZ), 67 Apollo Drive, Rosedale, North Shore, Auckland 1311, New Zealand (a division of Pearson New Zealand Ltd.)

Penguin Books (South Africa) (Pty.) Ltd., 24 Sturdee Avenue, Rosebank, Johannesburg 2196, South Africa

Penguin Books Ltd., Registered Offices: 80 Strand, London WC2R 0RL, England

Copyright © 2004 by Roberta Temes, Ph.D.

International Standard Book Number: 978-1-59257-271-7
Library of Congress Catalog Card Number: 2004106750

10 09 08   10 9 8 7

Interpretation of the printing code: The rightmost number of the first series of numbers is the year of the book's printing; the rightmost number of the second series of numbers is the number of the book's printing. For example, a printing code of 04-1 shows that the first printing occurred in 2004.

Printed in the United States of America

Most Alpha books are available at special quantity discounts for bulk purchases for sales promotions, premiums, fund-raising, or educational use. Special books, or book excerpts, can also be created to fit specific needs.

For details, write: Special Markets, Alpha Books, 375 Hudson Street, New York, NY 10014.

Publisher: *Marie Butler-Knight*
Product Manager: *Phil Kitchel*
Senior Managing Editor: *Jennifer Chisholm*
Acquisitions Editor: *Mikal Belicove*
Development Editor: *Jennifer Moore*
Production Editor: *Janette Lynn*
Copy Editor: *Keith Cline*
Illustrator: *Chris Eliopoulos*
Cover/Book Designer: *Trina Wurst*
Indexer: *Brad Herriman*
Layout: *Becky Harmon*
Proofreading: *Donna Martin*

Contents at a Glance

Contents

Foreword

Hypnosis: It happens to us all, young and old, in everyday life and on special occasions. It is a state of being fully absorbed and attentive to such a degree that occurrences in the outside world become less important. It feels good to be in hypnosis. Besides, hypnosis can be used successfully to reduce fears, anxieties, and pain; to overcome undesirable habits; and to pursue self-set goals. Hypnosis provides the means to accept the stresses of the modern world more easily.

Dr. Temes has accomplished an admirable task, explaining in easily understood terms the nature, uses, and potential benefits of hypnosis. Beyond that, there are gems for those experienced in hypnosis; useful hints and wordings for the health-care professional who applies hypnosis; and for the consumer, guidance in avoiding mishaps in the exploration of the hypnotic state and selecting the appropriate professional to apply the process.

The book is easy to understand, using enlightening stories about resolution of clients' problems, and all in plain English. I found the reading of this book to be relaxing, instructive, inspiring, and absorbing—in a word, hypnotic.

—Elvira V. Lang, M.D.

Elvira V. Lang, M.D., is associate professor of Radiology at the Harvard Medical School, and is the Chief of Interventional Radiology at the Beth Israel Deaconess Medical Center in Boston, Massachusetts.

Introduction

Hypnosis is amazing. For centuries hypnosis has gone in and out of vogue. Now, in the twenty-first century, there's finally sufficient scientific evidence, real hard data, that proves its effectiveness. So, at last, it's here to stay. I've seen my clients use hypnosis successfully for everything from conquering stage fright, to having a painless tooth extraction, to winning a tennis match. There's even some recent research that suggests that hypnosis may strengthen your immune system. Please use this book to discover all the ways that hypnosis can enhance your life.

How to Use This Book

Are you curious about hypnosis? Read **Part 1, "What Is Hypnosis?"** to find out what hypnosis really is—and is not. Your questions will be answered. You'll find out what it feels like to be "under," and why you cannot get stuck in a trance.

Part 2, "You're On Your Own," teaches you how to hypnotize yourself and how to impress your friends with your new knowledge. Follow these instructions and you'll be able to put yourself into a hypnotic trance whenever you want to reach a new goal.

Want better health habits? **Part 3, "The Healthy You,"** tells you how hypnosis can help you quit smoking, stop biting your nails, and get rid of other unwanted habits and phobias. You'll learn how to use hypnosis to get a good night's sleep and to stop drinking, drugging, or overeating. Yes, hypnosis can get you to lose weight, too!

If you're looking for self-improvement, see **Part 4, "The New You."** Hypnosis can help you improve your golf game, your sex life, your social life, and more. You'll never again be nervous before taking a test or making a speech. If you're a parent, you'll be pleased to find out that hypnosis can help your children, too.

Don't even think of having an operation, or any other medical procedure, before reading **Part 5, "Get Well Soon—and Stay That Way."** It brings you up-to-the-minute medical information from the research labs. You'll learn how to use hypnosis to heal yourself. You'll find out how to use hypnosis when you go to the dentist.

Part 6, "Another Side of Hypnosis," reveals the secrets of the hypnotists you see on TV, and also explains how hypnosis is used to dig up old memories.

I know you'll benefit from reading this book. Good luck.

Extras

Hypnosis is fascinating and, well, it's mesmerizing, too. You'll discover even more about hypnosis when you read the sidebars. Every chapter has many, many sidebars, and you'll see four different types:

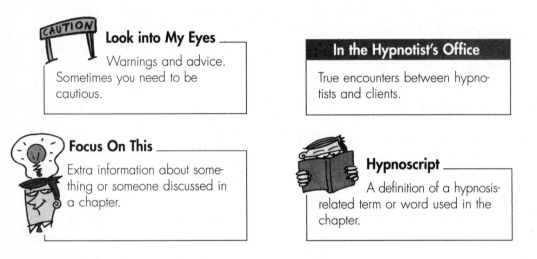

Look into My Eyes

Warnings and advice. Sometimes you need to be cautious.

In the Hypnotist's Office

True encounters between hypnotists and clients.

Focus On This

Extra information about something or someone discussed in a chapter.

Hypnoscript

A definition of a hypnosis-related term or word used in the chapter.

Acknowledgments

Special thanks and sincerest appreciation to (in alphabetical order) Mikal E. Belicove, acquisitions editor; Sheree Bykofsky, literary agent; Doris Cross, development editor; Melvin Gravitz, Ph.D., hypnosis scholar and historian; David Lyons, husband extraordinaire; and Jennifer Moore, development editor.

Special Thanks to the Technical Reviewer

The Complete Idiot's Guide to Hypnosis was reviewed by an expert who double-checked the accuracy of what you'll learn here, to help us ensure that this book gives you everything you need to know about hypnosis. Special thanks are extended to Samuel Perlman, D.D.S.

Trademarks

All terms mentioned in this book that are known to be or are suspected of being trademarks or service marks have been appropriately capitalized. Alpha Books and Penguin Group (USA) Inc. cannot attest to the accuracy of this information. Use of a term in this book should not be regarded as affecting the validity of any trademark or service mark.

Part 1

What Is Hypnosis?

Curious about hypnosis? Scared of hypnosis? Want to know what it's all about? These chapters are for you.

You'll find out exactly what goes on in a hypnosis session—what it feels like, what you do, and what the hypnotist does. The mysteries of the hypnotic process are revealed and completely explained.

Mind Over Matter

In This Chapter

- Reaching your goals with hypnosis
- Hypnosis as mind/body medicine
- Can you be hypnotized?
- Understanding how hypnosis works
- Find out how hypnotizable you are

Fifty years ago hypnotists were entertainers who persuaded your Uncle Bill to quack like a duck in a nightclub. One hundred years ago hypnotists were called charlatans, and during the Middle Ages hypnotists were considered witches.

Today's hypnotist is likely to be a physician, a psychologist, a university researcher, or a nurse, and to be employed in the emergency room of Jefferson Hospital in Louisiana, at the figure skating pavilion in the Olympics, or at the local weight-control center. Today, hypnosis is a respected technique.

Although it's a serious therapeutic technique, hypnosis is also a pleasant and calming experience, and you'll be delighted when you realize that it can help you transform yourself.

Why Would I Want to Be Hypnotized?

Hypnosis can help you reach your goals.

- **In your personal life.** Perhaps you want to stop smoking, or maybe you need motivation to start exercising?

- **In your work life.** Thinking about making a dynamic sales presentation, or do you need help so you won't arrive late at meetings?

- **In your family life.** Perhaps you want to have more patience for Suzy, or do you want to remember to take out the trash every night?

- **In your recreational life.** Do you want to improve your golf game or concentrate better at bridge?

Hypnosis Can Help You Have Better Health

Hypnosis is often the treatment of choice for certain health and emotional problems because it is noninvasive (nothing gets inserted into your body), it is not a drug (therefore no side effects), and it is relatively inexpensive because one or two sessions can usually do the trick. Health-maintenance organizations and other managed-care groups are finally getting the idea that hypnosis should be the first treatment to try, not the last.

Hypnosis is the original mind/body medicine. During hypnosis a health professional suggests that you experience particular changes in your ideas or your future actions. The suggestions that are spoken to you are called hypnotic suggestions.

A dentist may use hypnosis to calm a fearful patient, ease dental surgery, and stop nighttime tooth grinding. I use hypnosis in my psychotherapy practice when a client wants to stop an unwanted habit. Smoking and nail biting are the two habits I'm most often asked to eradicate, but eating too much junk food comes in as a close third. Clients also request hypnosis to fall asleep easily or have peak performance during an athletic competition.

I discuss all these situations, and more, in later chapters of this book.

Clinical hypnosis helps you to regulate your behavior, alter your thoughts, and use your mind to control your body. Try it to treat your stress, or phobia, or pain—you'll wish you had tried it earlier. Clinical hypnosis is a much-underutilized therapeutic tool.

Focus On This

Dr. Gerard Sunnen of the New York University School of Medicine calls hypnosis "the most potent nonpharmacological relaxing agent known to science." He will prescribe hypnosis before prescribing a tranquilizer!

In the Hypnotist's Office

Last week was a typical week in my office. I hypnotized the following people: a pregnant woman to help her get through childbirth; a businessman who was nervous about delivering a sales presentation; a teenager who was afraid of elevators; and an attorney who wanted to improve her concentration and memory. All these uses of hypnosis fall under the category of clinical hypnosis, which is a procedure practiced by a health professional, using words only, to encourage a patient to make a specific change in behavior or attitude.

What Exactly Is Hypnosis, Anyway?

Now that you know how wonderful it is, you want to know what it is and how it works, right? You are not alone.

Researchers at the National Institutes of Health (NIH) in Washington, D.C., are conducting studies to figure out how and why hypnosis works, and exactly what it is. There are many theories and, as in other areas of human research, some theories contradict others. No one really knows what hypnosis is. But we do know what it is not.

Hypnosis Is Not Meditation

Here is a list showing the differences between meditation and hypnosis:

	Meditation	**Hypnosis**
Motivation:	To focus on yourself	To focus on some thing outside yourself
Goal:	No goal	To enjoy a new behavior
Process:	Enter an altered state and then focus on yourself	Enter an altered state and then receive suggestions

In hypnosis you get to the meditative state and then go ahead to do some work on yourself by changing a thought, idea, or behavior. In meditation you simply stay in that meditative state.

Hypnosis Is Not Psychotherapy

Hypnosis is a technique—it is not a therapy. *Hypnotherapy* is psychotherapy that uses hypnosis as part of its treatment in an effort to uncover events from your past that may be influencing your present thoughts. Hypnosis is not hypnotherapy.

Hypnoscript

Psychotherapy that uses hypnosis as part of the therapeutic process is called **hypnotherapy**.

Hypnosis Is Not Relaxation

Contrary to popular belief, it is not necessary for you to be relaxed during hypnosis. Although most clients like to feel rested and comfortable during their sessions, occasionally someone comes in for hypnosis who warns me, "I hate to relax. Don't ask me to slow down." I then stay away from all words having to do with relaxation, and instead talk about the adventure of hypnosis and the fun of going places and having new experiences. It's easier for the hypnotist if you're calm, but hypnosis can be accomplished quite successfully while you're tense, upset, or unhappy.

Hypnosis Is Not Sleep

Hypnos is the Greek word for sleep, so we know that centuries ago hypnosis was thought to be a sleep state. The differences and similarities between sleep and hypnosis are shown in the following chart.

Sleep	Hypnosis
Eyes closed	Eyes may be closed, but can remain open
Body relaxed	Body usually relaxed, but can be instructed to become tense
No attention paid to surrounding environment	No attention paid to surrounding environment
Will not hear conversations	Will hear hypnotist's voice
Usually move around	Remain still; too much effort to move
No ability to concentrate	Extremely high ability to concentrate
EEG studies show brain waves of sleep have little alpha activity	EEG studies show brain waves have high alpha activity, indicative of alertness

During sleep you drift off, whereas during hypnosis you are alert and interested in the mental adventure you are having. Hypnosis may look like sleep because you might be asked to concentrate on an image in your mind and it is easier to do that if you close your eyes. But, even though your eyes are closed and you are sitting motionless on the chair, you are actually extremely alert—the opposite of sleep!

Positron emission tomography (PET) scans of the brain show that hypnosis produces a very specific pattern of brain activity. A PET scan is a medical imaging technique that measures cellular activity in the brain. It is different from a CAT scan, which takes pictures of tissues from different angles for diagnostic purposes.

Focus On This _____

Frankenstein was right! The brain does need electricity. In Mary Shelley's story, Dr. Frankenstein took parts from dead people to create a body, and then used electricity to charge the brain, bringing the body to life. Today we know that your brain continuously gives off electrical impulses called brain waves, which can be recorded with a device called an electroencephalograph, better known as an EEG machine.

Hypnosis Is a Tool

We may not know what the neurology of hypnosis is, but we do know that it is a powerful tool. Just as a surgeon's scalpel may save your life or kill you depending upon the skill of the surgeon, so the hypnotic process is only as good as the ability of the particular hypnotist you've chosen. I explain how to check out your hypnotist later on in Appendix B.

Can I Be Hypnotized?

You're convinced—hypnosis is wonderful. But, you may be thinking …

- ◆ I'm a control freak.

- ◆ I have a strong mind.

- ◆ I'm stubborn.

Do you suspect you'll never be able to go under? I have a surprise for you—you've probably already been hypnotized! You may have inadvertently hypnotized yourself. Most people do. Have you ever …

- ◆ Been engrossed in a book to the extent that when someone called your name you did not hear him or her? And then when you did hear, the voice seemed so far away, so unimportant, so irrelevant to the world you were in (the world of the book) that you had to be called many times before you responded. You were focused intently, ignoring the outside world, and thoroughly absorbed in what you were visualizing—that is hypnosis!

- ◆ Driven to your destination and then wondered how you got there? You put your driving on automatic while you paid attention to your inner world. You were oblivious to your surroundings—you were hypnotized!

- ◆ Concentrated on a project with such focus that you didn't hear the doorbell or the telephone? The project may have been at your desk, or in your workshop, on the computer, or at your easel. You were simply doing your thing, and when it was over you were incredulous. You might say, "It can't be 6 o'clock already. That would mean I was working for 4 hours; I thought I was there for 20 minutes." Deep absorption in the task at hand and time distortion are both indications of hypnosis.

- ◆ Watched television with such intensity that you felt part of the action? Earlier, I mentioned that relaxation is not absolutely necessary for hypnosis to occur. You are probably not relaxed when watching the Super Bowl, but you might be hypnotized if you're glued to the screen and oblivious to everything around you.

The essence of hypnosis is your intense concentration on one small thing to the exclusion of everything else. When the one thing is your hypnotist's voice giving you useful instructions, then hypnosis becomes a powerful, beneficial experience.

The hypnotist helps you get into an altered state of consciousness, or *trance*, just like when you're intensely watching television, reading, or driving. You are more able to absorb suggestions when you are in that state of deep concentration.

Hypnoscript

A **trance** is a state of heightened mental alertness and diminished physical movement. It is a state of susceptibility to suggestion.

There is another form of inadvertent hypnosis, and that is the hypnosis that occurs when you overhear someone else's hypnotic session. Nine-year-old Jennifer came to my office for hypnosis to help her cope with the kids in her class who teased her. Her mom was with her and wanted to observe the session. Within five minutes both Jennifer and her mom were in a trance.

Years ago there was a popular TV show called *Marcus Welby, M.D.*, starring Robert Young as Dr. Welby. On one episode Dr. Welby hypnotized a patient as part of her medical treatment. When the show ended, the NBC switchboard was flooded with calls. "Help, my husband is stuck in a trance," and "What should I do, my daughter is on the couch staring at the television screen?" were typical of the viewers' alarming reports. Of course, no one had any need to worry. All the family member had to do was say, "Wake up now, open your eyes and come out of it. Time to get back to normal." Just a nudge, or a suggestion to become alert, would have been sufficient to rouse the easily hypnotizable folks who responded to Dr. Welby's suggestions for hypnosis.

The scriptwriters would have been well advised to include the conclusion of the hypnotic session—the part where the doctor instructs the patient to awaken. Uninformed people caught up in the mystique of hypnosis believe it's a very mysterious process and that there's no room for common sense. That's why the viewers panicked, instead of simply telling their hypnotized family members to get up.

Still Unsure If You Can Be Hypnotized?

There's only one way to find out, and that's to try. The ability to be hypnotized correlates with nothing; it's an aptitude in and of itself. It doesn't matter if you're strong willed or very gullible, smart or slow. You're simply born with a talent for hypnosis. How talented are you? You may be like the 15 to 20 percent of the population born with exceptional talent for hypnosis. If you are in that lucky group, then a hypnotist's voice is the only anesthetic you'll need during surgery. If your talent is minimal, like the 15 to 20 percent of the population at the other end of the scale, you'll be able to use hypnosis to get rid of a bad habit, or to increase your self-confidence. But when you're about to have an operation, you'll definitely want an anesthetic dripping into your vein.

Until you try hypnosis, you won't know the extent of the talent you were born with. It's a little like playing the piano. You might need only one lesson to be on your way to Carnegie Hall, or you might struggle with years of weekly lessons and daily practicing and remain mediocre. Until you sit on the piano bench and begin to play, you'll have no clue about your potential. After one session of hypnosis, you'll know whether you're like the majority of people—somewhere in the middle—or whether you have very great or very little hypnosis talent.

Focus On This

Hypnotizability is the inborn talent you have for hypnosis that determines how deeply you go into an altered state of consciousness during the hypnosis process. How hypnotizable are you? Some researchers suspect that people who are passionate and emotional can achieve deeper states of hypnosis than people who are analytical and critical.

For you to be hypnotized, you must be smart enough to achieve concentration, and clever enough to know what's good for you. Your unconscious mind will not permit the acceptance of suggestions that are dangerous. Except in the rarest of circumstances—which are discussed in Chapter 26—you will do only what is consistent with your belief system. If there's a suggestion that is alien to you and against your values, you'll either get up from the trance or simply not hear that suggestion—your mind will block it out. Throughout the hypnotic procedure, you are a willing participant being guided into and through a safe section of your mind.

Although there is no particular personality type that becomes deeply hypnotized, some researchers believe there is a way to predict your hypnotizability. They've identified a biological marker—something about your physical self that remains the same in all circumstances—that they believe can predict your ability to go into a trance. The fixed biological marker is the white of your eyes! Experiments indicate that if you can roll your eyes way back into your head so that only the whites are visible, you'll turn out to be very susceptible to hypnosis. The more white in view, the more likely that you'll become deeply hypnotized.

Who Cares How Hypnotizable I Am?

Scientists need to know how hypnotizable their subjects are in order to evaluate their research results. Hypnosis researchers use tests called susceptibility scales to determine the extent to which a person can be hypnotized. The people who agree to participate in the research studies are called subjects. Good subjects are those people who can achieve very deep hypnosis. Hypnosis research is conducted to determine the usefulness of hypnosis for pain control, appetite suppression, and every other behavior mentioned in this book. Claims can be made for the effectiveness of hypnosis only after proper scientific study.

Do you have a very strong mind? Good. It will make it easy for you to accomplish your goal under hypnosis. Hypnosis is a cooperative endeavor. It is not adversarial. Larry blustered into my office saying that he might never "go under" because he's too stubborn. We talked awhile, and Larry realized that he and I both wanted the same thing—we both wanted him to remember to carry his inhalator with him so that he could avoid trips to the emergency room brought on by acute asthma attacks. He finally realized that his strong mind could work to his advantage. He is in charge of determining where he wants to go in hypnosis, and I am his coach helping him to get there. His willingness and consent are necessary for the procedure.

How Does Hypnosis Work?

During hypnosis you are given suggestions that will change your life. Before we do the actual hypnosis, I work with my patients to develop a list of suggestions that we agree will be helpful. When you choose the suggestions that you want the hypnotist to say to you, you are more likely to choose to respond. I like to think of myself as a coach who is gently guiding the patient.

Hypnosis manages to change the way your brain interprets experiences. Hypnosis can change your perceptions, your thoughts, your behaviors, and your feelings. When Larry left my office, he wanted to know that his inhalator was near him. He developed a need to have it in his pocket or his briefcase or next to him in the car. How did that happen? Scientists are not really sure. Somehow, the words I said to him while he was in an altered state of consciousness changed his way of thinking about asthma, or about inhalators, or about himself and his responsibility for maintaining his health. Larry would not have accepted my suggestion if he truly wanted to remain ill, or if he had no interest in taking responsibility for his care.

When you're in the hypnotic state, you're in a state of deep concentration. You are extremely focused and paying attention to the hypnotist's words while ignoring everything else going on around you.

After the hypnotist has used words to help you enter hypnosis, you become extremely suggestible. It is at this point that the hypnotist introduces new ideas to you. Those ideas are absorbed by your unconscious mind and become part of your thinking. While you are in that suggestible, absorbable state, your guard is down. Ideas you might ordinarily object to are easily transmitted into your mind. It's as if your intellectual, critical censor is turned off, and it becomes easy for you to say "yes." You will not reject new information, information that you might ordinarily be wary of. Your conscious mind likes to analyze and criticize. Your conscious mind can judge and reject. But now your conscious mind is out to lunch, and your hypnotized mind wants to absorb information without questioning it.

After the new ideas are implanted and you've had a chance to visualize them, the hypnotist will gently guide you back to your regular state, and the hypnosis session will be over.

> **CAUTION**
>
> **Look into My Eyes**
>
> If a hypnotist tells you that you need not know the suggestions in advance, and that you should simply trust him or her, gather your coat and walk out the door. No matter how many degrees a professional may have, that person still must earn your trust. Do not assume that the hypnotist will say the right thing to you if he or she is unwilling to go over it ahead of time.

Throughout the hypnotic experience you are totally in control of yourself. You can speak, you can hear, you can move, and you can come back to your ordinary state of being whenever you wish. It is not possible to remain hypnotized any longer than you want to be.

In the Hypnotist's Office

H. K., the owner of a small lamp factory, consulted me when he had trouble learning a new computer system. "I'm the boss," he wailed, "I should be able to do what my employees are doing, but whenever I sit in front of the computer I feel nervous. When my company trainer came to give me a lesson, I was so tense that I never heard a word she said." I gave Mr. K. the hypnotic suggestion: At his next computer lesson the trainer's words would be easy to follow, and he would be motivated to spend one hour each day comfortably fooling around with his computer. One week later Mr. K. called to thank me—he was doing spreadsheets with ease.

Reframing: Making Old Pictures New

You may think that the old oil painting in the black picture frame that's hanging on Mom's living room wall is dreary. But, when that same painting is reframed in yellow, you begin to see the yellow in the background—it was always there, but you never before noticed it—and then the entire scene suddenly appears more lively. Hypnosis gives you a new frame for …

◆ Your thoughts about yourself.

◆ Your ideas.

◆ Your attitudes.

Hypnosis can give new meaning to an old situation—yes, you really can develop a strong desire to exercise, to stop midnight snacking, or to fall asleep promptly.

Sometimes it's too difficult to reframe a situation by yourself. That's when you need a boost from hypnosis. After one session, you can change your perception of a situation as one of hardship to one of pleasure. Hypnosis gives you the advantage of looking at a particular experience from a new perspective.

Imagine that you're on a trip across the desert and your car breaks down. You're very hot, you become irritable, and when help finally arrives after 35 minutes, you're in a bad mood that lasts for hours. Now, imagine that you're on a wonderful vacation. You're at a Caribbean beach resort and waiting for your friend to join you on the sand. You have to wait in the hot, hot, sun for 35 minutes. You are thrilled to be in Martinique; your good mood lasts for hours after your friend arrives. Why can you tolerate the heat in one situation and not the other? When you tell yourself a story that reframes an event from the negative—"the car broke down"—to the positive—"I'm finally in Martinique"—you are changing your attitude by using words.

In the Hypnotist's Office

A mother and her son are worrying because the child is experiencing pains throughout his body. The mother anxiously awaits the pediatrician's evaluation. Finally, the pediatrician enters saying, "All the blood work is normal. Paul is having 'growing pains.' They won't last much longer." Paul is happy to have growing pains; he is hoping to gain a few inches before seventh grade. Mom is relieved. The doctor reframed the situation with words. The pain is still there, but mother and child are no longer upset. In fact, Paul hardly notices the pain anymore. Mother and son did not need formal hypnosis; the pediatrician reframed the situation for them quickly and easily.

A hypnotist reframes situations for you that you are unable to reframe for yourself. Hypnosis can get you to believe that broccoli is delicious, that tomorrow's math test is nothing to be nervous about, and that becoming stuck in rush-hour traffic is fun. You are in charge of deciding what it is you want to accomplish during your hypnosis session.

You will be amazed at all you can achieve with hypnosis.

Take This Quiz

Some researchers say that certain personality characteristics help determine your hypnotizability. Those researchers would ask you to take this quiz to see if you are extremely hypnotizable, slightly hypnotizable, or somewhere in the middle. Other scientists, though, say that the answers to these questions make no difference—it's just the whites of your eyes that matter. And then there's me: I think with a good hypnotist you'll do just fine, no matter what.

Let's have some fun, anyway. Answer "yes" or "no" to the questions in this quiz, and then see the scoring instructions following it.

How Hypnotizable Are You?

1. Do you often feel extremely emotional about a book or a movie? ___Yes __No

2. Do you often daydream? __Yes __No

3. Do you believe most everything your dentist tells you? __Yes __No

4. Do you, or are you tempted to, take in stray animals? __Yes __No

5. When you return from a trip you enjoyed, do you try to persuade those you love to take the same trip? __Yes __No

6. When you see a child crying, do you feel your own tears coming on? ___Yes __No

7. Do you sometimes wonder how you drove to a particular place? __Yes __No

8. Would you say that you enjoy most days of your life, without excessive worrying about the future? __Yes __No

9. Are you a good list maker? __Yes __No

10. Would you say that you enjoy most days of your life, without excessive worrying about the past? __Yes __No

11. Are you a good card player? __Yes __No

12. Does your mind wander when you sit down to read? __Yes __No

13. Do you become deeply absorbed in TV shows? __Yes __No

14. Are you very well organized? __Yes __No

15. Are you good at games requiring memory skills? __Yes __No

16. Do you often doubt your car mechanic? __Yes __No

17. Do you usually know what you'll be doing two weeks from Sunday? ___Yes __No

18. Do you enjoy debating ideas? __Yes __No

19. Would you say you are reasonable and steady in life? __Yes __No

20. When things go wrong, do you easily panic? __Yes __No

Scoring Instructions:

Give yourself 5 points for a "yes" to questions 1, 2, 3, 4, 5, 6, 7, 8, 10, 11, 13, 15, and 20.

Give yourself 1 point for a "yes" to questions 9, 12, 14, 16, 17, 18, and 19.

No points for "no" answers.

How did you do?

50 or more points: Watch out, you are so very hypnotizable you might go "under" from overhearing someone else's hypnosis session.

30–49 points: You are a good hypnotic subject and will go under easily.

20–29 points: You will enjoy hypnosis, but the hypnotist may have to work to get you there.

10–19 points: You can be hypnotized to some extent—enough to stop smoking, but not enough to have root canal work done with no anesthesia.

0–9 points: A good hypnotist will get you there; a mediocre hypnotist will succeed only if you are very motivated. You'll do well by practicing self-hypnosis, which is discussed in Chapters 5, 6, and 7.

Now that you know you have some talent for hypnosis, go to the next chapter to learn what it feels like to be under the spell.

The Least You Need to Know

- Hypnosis can help you improve your life.

- You were born with a talent—maybe great, maybe less so—for being hypnotized.

- Hypnosis is not meditation, psychotherapy, relaxation, or sleep.

- Hypnosis is a safe experience.

- Hypnosis helps you to see situations in a new way.

Chapter 2

You Are in a Trance

In This Chapter

- ◆ What it feels like to be hypnotized
- ◆ What you look like when you're hypnotized
- ◆ How suggestion works
- ◆ Will I quack like a duck?
- ◆ How will I know I was under?

Some movies and television programs have depicted hypnosis as a weird, eerie experience conducted by a strange figure on an unwilling victim. It's not surprising that you may have some concerns about getting stuck in a trance or obeying a cruel master. Read on and be reassured. Real hypnosis is not the stuff of the screen.

You'll actually feel good during and after hypnosis. You won't do anything to embarrass yourself or say anything to humiliate yourself. In fact, you'll enjoy the experience so much that you'll probably want to do it again.

What Does It Feel Like to Be Hypnotized?

You may feel as if you're in an isolation booth because you'll be concentrating on the hypnotist's voice so intently that you'll pay no attention to your environment.

Focus On This

A quiet room is not necessary for hypnosis. For two months there was noisy construction outside my office—bulldozers, jackhammers, and loud-talking workmen—and clients continued to respond as if my voice was all they could hear.

When you're not hypnotized, you're aware of everything your senses report to you. You know if you're warm or chilly, if you're in the mood for ice cream or thirsty for a drink. You know if you're hearing music, if you're smelling pizza, visiting the zoo and looking at a monkey, or at a hospital facing a nurse. When you're hypnotized you willingly shut off all feedback from your senses. With no distractions from your senses, you can focus more precisely on the words and images provided by the hypnotist.

Paying attention only to the voice you hear and the suggestions offered to you, you might experience the voice as if it's coming from far away. Paying no attention to extraneous, irrelevant stimuli, you become particularly cooperative and mellow. You have no interest in arguing, and no energy to put up a fight.

Most people feel physically relaxed and mentally alert while hypnotized. Some say it feels like meditation, others say it's similar to the high feeling induced by certain drugs.

During hypnosis you may have a distorted perception of time. Some clients assume a few minutes have passed when it's really much longer; others think they were hypnotized for hours when it was only minutes.

Your body may feel weighted down and heavy, or light, as if you're floating. Some people feel warm, and many feel tingling throughout their bodies.

When your hypnotist suggests that you experience certain feelings—perhaps relaxation or comfort—you'll readily comply. The suggested reality will seem more real to you than what you're actually feeling.

Every person experiences hypnosis in a unique, individualized fashion. Listen to these comments, made by my last 12 clients, just a few minutes after they opened their eyes at the conclusion of a hypnosis session:

- I feel like I just got up from a long, deep sleep.

- I was under for only 10 minutes? Can't be. I was out for hours.

- I feel like I do after a massage.

- This is weird.

- When can I come back again?

- Sorry, Doc, I wasn't hypnotized.

- Are you sure this is going to work?

- I am so groggy.

- My headache is gone, but I never even told you I had a headache. How did that happen?

- This was hypnosis?

- I want to go back to that calm scene on the lake.

- I can't wait to see if I'll skip dessert tonight.

Although some of my clients may feel quite ordinary during hypnosis, I know that they are hypnotized. How do I know?

I do a six-month follow-up of clients who have come to my office to stop smoking. I send them a form asking if they are still smoking and I ask them for comments they may have about their office visits for hypnosis. A typical reply card contains a version of the following:

> Dear Doctor,
>
> You were a nice lady so please don't be insulted when I tell you that I don't think I was hypnotized that day in your office. I know you tried hard, but I was aware of every noise and every movement during my session. I didn't feel spacey, and I drove home with no problem. By the way, coincidentally, that evening I decided, on my own, to give up my two-pack-a-day habit. I guess I didn't need hypnosis after all.
>
> Sincerely,
>
> Unhypnotizable

Hypnosis can change muscle tension, heart rate, oxygen consumption, blood flow, and skin temperature. When you're hypnotized, you usually receive suggestions to put yourself into a tranquil state, and you usually obey. Your blood pressure drops, your heart rhythm slows down a bit and becomes very regular, and all your muscles relax. Your heart, your muscles, your glands, and your blood pressure are all regulated by your *autonomic nervous system*. It's interesting to note that scientists have found that words have an effect on this system—a system that is supposed to function automatically. Hypnosis uses your mind to control your body.

Hypnoscript

Your **autonomic nervous system** controls your unconscious bodily functions such as your heartbeat, your blood pressure, and your digestion.

Vanity, Vanity

It's human nature to be skeptical of any situation that seems strange. It's normal to be hesitant about entering unfamiliar territory. As you read on and learn more about a hypnosis session, you'll become more comfortable with the idea of hypnosis.

In the Hypnotist's Office

Some years ago my dad had a serious heart attack and was in the ICU, attached to many machines, and fading in and out of consciousness. The cardiologist said hope was dim. A particular life-saving drug couldn't be given to Dad until his blood pressure dropped back to normal, and that seemed unlikely. The nurses and doctors agreed that Dad could not hear. Nevertheless, I began speaking directly into his ear, telling him that he was walking down a garden path and when he reached the yellow flowers he would pause, his body would relax, and his blood pressure would become normal. Within five minutes his blood pressure lowered and stabilized. He is fine today.

What Will I Look Like While I'm "Under"?

You'll appear extremely relaxed, as if your body is dead weight. Your muscles will relax so much that your mouth may hang open, with your bottom jaw sagging because it seems like too much trouble for you to hold it up. Some people find their mouths so relaxed that they drool a bit. Don't worry, it happens to the fanciest of clients; I simply keep a box of tissues handy.

Your breathing rate will be noticeably slowed down. Your eyes will close and your eyelids may flutter. Some clients get teary eyed (another use for those tissues). The tears are not because of a sad or sentimental journey they're taking in their minds. Tears are released because of the relaxation of the tear ducts during hypnosis.

Most people are motionless. Hypnosis encourages voluntary cessation of all activity, but occasional involuntary, jerky little shudders do occur. This is not true for children. Children tend to become deeply hypnotized but, throughout the session, wiggle and squiggle and open and shut their eyes (see Chapter 18).

What Will I Say While I'm "Under"?

"Will I be forced to speak the truth? Will I confess my sins?"

In most hypnotic sessions, there's little reason for the client to say anything at all. It's the hypnotist who does all the talking. If you're having hypnosis for habit control or to change a specific behavior, your sins are quite irrelevant anyway.

If you speak at all, it will be in a monotone, almost robotlike response, in slow motion. Most people, though, prefer not to speak. Talking breaks their perfect state of rest and seems like too much effort.

However, if you have a hypnotherapy session (discussed in Chapter 1) as opposed to a hypnosis session, and its purpose is to explore your inner attitudes, you might wind up talking and revealing some private thoughts. That's the point of hypnotherapy.

CAUTION

Look into My Eyes

Before you agree to be hypnotized, be certain you and the hypnotist have the same agenda. Clarify whether you will be prompted to speak. Discuss, ahead of time, the aim of the session—is it hypnosis or hypnotherapy?

What Will I Do While I'm "Under"?

"I don't want to embarrass myself and hop like a rabbit or quack like a duck."

You might embarrass yourself if you go to a stage hypnotist. Stage hypnotists are entertainers as well as hypnotists. Their job is to give the audience a good time. My job, and the job of other health professionals who practice hypnosis, is to help you change a behavior or an idea. That leaves you no opportunity to embarrass yourself, unless, of course, your purpose in going for hypnosis is to improve your hopping or refine your quacking!

Can hypnosis force you to do something against your will? The answer is no. In very, very, very, rare circumstances, *if* you're among the segment of the population that is extremely hypnotizable, *and* you happen to go to a hypnotist who is dishonest, unscrupulous, and a charlatan, then *maybe* you *might* respond to a suggestion that is not in your best interest. Even then, what you learn in this book will prevent that from ever happening to you.

For almost everyone, a suggestion works only if it's something that you believe in. Motivation counts. If you're ambivalent about stopping smoking, your success is less likely than if you strongly want to quit. If you're certain that you absolutely do not want to give up your cigarettes, I will not be able to hypnotize you to quit. During hypnosis you always have the option of rejecting suggestions that encourage you to do something that goes against your value system. You won't harm someone, commit an illegal act, or do something outrageous.

The exception to this is if an unethical hypnotist has increased your suggestibility by starving you, prohibiting you from sleeping, and has employed other brainwashing techniques, as well. Of course, this does not occur in your everyday hypnosis session, but might occur if you are kidnapped by a terrorist.

At any time during the trance, you can return to your regular state. Hypnosis makes it easy for you to absorb a suggestion, but it does not force you to accept that suggestion. (See Chapter 1 for more on trances and suggestions.)

What If I Get Stuck in a Trance?

Impossible. When the session is over the hypnotist will tell you to open your eyes. Presumably, the hypnotist has a day's work to do and is not interested in having a person in a trance hanging out in the office. To end the session your hypnotist will simply instruct you to leave hypnosis and come back to "ordinary."

"What if my hypnotist drops dead or has a stroke or gets paralyzed vocal cords before he or she gets to the part about me coming back to ordinary?"

Don't worry. You'll get the idea, all by yourself, that you should open your eyes and return to regular. It may take you a few minutes, but it will happen. You will become bored when you have no voice to listen to.

Focus On This _____

If you know you should change a habit (maybe you're always late to work), but you're not sure you really want to (maybe you hate your boss), schedule two hypnosis sessions—the first to hypnotize you to overlook your boss's mean personality, and the second to encourage you to arrive on time. Sometimes the first hypnotic session gets you ready to succeed during the second.

"What if there's an emergency—say, a fire—while I'm under?"

You'll respond in your customary way. You probably won't wait for your hypnotist to say something to you, but will open your eyes and get going on your own. Don't forget, you're not sleeping and you're not in a coma. You're conscious of everything around you, and awake and alert. Your autonomic responses may be slowed during hypnosis, but your mental awareness is acute.

Trance is a pleasurable state, and you'll prefer staying in one to responding to Aunt Ellen when she calls your name; but if Aunt Ellen calls your name to announce a fire, you'll immediately break your trance.

How Long Do Suggestions Last?

"Will I need to return to the hypnotist's office every few days?"

The lasting effect of hypnosis depends upon the …

- Particular behavior you want to change.

- Environment you live, work, and play in.

- Words the hypnotist uses.
- Rapport the hypnotist establishes.

Most of the time, for most people, the suggestions last beyond their expectations.

How Often Will I Be Tempted to Resume This Behavior?

Some behaviors are easier to eradicate than others. It's easier to get rid of a smoking habit than an overeating habit. When you stop smoking, you need not touch a cigarette ever again. Food, however, needs to be consumed several times each day, so, over time, a "no more overeating" suggestion might wear down and need a repeat session.

How Often Will Others Tempt Me to Resume This Behavior?

Your environment has an influence on how long your suggestions last. If an ex-smoker is married to a smoker and works in an office with smokers, it's possible that, over time, those environments will erode the effect of the hypnosis, and an occasional follow-up session might be in order.

In the Hypnotist's Office

I invite my clients to bring a tape recorder into their sessions with me so they can re-experience their sessions anytime they want, without paying for another office visit. Most often, though, the tape is unnecessary. A client will feel nice and secure having it, but, in fact, will rarely need to use it. If it is used, though, it's a pleasure to become hypnotized in the privacy of your own home, and not have to schedule an appointment in advance and then travel to the hypnotist's office. Hypnosis audio tapes are for sale in many bookstores, too. Although those tapes are not individualized, many of them are useful.

Is Your Hypnotist a Good Communicator?

Here is where the skill of the hypnotist really makes a difference. An excellent hypnotist decides which words to select to say to you based upon your particular personality and life experiences, and your vocabulary and speech patterns. The words and phrases used will make or break the success of your session and influence how long the suggestions will last.

I once had two clients come to my office on the same day with the same problem. Gregory, an artist whose name is often in the newspaper because of the famous people who buy his paintings, asked for help with his fear of public speaking. His agent insists that he accept invitations to dinner parties at the homes of people who have his paintings hanging on their walls. Once there, he's expected to be witty and charming. He prefers to be silent. He would rather be home in his loft painting.

Debbie, a high school basketball coach, led her team to victory and now must give the obligatory interviews to newspaper, radio, and television journalists. She is frightened and would rather be home in her backyard shooting baskets.

I hypnotized Gregory; I hypnotized Debbie. Can you figure out which of the following sentences I used with each client? In the following list, check off under each name the ones you believe I used.

	Gregory	Debbie
1. You will see yourself speaking clearly.	___	___
2. You will notice how good your eye contact is.	___	___
3. You will move right along to the next topic.	___	___
4. You will jump in with just the right comment.	___	___
5. Your speech will be full of bright sayings.	___	___
6. When you get a good idea you will run with it.	___	___

Gregory, the artist, of course is a visual person. He sees clearly (sentence 1); makes eye contact (sentence 2); and notices brightness (sentence 5). Debbie, the athlete, moves around (sentence 3); jumps (sentence 4); and runs (sentence 6).

Before beginning the hypnosis part of the session, your hypnotist should spend enough time talking to you to perceive your particular ways of relating to the world. If the hypnotist's words feel right for you, if they're comfortable and familiar, you'll more readily respond to the suggestions.

Is Your Hypnotist Using the Right Technique for You?

A hypnotist establishes rapport by matching behaviors; if you speak slowly, so should your hypnotist. Your unconscious mind will become engaged with your hypnotist's unconscious mind if you're both nodding, blinking, motioning, breathing, and speaking at the same pace. This hypnotic technique is called *pacing*. The good hypnotist will cross his or her arms if your arms are crossed, take a deep breath when you do, and clear his or her throat after you clear yours. When you're in sync with each other, you'll follow the suggestions you receive easily.

Some hypnotists are particularly skilled at couching their suggestions in just the right way, and their suggestions have been known to last a lifetime. Dr. Milton Erickson, a famous psychiatrist and hypnotist, once hypnotized a college student to help him solve a problem. The young man wanted tangible evidence that he was in a trance, so Dr. Erickson gave him the additional hypnotic suggestion that whenever they would meet each other the young man would feel the need to tug at his ear—his own ear, that is, not the good doctor's. Sure enough, the young man found that whenever he encountered Dr. Erickson on campus, his hand would automatically fly up to his ear lobe. Many years passed, and one day at a professional conference he noticed Dr. Erickson's name on the list of speakers. Soon he had a chance to reintroduce himself, and, to his amazement, watch his own hand rise up and tug at his ear.

"Will I have to stare at a swinging pocket watch?"

No, not necessarily. That idea is popular because it's easy to become hypnotized by staring at something. And a repetitive motion, such as swinging, is monotonous enough to lull anyone into relaxation. You may be asked to stare at something in the office or to close your eyes and visualize a particular scene in your mind.

I suggest that my clients stare at the desk drawer handle facing them when they sit opposite me. For those clients who prefer to be hypnotized lying down, I ask them to stare at a spot on the painting in front of them as they recline on the couch. Although I begin my sessions in that manner, most people do end up closing their eyes within five minutes.

> **Hypnoscript**
>
> An excellent hypnotist **paces** the client by recognizing and imitating that client's patterns in speech, movement, and behavior.

> **Focus On This**
>
> Milton H. Erickson (1901–1980) was a physician who championed the use of hypnosis in the United States. He formed scholarly hypnosis societies, mentored many hypnotists, and was an astounding presence, curing patient after patient with his unique hypnotic approach. Today, Ericksonian hypnosis is taught throughout the world.

How Will I Know If It Took?

After the session, how will you know if you were really under? Your success is your proof. If you accomplish your goal, then you were hypnotized. If you don't reach your goal, but almost get there, try a second or third session with the hypnotist. A partial response indicates that you are somewhat receptive to hypnosis and may just need some more practice. As with playing the piano, practice makes perfect.

You will remember the session—unless you ask the hypnotist to give you the deliberate suggestion for amnesia. There are no side effects to hypnosis other than feeling more relaxed than usual. Many people report that they fall asleep immediately and enjoy a long and restful sleep on the night of their session. The only other changes you'll see in yourself are the changes that you came to the session to achieve.

In the Hypnotist's Office

Suzanne is very hypnotizable and enjoys the feeling of being hypnotized. She comes in for a session even when nothing is bothering her, sometimes telling me that if I were not available she would have gone for a massage to get that same relaxation effect. When Suzanne walks into my office she invariably says, "Oh, I suddenly feel so sleepy," then she sits, closes her eyes, and puts herself into trance—with no help from me! I once gave her the suggestion that she would begin feeling hypnotized as soon as she walked into my office, and so she does!

Now that you know what it feels like to be hypnotized, let's proceed to the next chapter. You'll learn exactly what happens in the hypnotist's office, from the moment you enter until you leave.

The Least You Need to Know

- You can be hypnotized and not feel particularly "under."

- Hypnosis can help you use your mind to control your body.

- The skill of the hypnotist can determine the effectiveness of your session.

- You're in control of yourself during the session; you will not do anything against your will.

3

Look into My Eyes

In This Chapter

- ◆ Becoming hypnotized
- ◆ Staying hypnotized
- ◆ Enjoying the process
- ◆ Coming out of it

There are as many ways to hypnotize folks as there are hypnotists. The best hypnotists know several methods of helping a client go "under," and then several methods of conveying suggestions, and, afterward, many different ways of reawakening the client. You'll learn about many of these techniques in this chapter.

You'll eavesdrop on an actual hypnotic session, listen to the hypnotist (me!), greet the client, and learn about her life. You'll witness the interaction as I establish rapport, explain the process, and then go ahead and hypnotize her.

Welcome to Hypnosis

Judy is seated on a comfortable chair opposite me. We've exchanged pleasantries, and now I ask her why she's here.

Focus On This

Take to your hypnosis session any phone numbers or written instructions from health professionals. This ensures that the hypnotic suggestions will not interfere with medical processes and with healing.

Judy: *My physical therapist thought you might be able to help me since nothing else has worked. I had knee surgery, and after the surgery I could not walk down stairs. Now, my knee has healed and, according to the x-rays, I should be able to walk down a step. My problem is that every time I'm about to make that move, my knee stiffens and just won't go there.*

RT: *Oh, no. How awful for you. Before we proceed, please allow me to speak to your physical therapist and orthopedist.*

Judy's orthopedist gives me precise information about the muscle groups that need to be put into play. The physical therapist tells me that Judy must learn to bend her injured knee immediately after her other foot begins to go down to the next step.

After I get clearance from Judy's health team, she and I write three sentences specifying exactly what her knee must do. Then, we chat about her life—her family, her activity level prior to surgery, her future plans. She's a bit nervous, so I find topics that are easy for her to talk about, such as her new home and her son in junior high, and stay away from topics that seem to unsettle her: her husband and her inability to continue ice skating. Remember, Judy did not come to me for advice or counseling or psychotherapy. In about 10 minutes she seems much more relaxed, so I proceed as follows:

Hypnoscript

An **induction** is the technique used by the hypnotist to help the client relax and reach a state of suggestibility—the trance state.

RT: *I know you must be curious about hypnosis, so I'll explain the procedure to you and tell you what you can expect. Please feel free to ask any questions.*

(I use the word "curious" instead of "scared" to reframe Judy's feeling in a positive way. Judy leans back in her chair; I mirror her, and lean back, too.)

After we chat I begin the *induction*, which will get Judy into a receptive state so that my suggestions will "take."

You Are Going Under

I prepare Judy to be alert by using the word "interesting." I tell her that by doing a simple task that I know she can do—focusing her eyes—everything will go smoothly. I remind her that she and I are working together toward a common goal, by saying "we'll" proceed.

RT: *Hypnosis is an interesting experience. If you'll find something to focus your eyes on while I speak now, we'll proceed very smoothly. Most people like to stare at this drawer pull.*

Now I speak to Judy in a slow, quiet voice and explain the information that you already know:

- That she is in charge of herself during hypnosis
- That she cannot get stuck in a trance
- And most important for her, that her mind can control her body

Next, I give Judy suggestions for relaxing her body and her mind. I talk about the "slowing down" of her muscles. I use the words "comfortable," "calm," and "tranquil" several times during the one minute of sooth-ing phrases that I speak to her. Each time I say these words, I change my tone of voice and slow down my pace. I am not directly telling Judy how to feel. I am not command-ing her to relax! Calm down! Get comfort-able! Instead, there are suggestions *embedded* in my sentences. Some of my embedded sen-tences are as follows:

Hypnoscript

Embedded suggestions are emphasized words or phrases purposefully inserted into a regu-lar conversation. The listener gets the message in an indirect manner.

- *It feels good to make yourself comfortable.*
- *Have you noticed how tranquil the ocean is today? (We can see the Atlantic Ocean from my office window.)*
- *Some people feel calmed when they look at the ocean.*
- *I'm glad the phone stopped ringing in the waiting room. It is nice when things slow down.*

I notice that Judy's breaths are irregular, perhaps because of her anticipation of this new experience, so I mention that she might want to relax her breathing. I tell her that many people experience heaviness throughout their bodies, particularly their hands and feet, during hypnosis. I wonder, aloud, whether she'll notice her hands becoming heavier than her feet, or her feet becoming heavier than her hands.

An induction is the process used to guide the client from the ordinary state of conscious-ness into the trance state. The combination of my rhythmic voice, her staring at one spot, and the relaxation suggestions, induces hypnosis.

Look into My Eyes

Inductions for hypnosis should use words, or sometimes music or art. Inductions do not require touching, massage, or other personal behaviors.

Judy seems to be concentrating on that drawer pull with great intensity. She is not moving, she is staring, although I notice her eyes blinking. I pace her by timing my words to the blinks of her eyelids. She blinks; I speak. She's paying careful attention to my words. At this point I remind her that we are about to accomplish something extremely beneficial for her, and then I say:

RT: *Please close your eyes when you're ready to begin.*

Judy's eyes close after about a 30-second delay. She is now somewhat hypnotized and I can begin the next part of the session, which is to give her the suggestions about her knee that she and I developed. However, I decide to *deepen* her hypnotic state. Deepening will …

Hypnoscript

Deepening occurs when instructions are given to intensify the hypnotic experience. Deepening usually engages the imagination in a vivid way.

- ◆ Increase her depth of hypnosis.

- ◆ Increase the probability of her unconscious mind absorbing the sentences I will read to her.

- ◆ Provide her with a more deeply felt experience.

- ◆ Provide her with a more interesting experience.

Staying Under

One of many possible deepening exercises involves a staircase. Because stairs are part of Judy's problem, and therefore solution, I use the staircase deepening device and instruct Judy as follows:

RT: *Please visualize a staircase. It can be a staircase from your imagination or from a movie or book, or it may be a staircase you know very well. Maybe it's outdoors and old and rickety, maybe it's inside your home. When you see that staircase, please see yourself standing on the bottom step. When you can clearly see yourself and the stairs please nod your head.*

In about 20 seconds Judy's head begins to nod ever so slightly. Her eyes are tightly shut, her breathing is slowed down, and her face is starting to sag. I continue:

RT: *Please see yourself walking up that staircase. With each step you take you will go deeper and deeper into the hypnotic state. When you reach the top of the stairs, you will be deeply hypnotized and ready to respond to the suggestions I offer you. The suggestions are for your good health, for your good life. Please walk up slowly. We have plenty of time. Just nod your head when you reach the top. Thank you.*

While Judy is walking up that staircase in her mind, I am repeating, in a slow, drawn-out rhythm:

RT: *More … and … more … hypnotized … more … and more hypnotized ….*

When she nods her head I read the *script*, the three sentences that we had prepared. I read them slowly and clearly, pausing after each. Then, I ask her to visualize herself walking down one step. She frowns, and starts to whimper. I repeat one sentence, the sentence that tells her exactly how to hold her foot and knee while walking down a stair. I ask her to watch herself as she follows those instructions. I speak very slowly. I ask her to repeat the stepping several times in her mind and nod her head when she feels she has mastered it. I wait about three minutes before I see the nod.

RT: *Good for you. You did it. Congratulations. Each staircase you walk down will be easier for you than the previous. Soon you'll be walking stairs effortlessly and swiftly.*

Hypnoscript

The suggestions and other words said to the client during the time she is "under" comprise the hypnotic **script**. Scripts should be prepared ahead of time, with input from both the hypnotist and the client.

Focus On This

During hypnosis it's a good idea to receive oral instructions and then to have an opportunity to visualize what is said. The more the senses are engaged, the more likely a lasting result will be achieved.

Coming Out of It

Judy did a good job and now I'll be getting her to return from hypnosis to her regular state.

RT: *Now it's time to leave hypnosis for today. Please see yourself walking down the staircase. And with each step you take you will be leaving hypnosis. When you reach the bottom step, you will be finished with hypnosis for today. You will return your mind and your body to their regular ways. Please take your time. We have plenty of time. Whenever you're ready you'll reach the bottom of the staircase.*

Everything you accomplished today will stay with you. Anytime you need to hear my words, they will come to you. My voice alone will be enough to remind you of everything you mastered here today. Anytime you hear my voice—in person, on the phone, on a tape, or on voicemail, you will immediately feel just like you feel right now. Please take your time. When you are ready, at your own pace, you will open your eyes and come back to ordinary. Take your time.

I wait about three minutes, which seems like an eternity in a silent room. Judy starts to fidget. Her eyes remain shut. She stretches out, moves her legs, and clenches and unclenches her fists. Her eyes are still shut.

RT: *You will know just when to open your eyes.*

Judy opens her eyes, appears a little dazed and sleepy, and smiles. She says nothing, but sits there contentedly.

RT: *I hope you enjoyed this. Please call me next week to tell me how you're doing with stairs. I expect you'll be walking then with no problem, so it is not necessary to make another appointment.*

Focus On This

It's a good idea for the hypnotist to incorporate any background noise into the induction. If there's a dog barking, the hypnotist can say that every time the dog barks the client will move into a deeper state of hypnosis. That way, noises can become assets and are not distractions.

Judy makes no effort to get up. She is mellow, sitting in my office as if it's her living room, so relaxed and unhurried. I hear my next client in the waiting room chatting with Jeanne, my secretary. Judy has settled in.

I tell Judy that most people feel very comfortable after hypnosis and wish they could prolong the experience. "However," I add, "it is necessary to leave the office now." I suggest she wait in the waiting room for 10 minutes. By that time any grogginess will have lifted. Judy reluctantly leaves my office. She calls in two weeks to announce that she is almost back to normal on stairs.

The Hypnosis Session

You observed a full session that consisted of ...

1. An interview.

2. Writing the script (also called suggestions).

3. Doing the induction.

4. Deepening.

5. Reading the script.

6. Coming out of the trance.

7. Encouraging the client to leave (only kidding).

Now that Judy has finally left the office, we can go over the parts of a session in detail.

Interview

The interview is your opportunity to tell the hypnotist who you are.

I like to find out about a client's interests in music, or work, or books, or family. Everything I learn about the person helps me select the right words for the induction and the script.

In the Hypnotist's Office

For an induction, I suggested that a client imagine he was walking in the woods. I encouraged him to see the sky and the trees, smell the flowers, hear the birds, and become engrossed in the scene. Suddenly, his eyes got all red and teary, his nose started twitching, and then the sneezing began. He had a vivid imagination. I hadn't asked the right questions during the interview, and the poor guy was having a serious allergy attack in my office because of the flowers, trees, and grasses in his mind.

Writing the Script

My clients work with me to write their scripts, and during hypnosis, I simply read the very words that they have selected. That way there are no surprises.

Induction

An induction can take 30 seconds to do, or 30 minutes, depending upon the talent of the client and the skill of the hypnotist. Hard-to-hypnotize clients need more time, whereas some very hypnotizable clients (remember Suzanne in Chapter 2?) just sit in the chair and they're out. All inductions are presented in a slow, soothing voice. I use only my voice for the induction, no bells or whistles or clapping or booms.

The induction I did for Judy is an eye-fixation induction. Other eye-fixation inductions include staring at a pendulum or crystal ball, or any handy object.

Sometimes an induction involves simply asking the person to recall a favorite place, a place of comfort and pleasure, and then requesting that the person see the scene in his or her mind's eye. I encourage the visualization of detail and the involvement of all the senses, so I ask the following questions:

- *What do you see there? Look all around.*

- *What sounds do you hear?*

- *Take a deep breath and become aware of the aromas you smell.*

- *What is the weather? Are you warm or cool?*

Another induction method that I often use, particularly with children, is called the coin drop. You can actually try this yourself when you want to experience the trance state.

Hold a coin between your thumb and index finger, with your arm out in front of you, your fingers facing downward. Focus on your hand, notice your skin, your nails, and just keep staring and staring at your hand. Tell yourself that when you're ready for a trance, your fingers will relax and the coin will drop. Your hand will go to your lap. When the coin drops, that's your signal that your eyes will automatically close and you'll enter a trance. Tell yourself that your suggestion will be that you will relax, and then open your eyes and come back to regular.

Focus On This

When a client has something to visualize, the mind has a place to go and something to do, so it will be too busy to reject suggestions.

Sometimes, for an induction, I request that clients fold their hands in their laps and stare at them. After some relaxation suggestions and slow talking, I give the suggestion that glue is all over their fingers and they will be unable to pull their hands apart. When I see them trying hard, but unable to separate their hands, I know they're in a deep trance and ready to respond to the script.

Progressive muscle relaxation is another popular induction. I go through the body, bottom to top, announcing that relaxation is occurring in each body part as I name it. I tell clients that soon after we get to their head, their eyes will close, signaling that they are ready to enter a trance. Read more about progressive relaxation in Chapter 6.

Some people go into an immediate trance if asked to picture a repetitive motion. I'll set up a scene for them in which they're swinging in a swing, or rowing a boat, or sweeping a broom across the floor. I choose the appropriate motion based upon the information I gathered in the interview. Then I encourage them to see the scene clearly in their minds while I repeat the words *"back and forth, back and forth, back and forth"* perhaps for several minutes.

In the Hypnotist's Office

Hypnotist Ann Damsbo happened to be seated next to a fearful passenger on a cross-country flight. Ann asked if he would be interested in hypnosis to help calm down. He said "yes," and she proceeded to induce a trance by having him stare at the "Fasten Your Seat Belt" sign. She then gave him the suggestion that whenever the sign was lit he would be extremely calm and sleepy. Ann had a good trip; her seat mate slept all the way home.

Imagine if you entered my office and I told you to …

Close the door, then open the door, then open the window, then close the window, take the orange out of the refrigerator, put the orange in the stove, now turn around, look for a grape-fruit and sit down.

If I went on and on for four or five minutes giving you instructions that made absolutely no sense, what would you do? Probably, you'd stop trying to make sense out of my words and give up. That's what happens when hypnotists use the *confusion induction*. Some clients are so rigid and analytic that the best way to induce hypnosis is to get them to stop thinking so much.

A client, Herbert, was the analytic type. He kept interrupting my induction by asking "what if?" and "why?" and "how?" His intellectual approach would not move out of the way to make room for an induction, so I deliberately confused him with rapid-fire talk that made no sense. Finally, he stopped struggling to understand the process and just relaxed. At that point I easily induced hypnosis.

Hypnoscript

The **confusion induction,** which is a bombardment of bewildering terms and instructions, rattles clients so much that they let down their guard and go with the flow.

Deepening

Imagining a staircase as Judy did is but one of many deepening techniques. I may be the only hypnotist who uses the top of the staircase as the place of deepest trance. Most hypnotists say "deep" means "bottom," and they have their clients visualize themselves walking down to become hypnotized. When clients are in suggestible states, they will suspend disbelief and go along with the program. My clients are just fine climbing *up* to go deeper *down.*

Sometimes I use silence as a deepening technique. I suggest that the client enjoy the quiet experience of hypnosis, while silently going more deeply into the state.

Other times I help clients go deeper by increasing their sensory awareness. I encourage them to use all their senses while experiencing whatever they are visualizing in their mind. Or I suggest they follow my instructions for hallucinations to stimulate their imagination.

Hallucinations

Hypnosis can help you experience alterations in all your senses. When you see, feel, hear, taste, or smell something that is actually not there, you are hallucinating.

Hallucinating under hypnosis is appropriate and expected. To help you hallucinate, I stimulate your imagination by altering your senses.

Usually I select one or two from the following list; some folks benefit from going through all of the items:

- **Room temperature.** I suggest either a very hot or very cold room. Good subjects will begin to either perspire or shudder. (Remember our discussion on good subjects in Chapter 1? They're the ones who are easily hypnotizable.)

- **Eating.** I suggest you imagine yourself sucking on a lemon. This is another reason why, during the interview, I may inquire about food likes or dislikes and about allergies. Good subjects begin to pucker their mouths as soon as they get this suggestion. Are you doing that now while you're reading this?

- **Change in skin temperature.** I suggest that there's an ice cube sliding down your arm. You may respond by feeling changes in your skin. Is the hair on your arm bristling? Is your skin getting red? Do you want to wipe up some drips you're feeling?

- **Visualize beauty.** Imagine walking through a beautiful garden in springtime. Smell the fragrances, see the bright colors, feel the warmth of the sun. Does your heart rate slow down? Are you smiling?

- **Be in the audience.** Depending upon your lifestyle and special interests, I suggest that you're watching either a ballet, a World Series game, or your child's school play. Are you apprehensive? Excited? What's your facial expression? The idea is for you to become absorbed in the performance.

- **Music.** Some people are easily transported by music. If during our interview you mention that you're a Metallica fan, I'll give you a different suggestion from the one I'd give if you're a classical pianist. Most people are capable, while hypnotized, of creating music in their minds that sounds absolutely real to them.

Look into My Eyes

Even if you think it's irrelevant, you should inform your hypnotist of any physical problems, allergies, phobias, or sensitivities. If you turn out to have a great talent for hypnosis, some suggestions might inadvertently cause minor discomfort.

I once gave a client a deepening suggestion that involved basking in the sun while on a raft on a lake. Did I know that she was water phobic? Or that her father had drowned in a boating accident on a lake? No, I did not. She awakened out of her trance to inform me that the lake was not a good idea, and I immediately chose other images. During the interview, I asked if she enjoyed going to the country, and because she had a tan I assumed she liked sunning herself. I should have questioned her about the lake because I was planning to use it in her suggestion.

Reading the Script

This is the most important component of the entire hypnosis procedure. Here is where you'll accomplish what you came for. Now you will receive the suggestions.

The script you helped prepare will be read to you, perhaps several times, and then you may be asked to visualize everything that was said. During the interview I silently determine if you would respond best to commands or choices depending on what you say and how you say it. I figure out if you tend to react to group pressure or to your own internal values. My observations help me choose the best words for your script.

In the Hypnotist's Office

Debbie was an eleventh grader who came to me for help with test anxiety. She had terrible nervousness during the PSATs and was fearful of the next year's SATs. She described herself as rebellious at home, so I did not want her to experience hypnosis as coercive. I used the phrases "When you decide to ..." and "You will determine, on your own ..." because Debbie needed choices, not commands.

When I hypnotized Judy I told her that most people sitting in her seat stared at the drawer pull. I did not command her to stare at that spot; instead, I gave her an *indirect suggestion.*

Here are some other examples of indirect suggestions:

♦ *Many people want to read this book.*

♦ *Won't you be happy when you finish this book?*

♦ *Reading this book will change your life.*

♦ *I wonder when you'll buy this book.*

I'm not commanding you to run to the bookstore or immediately click on to Amazon. com, but you get the idea.

People who do best with indirect suggestions are those who are skeptical of hypnosis, or unwilling or unable to respond to direct suggestions. A direct suggestion is a simple goal-directed command. "Please close your eyes," is a direct suggestion. "Buy this book," is a direct suggestion.

Hypnoscript

Indirect suggestions are hints that prompt the listener to think about a specific situation and the subtly suggested course of action.

Charles, a 40-year-old plumbing contractor, was a client to whom I said, "Close your eyes," and got absolutely no response. His eyes remained open. It is possible to do hypnosis with open eyes, but it is a much better experience for the client if his eyes are shut. After one or two "Please close your eyes" statements, I knew I had to say something else to Charles. I tried the following indirect suggestions, interspersing each of them with comments about the weather and other unimportant observations:

- *I wonder if you'll be able to close your eyes.*

- *People who get good results with hypnosis usually close their eyes within a few minutes of sitting down.*

- *Sometimes it's enjoyable to close your eyes for a while right in the middle of the day.*

- *It will be interesting to notice when your eyelids will decide to shut.*

Similar to the indirect approach is the permissive approach. This is an Ericksonian technique that offers the client possible alternatives. Dr. Milton Erickson, the famous physician/hypnotist, used permissive, indirect suggestions. Examples of permissive suggestions include the following:

- *You may decide to allow yourself to close your eyes.*

- *You may give yourself permission to figure out how to enjoy closing your eyes.*

- *I don't know if your eyes will close now, or in 30 seconds, or in 2 minutes.*

- *I wonder if you know that when you close your eyes you'll have a more worthwhile experience.*

- *When the time is right, you'll probably want to close your eyes.*

Maybe you think it would be fun to be a hypnotist. It is, but as you can see, hypnotists need a lot of patience.

Familiar Words

Clients do best when they feel understood by the hypnotist. Part of that understanding is knowing the vocabulary and speaking style of the client.

Focus On This _____

During hypnosis a command is an authoritative or direct suggestion, and a choice is an indirect or permissive suggestion.

Bill, a police officer, came in for help a few weeks after a violent encounter. He was still upset and jumpy. When I wrote his script I was sure to incorporate the words "team" and "protect" and "partner" into his script. I knew he'd feel comfortable with words that reminded him of his daily work. Your hypnotist's choice of words is extremely important.

Forced Choice

Sometimes, parents who are at their wit's end with their child's eating habits present a choice: You may eat either the spaghetti or the ravioli; it's up to you. Presumably, the child feels in control; he or she has a choice. Actually, the parents feel victorious because either choice is good for them and for their child.

Giving a hypnosis client a forced choice can be a winning idea. One of my favorites is …

You may go into a very deep hypnotic state, or you may go into a moderately deep hypnotic state. The choice is yours.

Posthypnotic Suggestions

Most clients come to hypnosis to learn a new behavior. It is mandatory that the hypnotist help the new behavior become a reality, not only in the client's mind and during the hypnosis session, but for eternity. Well, maybe that's pushing it; if not eternity, at least the next few weeks, or months, or years.

Posthypnotic suggestions accomplish the carrying out of the new behavior. They are usually in the form of: When A occurs, you will do B. Here's a list of examples.

Hypnoscript

Posthypnotic sugges- **tions** are given to clients while they're in a trance. The purpose of the posthypnotic suggestions is to extend the suggestions to future behavior.

A	B
When you are hungry	You will eat vegetables
When you are driving	You will observe the speed limit
When you feel scared	You will do deep breathing
When you want a cigarette	You will drink water

I use the following props with some of my posthypnotic suggestions:

◆ **Bottled water.** I give bottles of water to certain clients when they leave the office. They're the ones who get the posthypnotic suggestion that, when they drink bottled water, their urge (to drink alcohol, use drugs, overeat, whatever it may be that they came to hypnosis for) will disappear. Never mind that Vinnie at the A&P checkout counter thinks I have a very thirsty family.

- **Red pen.** I buy shiny red pens in bulk, and use them as part of certain suggestions. Clients are told that if they see the pen, have it near them, or use it, it will reinforce everything that was said at our session. It's particularly useful as an anti-anxiety tool. These clients are told that the pen will calm them. An actor kept it in his pocket while he was on stage, and a mother once took it to the hospital to hold during her daughter's appendectomy.

Reawakening

After the induction, the script, and the posthypnotic suggestions, it is time to come out of the trance. Like Judy, most people don't want to come back to reality. The pleasantness of hypnosis is soothing and seductive, but, alas, all good things must come to an end.

You've probably seen an entertainment hypnotist who snaps his fingers and the person promptly comes out of the trance. I don't recommend that approach. I prefer to use words—no sound effects, no harsh commands. I announce that it's time to leave the scene in your mind; I encourage you to come back to regular; I instruct you to open your eyes whenever you feel ready to do so. Of course, I could tell you that when you hear me snap my fingers you'll immediately leave the hypnotic state and open your eyes. That would work, but I think it's too abrupt. I prefer gentleness. I prefer that my clients come back from hypnosis gradually, at their own pace. Of course, my method takes a while, and would be much too boring for a segment on *60 Minutes*.

You are now practically an expert on hypnosis, but there's even more to this fascinating endeavor. The next chapter is about special hypnotic phenomena.

The Least You Need to Know

- Hypnosis begins with some talk between you and the hypnotist.
- An induction gets you into hypnosis.
- While in hypnosis you receive suggestions.
- You are entitled to have input into those suggestions.
- Hypnosis is an enjoyable state, but you cannot stay in it forever.
- If done properly, your posthypnotic suggestions may last as long as you do.

Chapter 4

Strange Things Are Happening

In This Chapter

- Using hypnosis to see your future and examine your past
- Being here and there at the same time
- Healing from past traumas
- Overcoming unwanted habits
- Moving automatically

During hypnosis your mind can do interesting things. If you and your hypnotist decide to explore some tricks of the trade, you may find yourself acting like a baby, talking like an old man, imagining you're at a ball game, thinking it's yesterday or tomorrow, and wiggling your little finger instead of speaking. These events will happen only if you tell your hypnotist you want them to, and only if they will help you accomplish your goal. Yes, there is a purpose to each of these hypnotic phenomena. You can use any one of these techniques to become happier and healthier.

Think there's no way your pinkie can contribute to a new way of life? Read on and change your mind.

Seeing the Future

Marie's doctor wanted her to follow a low-salt diet. Marie was feeling fine. She said, "It's only my blood test that's abnormal, not me. Why do I need to torture myself?" I spoke to her physician, who assured me that if Marie did not change her eating habits she would soon be terribly ill.

Marie's doctor spoke to her, Marie's husband tried convincing her. Her children, her sister, her neighbors, and her co-workers all attempted to knock some sense into Marie—nothing worked. As usual, hypnosis was the last resort. It was actually a threat, as in, "If you don't shape up, we'll take you to a hypnotist."

Marie did not shape up; the family followed through with their threat, and now she's in my office saying:

Marie: *I thought a hypnotist couldn't make me do something I don't want to do, so why am I here?*

RT: *Good question. You are here because there is a possibility that you can encourage yourself to want to do this, to want to make this change in your life, to want to eat in this new way.*

Marie: *I doubt it. If I wanted to, I would have already. I'm a strong person, you know; if I want to do something, I do it.*

RT: *Have you ever changed your mind about something? Sometimes people get new ideas and new viewpoints. Sometimes these new ideas and new viewpoints begin during hypnosis.*

Focus On This

Health professionals agree that hypnotists should be consulted earlier in the health chain, but no one has figured out a way to make hypnosis less scary and more accessible. Any ideas? Tell your doctor.

Look into My Eyes

Insist that your hypnotist take the time to learn about you and your lifestyle. Even if the hypnotic induction is excellent, a rushed session may not be useful. The more the hypnotist knows about your daily life, the more relevant the script will be.

We talked, and I learned that Marie is a wonderful cook and an accomplished baker. She likes to dance, and is in a weekly tennis game. She wasn't kidding when she said she feels fine. She has no sign of the impending kidney disease evident from her blood tests, blood tests that were repeated several times with the thought that there might be a lab error. No error—there is a problem.

Marie has a married daughter and a son who is engaged to be married. She didn't like her son-in-law at first, but now is very fond of him. I asked how she got herself to change her mind, and she said she saw that he tried hard to please her daughter, and he agreed to change his hairstyle (from ponytail to short) just to please Marie. Also, he really appreciates Marie's Sunday cooking.

Marie appears to be comfortable now. She no longer has her arms crossed in front of her chest, and she agrees to give "this crazy thing a chance."

To my delight, Marie has a great talent for hypnosis, and in a few minutes is deeply involved in a scene in her mind. And that is when I introduce the idea of seeing the future, and we begin the process known as *age progression*.

Hypnoscript

Age progression is the hypnotically induced process of seeing yourself in the future with a current behavior, and then with a new behavior.

RT: *You are such a good visualizer that I wonder if you can see yourself and your husband playing doubles with your daughter and her husband. Please nod when you do. (Marie nods.) Good, now watch what good moves you make. Enjoy watching yourself play a great game. Let me know when you stop playing.*

Marie's eyes are shut and seem to be rapidly moving, probably following the ball. She nods, even though, this time, I had not specified how she should communicate to me.

RT: *Now, I would like you to see yourself on the tennis court in a couple of years. Maybe your daughter and son-in-law have a baby in a stroller on the side of the court. Watch yourself playing, and, oh, just remember that your doctor said you may have some trouble in a couple of years. Nod, please, when you're finished watching the game.*

Marie does not nod. Instead, after one or two minutes, tears stream down her cheeks.

RT: *I see that you're unhappy. Before we talk about your unhappiness please leave the tennis court for a moment, and use your good imagination to see yourself dancing at your son's wedding a year and a half from now. Listen to the music, see all the guests, see the bride and groom, and now see yourself and your husband dancing. And, please remember that your doctor said you might be in for some trouble at about that time. Enjoy the wedding, and when you finish watching yourself dancing, please nod.*

 Focus On This

Some people get teary eyed from the relaxation that is part of the hypnotic process. Tears from visualizing something sad always come from both eyes and are usually a steady stream. Tears from relaxation of tear ducts are sparse and may be from only one eye.

Marie is crying now; her eyes are shut; she has a strained look on her face. I talk to her about feeling sad, and ask if she's sad because she sees herself ill and somewhat incapacitated. She nods. I ask if she would like to change the future. She nods, and I proceed:

RT: *You have imagined your life in the future, with your current eating habits. Now, let us say that you just happen to decide to eliminate salt from your food. Let us say that you begin this new food habit sometime soon, perhaps in a few days, or one day next week. Now, knowing that you'll soon start eating differently, please visualize your daughter and son-in-law with their new baby. Look how happy they are. They are walking toward you and your husband; you're waiting for them on the tennis court. Please watch how they attend to the baby, who is sleeping, and then come onto the court to greet you and then play tennis with you. Please watch yourself playing. Remember, you started a new food habit more than a year before this tennis match. Enjoy your game. Please nod when you are finished.*

Marie's eyes dart around, she smiles, she's having a good time. No evidence of tears. After about three minutes, she nods. (I told you hypnotists need patience.)

RT: *Now let's go to your son's wedding and get out on the dance floor. Listen to the music and watch yourself go. You are a terrific dancer. It was a good idea that you started that new food habit a couple of years ago. You're having a wonderful time. How youthful you look, how vigorously you're dancing. Good for you. Let me know when this dance is over, please.*

Marie nods. She is smiling, and she is still deeply hypnotized. Now I continue with the idea of seeing the future, and I suggest:

RT: *Please visualize yourself 10 years from now. See yourself very clearly on a TV screen in your mind. Now, split the screen in half. On the other side, please see yourself as you are now. The older you is looking at the present you, you as you are right now. If you listen carefully, you will hear the older you speaking to the current you. I think she may be thanking you.*

Again, I must be patient. Two or three minutes pass. When Marie nods (without my having told her to), I ask if her older self was appreciative of her current self. She nods again, and I suggest that she must be very proud of herself. She smiles. I speak to her about her son-in-law and how she likes him now, and then, slowly we begin to disengage from hypnosis. In 10 minutes Marie is awake and her age progression is finished.

Focus On This

Dr. Michael Yapko, clinical psychologist and authority on hypnosis, says that the beauty of age progression is that "It encourages hindsight while it is still foresight."

Marie's husband is in the waiting room, and when she joins him, he asks her how it went. I overhear her answer: "It was great, but the only thing is, I have to wait until Saturday to begin the no-salt diet."

I did not command Marie to begin her new food program on a particular day. She has resisted coercion in the past, so I hinted that she would soon find the right time to begin. I never mentioned Saturday, but she must have planned it as her start date while hypnotized.

You'll benefit from age progression because it gives you positive expectations and optimism about your accomplishments. Also, it's fun to see yourself at future events and family celebrations.

Examining the Past

Hypnosis can help you go back in time. Why would you want to? There are two main reasons:

- ◆ To undo a trauma
- ◆ To remember forgotten feelings

This is all accomplished through the process of *age regression*. In age regression, the hypnotist guides you back in time and helps you picture events in your past. There are hypnotists who will guide you way back to a time before you were born. (Read about hypnotists who believe in past-life regression in Chapter 26.) I don't do that. I'm content that my clients go back to childhood—going back to the womb, or to colonial times, is not necessary.

Hypnoscript

When a hypnotized client is instructed to go back in time and visualize and actively experience a past time period, that is **age regression**.

You probably have done age regression on yourself. Have you ever …

- ◆ Looked into a box of old photos and immersed yourself in memories?
- ◆ Heard songs from years back, and suddenly felt younger and more energetic?
- ◆ Smelled an aroma from years ago—perhaps Aunt Clara's perfume, or your mother's vegetable soup, or the smell of the attic—and then thought about childhood?
- ◆ Tasted a food that transported you back to a particular time and place?

When your senses are stimulated it is easier to remember past experiences.

Undoing Trauma

Age regression can take you back to your past, to a terrible, traumatic event, and help you finally get over it.

Before you begin visualizing the event, you and the hypnotist decide how you will be protected. Maybe …

- You will be an observer and not a participant.
- You will have a weapon with you.
- You will say something you were not able to say at the time.
- You will take a certain course of action that will change the outcome of the event.

When you're feeling safe and secure, your hypnotist will hypnotize you and then you'll prepare for going back in time by taking the following steps:

1. Visualizing yourself a month ago, then a year ago, and finally, right before the time of the traumatic event.

2. Reminding yourself of how safe you are, sitting in a cozy office with a protective hypnotist.

3. Using the agreed-upon technique to help you visualize the trauma.

4. Talking to your hypnotist about the new way that you're seeing the traumatic situation. You may accomplish this both in and out of a trance.

Age regression is useful in hypnotherapy when the therapist wants you to work through the feelings and memories you have of a traumatic occurrence. During age regression you relive a part of your past, not as a memory, but as if you were there again, in the original context.

Remember our old friend, reframing? Age regression provides an opportunity to reframe.

Phil came to my office very upset. He cannot forget the day, following his divorce some years ago, that he moved out of the family home. His son was very angry and agitated, and Phil has since been unable to forgive himself for the divorce and the rupture of the family. He and his ex-wife are both remarried, and the boy seems to be doing fine. But Phil is awakened at night by the anguish of reliving that departure scene in his dreams.

When he revisits that scene during age regression, I tell him that his son's response is normal and appropriate. I reframe the agitation and anger by saying that the boy's strong feelings demonstrate the strong attachment feelings he has for his dad. Phil accepts that suggestion, awakens relieved, and calls to thank me some weeks later. He reports that his sleep has returned and his son has thanked him for "being easier to hang out with, lately."

Remembering Forgotten Feelings

During age regression you can access the feelings you had at an earlier time. Sylvia was suffering from serious depression and was feeling hopeless now that her medication had stopped working. She did not want to try a new antidepressant, saying, "What's the use? I never was content, I never will be."

During age regression Sylvia was able to recall just how content she had been some years back. She gave herself ample proof that she's capable of joyful moments and depression-free days. She relived all the feelings of a particularly happy weekend. She remembered everything, all details. Sylvia's intense recall while hypnotized is called *hypermnesia.*

Sometimes clients want to recall a very early memory. I help them do that by asking them, when they're in a trance, to recall …

- Their birthday parties, starting at an older age and working down.

- The first day of school of each school year.

- Significant family events: births, deaths, moves to new neighborhoods.

Hypnoscript

The phenomenon of rekindling memories of an event from long ago and vividly remembering details while under hypnosis is called **hypermnesia**.

In the Hypnotist's Office

Some hypnotists report that when they age regress adult clients who were born in another country, or come from families that did not speak English at home when they were children, the clients will begin to speak in their original family language, not English. My client Tim wanted to recall several childhood events and during hypnosis he was age regressed and clearly visualized himself seated at the kitchen table in the family home in Hungary. When I asked who was sitting with him he answered—in Hungarian! I told him that when he awakened he'd remember everything he said in Hungarian and translate it for me. He did.

Sometimes adult clients will regress to childhood, and if they're very good subjects, will be completely immersed in their earlier lives.

Joan was such a client. She wanted to explore the circumstances of her dad's death in a car crash. She was six years old when it happened. Joan decided beforehand that she would speak during her trance; she had particular questions that she wanted me to ask her when she was regressed. I began by establishing her whereabouts:

RT: *What is your name?*

J: *Joanie Koff.* (She utters her childhood nickname and her maiden name in a soft, babyish voice.)

RT: *Where are you now?*

J: *In Granny's house.*

RT: *Why are you there?*

J: *I don't know. Mamma had to go somewhere. The police called our house and Mamma brought me right over here. Mamma was crying, and now I want to cry, too.*

RT: *It is permitted.*

J: (Starts to weep.) *Are you sure it's okay?*

Joan spoke and behaved as if she were six years old the entire time she was in a trance. Her posture changed, her voice changed, her vocabulary changed. When she awakened, she promptly resumed her adult voice and demeanor.

Joan was able to clarify the events of that fateful day, so many decades ago, and recall that her grandmother forbade her to cry. In her adult life Joan has had difficulty crying and to her dismay she gets very angry at her children when they cry. She reported to me, several months after her age regression, that her attitude about tears was now remarkably different.

During an age regression to a time of trauma, I sometimes use the following indirect suggestions:

◆ *You might decide it's no longer necessary to think about this memory.*

◆ *You might decide to talk about this memory one more time and then be finished with it.*

◆ *Maybe tomorrow, maybe next week, you'll put this incident behind you.*

There is no coercion to quickly get over the trauma. The implicit assumption is that when the time is right it will be a part of the past that is rarely, if ever, revisited.

Crossing the Affect Bridge

Do you ever feel uneasy or uncomfortable, and you can't figure out why? Do you have a persistent feeling of fear or dread that doesn't go away? Sometimes age regression can help.

The affect, or feeling, you have now might have started a long time ago. In hypnosis, you may be able to recall the first time you had this feeling. When you connect the feeling you have now to the incident that provoked it for the first time, that connection, or bridge, is called an *affect bridge*. The affect bridge is a useful tool in hypnotherapy. It was during an age regression exercise that Toni realized that her aversion to ketchup had started when she was at summer camp and some bunkmates had put ketchup on her bed sheets as a joke.

Toni was having hypnosis to remember that summer more clearly. It was the summer her sister was born, but the ketchup incident had popped right up; she had not thought of it since the day it had happened. She left my office and went straight to McDonald's for a burger with lots of ketchup.

Hypnoscript

Hypnotherapists use an **affect bridge** to make a conscious connection between a long-ago circumstance that created a feeling in you, and that persistent feeling today.

Here and There

Do you sometimes get hypnotized while driving? You know, that feeling of not paying attention consciously, but still arriving at your destination? It's as if you're having two simultaneous experiences and are aware of one, but not the other. At the same time, you're "here," and you're "there."

When certain aspects of thoughts or behavior operate independently and don't seem related to the other aspects of your personality, you have *dissociated*.

Geena Davis, the actress, interviewed Helen Hunt, the actress, about winning an Oscar. Davis asked Hunt, "Did you have the same experience I did, that when they called your name you went, like, out of body?"

Geena Davis was thrilled, and part of her mind was so absorbed in the excitement of the moment that she suspended her usual awareness of the surrounding world. Geena Davis dissociated.

Hypnoscript

Dissociating is the process of separating the conscious part of your mind from the unconscious part. It occurs when you pay attention to one aspect of what you are experiencing and ignore the rest of the experience.

Dissociation helps you reach your goals in hypnosis. Some hypnotists believe that when you're dissociated you have a little observer inside you, called the _hidden observer_, that is always aware of what's going on. That hidden observer registers information, processes it, and stores it in your brain—without your knowing a thing about it.

Hallucinations

You know all about the ways in which a hypnotist can deepen your hypnotic induction by stimulating your senses. Remember smelling flowers, sucking a lemon, hearing music? All those suggestions can enhance your hypnotic experience.

I can also use hallucinations to give clients a very deep, rich, spiritual experience.

When Mark came to my office to stop smoking, he told me that his father had died of lung cancer, and on his death bed had begged Mark, his only child, to give up the habit.

Mark went into a trance, and I did my usual stop-smoking script (see Chapter 10). But then I added an hallucination. I asked Mark to visualize his father coming back to life to deliver a message to his beloved son. I suggested that he listen carefully, and hear very meaningful words. I suggested that he look around in his mind's eye, because you never know where a deceased relative will appear.

Mark was profoundly shaken. It was many minutes before he gave me our prearranged response, a thumb's up, to let me know his dad had left. When Mark awakened, he said, "Pop said it like it is. He told me he'll beat my brains in if I don't stop today. And then Pop said he loved me; he held me, and he slowly disappeared."

The hallucinations that work best for my clients are seeing and hearing …

- A deceased relative.

- A religious figure.

- A rock star or famous actor (particularly good for teens).

- A baseball player (particularly good for kids).

- A former teacher.

- A former coach.

Impressive people make good impressions on the hypnotized mind.

It's What Time?

In real life, outside of hypnosis, when you're with someone you love, time flies; when you're on a blind date with Aunt Margaret's next-door neighbor who just got divorced, time drags.

During hypnosis your sense of time becomes distorted without any help from the hypnotist. Just the process of closing your eyes and concentrating on your own thoughts makes it difficult for you to guess how much time has passed. If you receive suggestions about time slowing down or speeding up, you surely will experience an altered time clock.

Brian is an actor who performs regularly on Broadway. This season he's in a musical where he sings and dances six evenings and three afternoons a week. Wednesday matinee gets to him, and by Wednesday evening he's exhausted, and often feels he cannot go on. I checked with his doctor, who assured me that Brian's health was excellent, before I began hypnosis. I wanted to know that the fatigue was normal (Who wouldn't be fatigued working with that schedule?) and not because of an underlying health problem.

Brian does very well with time distortion. He comes to my office on Wednesdays, after the matinee. I give him the hypnotic suggestion that every minute he spends in hypnosis will replenish his body as if it is one hour of sleep. He stays hypnotized for eight minutes, and awakens refreshed and ready to perform.

Look into My Eyes

One way most people know they have truly been "under" is that when they leave their hypnotist's office, they have no clue what time it is. Be sure to wear a watch to your appointment.

Freeze!

When I was growing up, we played a game in our neighborhood where all us kids would run around, and then someone would say, "Freeze!" and we would have to pretend to be statues.

The first to move was out of the game, and we would then play another round, until there was only one person left—the winner.

Hypnotized people would do well playing statue. When most people enter hypnosis, all their bodily functions slow down. By the time they're well into their session, they are so slowed down that they may drool, because it's just too much effort to swallow their saliva. They may also find it too difficult to think of moving, even one inch.

At the time they enter hypnosis, some people may happen to have an arm or leg, or maybe their head, in an unusual position. And because hypnotized people tend not to move when they're under, these are the folks who awaken saying, "Boy, do I have a stiff neck. I was uncomfortable all through that session." When I ask why they didn't adjust their position, they look at me strangely. Movement is simply not an option, because during the trance they are cataleptic. *Catalepsy,* another hypnotic phenomenon, makes voluntary movement impossible.

Hypnoscript

Catalepsy is the inhibition of all voluntary movement because of intense focus on an alternative reality. The body seems stiff and rigid.

Suggestions for catalepsy are good for skeptical clients because it gives them proof that they really did experience hypnosis. When they awaken they note their contorted position, or comment on the fact that they could not swallow. Suggestions for catalepsy deepen the hypnotic state.

Finger Talking

How can your pinkie, or any other finger, help you in hypnosis? Your finger can do your talking when you are too deeply hypnotized to want to be bothered with words.

Sometimes, without any help from you, your body reacts to words you hear or things you see. Sometimes your body reacts in ways you wish it would not, ways beyond your conscious control. Have you ever blushed? Have you ever been physically attracted to someone? Those automatic bodily reactions are called ideodynamic responses. During hypnosis, hypnotists are interested in a particular type of ideodynamic response, called an *ideomotor response.* Ideomotor movements are subtle muscle movements that occur when a person is thinking or visualizing.

I encourage my clients to use ideomotor signals in trance. They help me to know what's going on, and assure me that the patient is listening to me. We often agree ahead of time that we'll use a finger signal:

- Raising the index finger means "yes."

- Raising the pinkie means "no."

- A thumbs-up sign means "yes." (Youngsters usually prefer this.)

Hypnoscript

An **ideomotor response** is a subtle muscle movement that you do not control. It simply happens automatically, in response to a thought or a feeling.

The ideomotor response is an automatic response to an internal experience. It's the body's answer to a thought or an idea. One client will automatically nod her head (remember Marie?), another may blink his eyes, and still others may alter their breathing rates. The response is so slow and studied that it seems mechanical.

No Feelings

During hypnosis you can believe that you have no pain in a particular body part; that is called analgesia. Or you can be hypnotized to believe that you have no feelings or sensations anywhere in your body; that is called anesthesia. People who are extremely hypnotizable are capable of having surgery with hypnosis as their only anesthetic.

Chapter 23 covers the many techniques for pain control available through hypnosis. For now, though, just remember that hypnosis gives you the opportunity to change your feelings in your body so that you have more self-control. Hypnosis permits you to stop being a victim of forces you cannot control.

The Least You Need to Know

- Age progression under hypnosis can help you change behavior.

- Age regression can help you get over a trauma, even if it was a long time ago.

- If you don't wish to speak while in a trance, you can communicate nonverbally with your hypnotist.

- Hypnosis helps you deal with forces you cannot control.

Part

You're On Your Own

Welcome to Part 2, where we'll peek in at a few professional hypnotists and see how they use hypnosis in their personal lives.

Also in this Part you will learn some amazing feats—how to hypnotize yourself just like a pro, and how to impress your friends with your new knowledge about hypnosis.

Chapter 5

The Value of Self-Hypnosis

In This Chapter

- What you can expect from self-hypnosis
- Amaze your friends
- Your mind controls your muscles
- Everyday uses of self-hypnosis

Hypnosis is fun and it is useful. You can go to a hypnotist or you can do it yourself. Do-it-yourself hypnosis is a skill that can be learned, and you can learn it!

You'll be in good company when you learn self-hypnosis. Many successful people say that hypnotizing themselves helped get them where they are.

It's Not Magic

Are you fascinated by the idea of self-hypnosis? Lots of folks are intrigued by the idea of putting themselves into a magical trance. They believe that when they're in that trance they'll be able to accomplish feats of wonder. They'll cure their depression, overcome their learning disability, lose all excess weight, and easily tolerate their most annoying relatives—maybe they'll even grow a few inches!

The Truth About Hypnotizing Yourself

Sorry, guys. Those ideas about hypnosis are not valid. Self-hypnosis can work and it can work well. But, it is not magic. And, learning how to hypnotize yourself is hard work. Self-hypnosis is a skill that requires instruction and then practice and more practice.

After you know how to put yourself into a hypnotic state, though, you have that skill for life. You will always be able to use it whenever you need it, wherever you need it. Self-hypnosis is worth learning.

Some Bad News

The downside to learning how to hypnotize yourself is that it is a time-consuming endeavor. Your family and friends may resent the time it takes for you to practice; and if there are young children in your family, they may resent having to be quiet while you are learning your technique.

> **Look into My Eyes**
>
> Hypnosis is not a game. It's a serious technique. Never hypnotize your friends, your family, or your next-door neighbors. Find a hypnotist for them to go to; don't put them into a hypnotic trance yourself.

The other negative of learning hypnosis is that other people may want you to hypnotize them. Please do not even consider that as a possibility. Unless you are a mental-health professional and you are also a graduate of a hypnosis program, you are not equipped to hypnotize anyone but yourself.

Hypnotizing Your Friends

If your friends insist upon a demonstration of your new hypnosis ability, here is a presentation that you can do to prove that you know hypnosis. It's not true hypnosis, but it's close enough. It does use hypnotic principles and it is fascinating. They'll think you are amazing.

The following explains how to hypnotize your friends.

Hands Up

Arrange your group so they are all facing you. Ask them to put their arms out in front of them at shoulder level. Their palms should be facing down, their arms straight.

Request that they close their eyes. Explain that this will take less than one minute.

In a soothing, but authoritative voice, say the following:

Your right hand is feeling very heavy.

Imagine that there is a heavy book being placed upon your right hand.

Now visualize another book on top of that book. And then a third book.

Your right hand and arm are heavy, heavy, heavy.

The heavy books are pushing down your arm.

Feel the heaviness.

Feel your arm moving lower and lower.

Simultaneously, your left hand is slowly drifting upward.

Your left hand is being pushed up—higher and higher

Your whole arm is rising.

There is a force under your left palm that is pushing it up.

Your left arm feels so light and airy. It is going higher and higher.

Your left arm is up; your right arm is down.

Keeping your arms and hands in exactly the position they are in right now

Please open your eyes.

Note the position of your arms.

Are they exactly as they were before you closed your eyes and began this exercise?

Are they slightly—a couple of inches—apart?

Are they very much apart?

(At this time, draw attention to those members of the audience who have one arm raised very high and one arm pretty low down.)

Good. Shake out your arms and let's talk.

Speak to Your Fans

This is the time to explain to your incredulous audience that …

- ◆ The average person, with average hypnosis ability, will notice a slight, minute difference between the levels of each outstretched arm.

In the Hypnotist's Office

Whenever clients come to my office to be hypnotized I explain that although I help them reach a trance state and I choose the words to say to them, they are really doing all the work. I simply provide the environment in which they can succeed. Without their willingness there would be no hypnosis. So all hypnosis is really self-hypnosis.

Hypnoscript

When a person attempts to move a pendulum that's in his hand by focusing on the idea of movement but keeping his hand and arm perfectly still, we say that he is enacting **Chevreul's Pendulum.**

- The very talented person who is born with extraordinary hypnosis ability will have his or her right arm very low and left arm very high.

- Those who are very talented have just discovered an inborn gift that they can use to make their lives richer.

Good for you. You've demonstrated your ability as a hypnotist and you've given your friends the opportunity to determine if they are particularly talented at hypnosis. Best of all, your friends have had the chance to experience a light hypnotic feeling for a few seconds.

Congratulations. With family and friends out of the way, we can get on to our business of learning self-hypnosis.

What? They want more? They say they don't believe in hypnosis. They say they don't know if the mind can really control the body.

Well, here's an astonishing demonstration you can show your friends that will prove there is a connection be-tween mind and body. It will prove that you can use hypnosis to control your actions. The name of this demonstration is *Chevreul's Pendulum*.

Teeny, Tiny Movements

First, this amazing fact: When you think about a movement, your thought can create a tendency for your muscles to perform that movement. Even though you have not directed your muscles to move they will move anyway, ever so slightly, because of your thoughts.

All you need to do is concentrate. Extreme concentration is not necessarily true hypnosis, but it is all that is necessary to perform this exercise. Thinking about an image or a movement or a task creates a picture in your brain. It is that picture that propels your muscles to practice that movement within your brain. Although you've not instructed your muscle to really move, often a slight motion occurs anyway. This movement is the ideomotor action discussed in Chapter 4.

Before you entertain your audience and have them try Chevreul's Pendulum, it's a good idea for you to do it yourself. Let's begin. Sit in front of your desk or table and we'll get started. Just follow these steps:

1. Take a piece of thick sewing thread or thin string and tie a small weight to one end. Most people use a button or a paper clip because they're easy to attach. The string should be about a foot long. You've just made your pendulum.

Focus On This _____

Michel-Eugene Chevreul was born in France in 1786 and lived until the age of 103! He was an accomplished chemist and physicist, and also was an expert in the analysis of color and thus became an influential person in the art world, too.

2. Sit with one hand in your lap. The other arm is upright with your elbow on the surface in front of you. Your palm is parallel to the surface.

3. Allow your wrist to bend and pick up your pendulum by grasping the string between the fingertips of your thumb and index finger. The weight is at the bottom of the string barely touching the tabletop.

   Good, you've created a fine pendulum.

4. Now, lift your wrist a bit so the pendulum is not touching anything. You may need to touch it with your other hand to stop it from moving.

5. Keep your hand still.

6. Without moving any muscles in your arm, hand, or shoulder, think about the pendulum circling to the right. Think, think, think.

7. Look at your pendulum and imagine that it is going around and around in small circular motions.

8. Concentrate.

   What do you see?

   It is circling to the right!

9. Touch to stop it and then imagine it is circling to the left. Focus on it circling to the left. Concentrate.

   Amazing, isn't it?

10. Now, think of imaginary lines going from right to left and from top to bottom. Think of making that pendulum swing from right to left. Concentrate and focus and it will obey you.

You have just completed Chevreul's Pendulum, a famous and incredible demonstration of the power of thinking.

Strong Thoughts

So what is this all about? Apparently, the muscles in your hand and in your arm have moved because of your thoughts, your concentration, and your focus.

Focus On This

In the Middle Ages, pregnant moms foretold the sex of their babies by lying on their backs and holding a string, with a ring tied to it, over their bellies. If the string circled in one direction it was predictive of a girl baby, the other direction, a boy. Could this have been the forerunner of Chevreul's phenomenon? Maybe.

Invite your skeptical friends to engage in this exercise. When it is time for the pendulum to move, please use a strong voice as you command it to flow in a particular direction. You may wish to tell them that imaginary forces are pulling the string. Encourage them to visualize those forces at work. They will forever understand that mind and body are linked.

Michel-Eugene Chevreul was the first scientist to realize that mental processes, and not a supernatural force, cause the pendulum's movement. Thus, we call this demonstration Chevreul's Pendulum.

Experts Speak

Self-hypnosis, sometimes called *autohypnosis*, is available 24/7. It's a skill that is always with you. It permits you to experience certain ideas and images as if they are real. It permits you to benefit from those ideas and images.

After you know how to hypnotize yourself, you'll find yourself using it all the time. Here are some reasons why you might want to hypnotize yourself today. You might want to …

♦ Stop snoring at night.

♦ Awaken in a good and cheerful mood every morning.

♦ Overcome your fear of going on a cruise.

♦ Have a better memory for people's names when you are on that cruise.

Hypnoscript

When you do hypnosis without a hypnotist, it is self-hypnosis, or it may be termed **autohypnosis**.

♦ Pay your bills on time.

♦ Limit your shopping so you won't have so many bills.

You might prefer to keep your particular reason for hypnotizing yourself private. That's okay.

Docs Do It

Q: How do professional hypnotists make changes in their lives?

A: They use self-hypnosis.

Read about these interesting uses of self-hypnosis by folks who spend most of their days hypnotizing others.

Naomi Sarna

New York City hypnotherapist Naomi Sarna has several interesting approaches to self-hypnosis. Here are three of them:

- **Curling up.** Sarna uses a counting technique to hypnotize herself. When she says numbers aloud, she visualizes those numbers and then sees herself curled up within them. "I see myself nestling comfortably in the curve of a 5 or a 6 or a 3," says Sarna.

- **Whizzing by.** Sarna goes to many meetings and lectures that are boring. She does not like to sit through dull talks, so she's developed a strategy. Sarna now uses the technique of time progression when she is at a boring lecture. "When I want time to pass quickly, I hypnotize myself and say, 'Time is racing by. Every minute seems like one second.' I can tolerate any speaker for a few seconds."

- **Hello, operator.** Sarna has a unique way of hypnotizing herself when she's out in public. She doesn't want to draw attention to herself. She doesn't want people to think she's talking to herself. But, she does want to use words to put herself into a trance and to give herself suggestions. What to do? She whips out her cell phone and pretends she's talking to someone. Within a couple of minutes she's deeply hypnotized and no one is the wiser.

Karen Olness

"If health-care professionals are to ask patients to try self-regulation techniques, then they too must experience them firsthand," says Dr. Olness. And she apparently meant *firsthand* literally, for she used self-hypnosis as her only anesthesia during hand surgery. Dr. Olness had a 45-minute procedure done to stitch the ligament in her thumb after a skiing accident. The suggestions she gave herself were sufficient for successful pain control.

Marc Oster

Dr. Oster talks about his recent root canal. "I had the whole two-hour procedure done in one sitting. In order to easily tolerate that and to have a more peaceful recovery, since I'd be seeing patients afterward, I used self-hypnosis. The dentist noticed I was contentedly sitting there feeling nothing. He was puzzled and asked, 'Mr. Oster, are you sleeping through a root canal?' When I left his office and headed for work, it was as if nothing had been done that morning. I had no discomfort, no headache, and no pain."

Chris Haskins

Chris Haskins is an operating room nurse in a plastic surgery practice. When he needed to have plastic surgery on his upper and lower eyelids, he was concerned because he had seen many complications due to anesthesia. So he embarked upon a course of hypnotherapy and became proficient at self-hypnosis, too.

Chris says, "I was intrigued with the idea of having awareness during surgery, not needing chemical anesthesia and narcotics, and maintaining some control over my own surgery."

Listen to his description of the surgery:

> Throughout the procedure I was aware of my surroundings. Music that I chose ahead of time was playing. The sensation of pain was absent. I felt no pain or anxiety as I listened to the usual OR table manners while equipment is requested and passed. When the surgery was completed, I was told to return to full consciousness. I then sat up, hopped down, and walked into the lounge where I pranced around in triumph. Half an hour later I had dinner with a colleague and then drove myself home.

> Due to the posthypnotic suggestions given prior to surgery, I had no post-op discomfort and little swelling. On postoperative day number three I returned to work, assisting in a full day of surgeries.

You can use self-hypnosis, too. You don't have to be a professional hypnotist to become really good at it. In fact, some professional hypnotists are excellent at hypnotizing their clients and not so good at hypnotizing themselves.

Paul Gustafson

Hypnotist Paul Gustafson considers himself a tour guide. He says that the wonder and mystery of every hypnosis session originates within the client and it is the hypnotist who points the client in the appropriate direction. It is always up to the client to decide if he or she wants to go in that direction or not. If clients decide to go there, it is their choice to decide what they want to accomplish when they arrive. Thus, according to Gustafson, all hypnosis is self-hypnosis.

If you were taking a tour of yourself—your thoughts, your ideas, your values, or your personality—where would you stop along the way? Which aspects of yourself might you want to develop? Which parts of yourself would you like to get rid of?

During the last few months I've asked my colleagues to tell me every time they've practiced self-hypnosis. I've kept a record of the reasons why they hypnotized themselves so that you could see the diverse uses of self-hypnosis.

Look into My Eyes

CAUTION

Remember, it's always up to you to decide about going ahead to the next level of hypnosis. If you are not ready to explore a new part of yourself, your hypnotist should respect your decision. A slower pace is often the correct pace.

Here is that list:

- To eat slower, chew my food more slowly.
- To have a better memory for the cards played during my weekly bridge game.
- To stop being squeamish about putting in contact lenses.
- To feel brave when I make the speech at my daughter's wedding.
- To stay calm at the airport next week.
- To remember to take my vitamins every morning.
- To stop biting my nails.
- To hang up my keys on the key nail as soon as I walk into my apartment.
- To call my father every Sunday and be nice to him.

What could you accomplish with self-hypnosis? What would you like to do differently in your life? What habit needs to be eliminated? Or what new habit would you like to develop? You can hypnotize yourself to get you where you want to go.

Interview Yourself

You'll recall from Chapter 3 that a full hypnosis session consists of an interview, an induction, and then suggestions. The induction and the script writing, which includes suggestions, will be taken care of in the next two chapters. What about the interview?

In self-hypnosis there is no hypnotist to interview you. You must become your own interviewer. Before you learn to induce hypnosis and put yourself into the trance state, it is necessary to take some time for reflection.

Spend some time figuring out what you want to change and why you want to change it. Do a bit of self-examination to be certain that you are attempting to accomplish something that is in the realm of the possible. Remember, you can change only yourself. You cannot change another person. You cannot make another person feel a certain way about you. You cannot make another person behave a certain way with you. Self-hypnosis is about you, not someone else.

And now read on and we will begin our self-hypnosis lessons.

Focus On This _____

When you plan your self-hypnosis session, think about including something that will make you happy. Enthusiasm and optimism will help you to live a healthy, long, fruitful life.

The Least You Need to Know

- ◆ Self-hypnosis helps you accomplish a realistic goal.
- ◆ Many people use self-hypnosis to improve their lives.
- ◆ With practice you will learn how to easily hypnotize yourself.

Chapter 6

Do-It-Yourself Inductions

In This Chapter

- Why should you hypnotize yourself?
- Choosing your induction
- Going deeper into trance
- Choose your hypnosis adventure

Imagine having the ability to feel good whenever you want to. Imagine being able to calm your nerves when everyone around you is uptight and freaking out. You can easily learn self-hypnosis, and you'll always be able to use your mind to control your body.

This chapter explains how to put yourself into a hypnotic trance and then go deeper and deeper into that altered state of consciousness where you'll be extremely receptive to suggestions—suggestions that you'll give to yourself.

Why Do It Yourself?

I think going to a hypnotist is a terrific idea. I also like the idea of using hypnotic tapes. But, sometimes *self-hypnosis* is the way to go. It's useful to know the skill of self-hypnosis because …

- You never know when you'll need to calm yourself instantly.

- You might want to reinforce a hypnotic session that you've already had with a hypnotist (that session in the hypnotist's office is called *hetero-hypnosis*, as opposed to self-hypnosis).

- You may live in an area where there are no hypnotists.

- You might want to save your money.

- You might need just a little boost in self-confidence before a new experience.

- It's fun to add a new ability to the repertoire of things you can do.

Hypnoscript

When you are your own hypnotist, the process is called **self-hypnosis**. When you are hypnotized by another person, the process is called **hetero-hypnosis**.

Please add your own reasons to this list.

Calm in a Jiffy

When her daughter accidentally cut herself with a kitchen knife, Julie thought she might faint. She looked at the blood, looked at her daughter, and knew she had to do something but couldn't quickly figure out what. Later that week she told me, "I did that 10-second hypnotic induction you taught me, commanded myself to focus and think, and then returned to regular. I opened my eyes in less than 15 seconds, and immediately got a towel to apply direct pressure, called the paramedics, comforted my daughter, and did everything right. If I hadn't known how to calm myself, I would've wasted time because I was in a fog at first, practically paralyzed."

Think of the times in your life when knowing how to focus yourself in the midst of a crisis would have been useful. Learn self-hypnosis for those unpredictable situations where keeping your cool is necessary, but not easy.

Enhance the Session You Had

Virginia was very successful in using hypnosis to stick to her food program. She was eating well and maintaining her new weight. But, she called for appointments once each month or so, prior to visiting her grandmother. Grandma cooked up a storm and was insulted if any food was left on the plate after the multicourse meal.

Virginia handled all other food predicaments well, including catered affairs, business lunches, and ice cream-in-the-freezer situations. But, Grandma's meals were not simply food issues. Virginia realized that she was brought up to be respectful and obedient and was saying to herself, "I should do what this loving old lady wants me to do, or she'll be insulted. Grandma will think I don't love and appreciate her if I don't eat the food she worked so hard to prepare."

We worked out a useful script so it wouldn't be necessary for Virginia to show up at my office for a session before each Grandma visit. Instead, Virginia learned self-hypnosis and now prepares herself for those visits from the comfort of her living room.

Where Do I Go?

If there's no hypnotist in your area, learn self-hypnosis before you travel to another city in search of a hypnotist. If you're talented at self-hypnosis and practice regularly, you'll see results and not need to find a professional. Some people do very well with self-hypnosis, others need an initial office session, and still others can accomplish what they want with a good hypnosis audiotape. You have nothing to lose by first trying to do it yourself.

Your Price Is Right

What a bargain! You can save the hassle of getting to and from an office and you can achieve results without paying a penny!

A Little Boost

Will called me from Europe. Before his promotion he'd come in twice for hypnosis to handle the public-speaking aspects of his new position. Now he was on the phone requesting telephone hypnosis for tomorrow's meeting during which he was to present his ideas to an impressive, but intimidating, group. At the end of his last session, I had briefly gone over the self-hypnosis process with him. So I reminded him how it works and told him to call me in an hour. Forty minutes later Will called to say he was fine about tomorrow's meeting.

Whether your situation is at work or at play, on the ball field or in the classroom, you'll benefit from knowing how to give yourself that extra boost of self-confidence. Self-hypnosis is particularly good for eradicating nervousness.

Focus On This

When you've given yourself an induction you'll be extremely relaxed, your heart rate and respiration rate will lower, and your blood pressure will lower. You will enjoy the serenity of hypnosis.

How Talented Are You?

Hypnosis is a talent, and self-hypnosis is a skill you can learn that will enhance that talent. When you succeed at self-hypnosis you'll know that you did so because of your practicing. The more you practice, the more you'll experience a deep hypnotic state.

Some researchers believe that hypnosis is a learned skill that anyone can master. Other researchers agree, but add that there are certain personality traits that can predict your inborn talent for hypnosis. They believe that if you were born with a great talent for hypnosis, your personality may cause you to …

◆ Feel pain when you see someone else in pain.

◆ React emotionally to daily events.

◆ Have an excellent memory.

◆ Have good concentration ability.

◆ Trust people in authority.

◆ Be nonjudgmental, not too critical.

They believe that if you were born with a lesser talent for hypnosis, you probably …

◆ Are highly organized.

◆ Remain aware of your surroundings, even when concentrating.

◆ Are logical and not overly emotional.

◆ Like to understand how things work.

◆ Are sometimes critical of others.

Look into My Eyes

If your mental or emotional state is shaky, do not practice self-hypnosis without consulting your psychologist or psychiatrist.

I believe that no matter your personality, you'll enjoy hypnosis. If you have a lesser talent, you'll simply need to practice a little more to bring yourself up to the hypnotic ability of those who were lucky enough to be born with tremendous talent.

When Not to Do It Yourself

When you work with a hypnotist, hypnosis is an excellent method of alleviating most problems. Self-hypnosis, though, can be a little tricky. Please don't think about learning self-hypnosis if …

- The problem you want to work on involves other people.

- Now, or recently, you've been in treatment for mental illness.

- You won't be able to practice. The skill of self-hypnosis develops by daily practice—several times a day.

- You want to use hypnosis to uncover your memories.

- You've tried many remedies and doctors and nothing's worked so far.

Don't set yourself up for failure. Instead, use self-hypnosis only when you know it will succeed.

In the Hypnotist's Office

People who come to my office for hypnosis tend to be highly motivated. Sometimes I think they're half-hypnotized by the time they enter the office, because they've been thinking about it so intently. But, twice in my career I've had clients who resisted hypnosis with me. They simply didn't go "under." Both of them had the same experience: They went to a hypnotist who gave them the posthypnotic suggestion that they must not allow anyone, ever, to hypnotize them. When I figured out that was the problem, I taught them self-hypnosis, and then shut up while they successfully put themselves into a trance and gave themselves the necessary suggestions.

Relationship Problems

You'll need the help of a hypnotist or more likely a hypnotherapist if you want to resolve issues that have to do with people in your family, co-workers, or others with whom you have regular contact. There are two sides to every story, and it's impossible for anyone to see an interpersonal relationship objectively. The therapist you go to will help you write the script for your hypnosis after evaluating the situation from your viewpoint and from the probable viewpoint of the other person.

Emotional Illness

If you are in a fragile condition, mentally, you'll require the expertise of a mental-health professional to work with you during hypnosis. The choice of words is very important, and your script should be written with the input of a trained person. Also, you want to reinforce your grip on reality and emphasize the here and now. Don't do self-hypnosis until your psychologist or psychiatrist thinks you're ready.

Practice Makes Perfect

Self-hypnosis is a skill just like hitting a ball with a bat. Only a few kids are lucky enough to get up on the ball field and have the ball and bat connect at the first shot. But everybody, with practice, sooner or later, can do it. Some people need more practice than others. The best professional ballplayers practice regularly. You must practice self-hypnosis daily, several times each day, to master the skill of self-hypnosis.

Hidden Memories

Don't go there. It's hard enough to find a hypnotist who can competently uncover memories; it's almost impossible to do it yourself. Don't look for trouble; your memories will make themselves known when they need your attention. (See Chapter 26 for more on hidden memories.)

Other Treatments

If you've tried to solve your problem with a variety of other treatments and they've all failed, you need an expert to guide you through the hypnosis process. An experienced hypnotist will evaluate the situation and determine whether hypnosis is the treatment of choice, and if it is, will then help you formulate the appropriate script.

Self-Hypnosis Success

What can you best accomplish with self-hypnosis?

- You can get rid of a habit that you're truly ready to give up.
- You can solve a problem if you can think of a one-sentence cure for it.

Plenty of other situations are amenable to self-hypnosis, but if you first try either of these you'll experience immediate success.

Do You Want to Stop Your Habit?

When you're ready to ditch that habit, self-hypnosis will work well. If you're attempting self-hypnosis because, for example, your spouse, parent, or child is bugging you to stop smoking, you're best off going to a hypnotist. You may require one session to explore your reluctance to give up the habit and one session to actually give it up. It's hard for hypnosis to get you to do something you don't want to do.

Just a Few Words

The one-sentence cure is interesting because it's a challenge to reduce your suggestion down to one sentence. Elliot wanted to have more patience when he was fixing his car. Every Sunday he'd lift the hood, start tinkering, and in no time he'd be cursing, stomping around, and slamming down the hood. He wanted to hypnotize himself to work on the car and not have his wife threaten to leave him.

It's too complicated for a beginner in self-hypnosis to instruct himself, all at once, to *have patience, stop cursing, be considerate of my wife, stick with a task, ask for help when needed, and be a good sport when things don't work out.* When we hit upon the suggestion *I will work on my car, calmly, for 10 minutes,* it was a perfect solution.

Elliot simply rehypnotized himself every 10 minutes. It took him less than one minute to go into a trance and say his suggestion, so it worked just fine. The second Sunday he changed his suggestion to 20 minutes.

In the Hypnotist's Office

Headaches are a frequent complaint of children who seek treatment at a pediatrician's office. The doctor first must determine the cause of the headache, before beginning treatment with hypnosis. When neurological diseases are ruled out, hypnosis can step in.

Dr. Karen Olness, professor of pediatrics and internationally known hypnosis researcher, taught self-hypnosis to 14 children who suffered from migraine headaches. Another group of 14 children with migraines was studied, but not taught self-hypnosis. The children who used self-hypnosis were able to reduce the number and intensity of their headaches.

Getting Ready to Do It

Hypnosis is a skill that you can practice on your own. Like other skills, you'll learn it best when you have a teacher or a coach to guide you. I thank you for allowing me to be your coach today.

Homework

As your guide, teacher, and coach, I'll be giving you a lesson and then some homework. It's the homework that determines whether you'll succeed at learning this skill. Self-hypnosis homework is called practice. The more you practice, the more you develop your skill.

You must practice every day. Some hypnosis scholars insist that their students practice going in and out of a trance at least 10 times a day. They suggest doing it for one or two minutes every hour during the day. Others recommend that you practice 2 or 3 times a day, for 10 minutes each. I'm not concerned with which practice model you follow, as long as you do practice at least twice every day.

You'll be taught how to induce hypnosis (the induction), and then you'll practice going into that state of trance. Create a log to help you maintain regular practice habits. Starting today, write down the time that you practice your self-hypnosis each day. Do this for the entire week, and then again next week, too.

Some people practice first thing in the morning before they get out of bed. Others practice when they get home from work. After you become proficient, probably within one week, you'll go into a trance in less than one minute. In Chapter 7, you'll learn how to give yourself suggestions and, eventually, the suggestions will take less than one minute, too.

Focus On This _____

You can practice self-hypnosis almost any time and anywhere, except while driving a car, of course. Some folks do it during TV commercials; others practice at the kitchen table.

Soon, when you want to accomplish something with hypnosis, you'll be able to do so in just a couple of minutes. You'll then be able to practice self-hypnosis anywhere. You can do a two-minute procedure on a bus or train and no one will ever know. You can even do it at your desk. As soon as you know the drill perfectly, it'll be easy for you to practice many times a day; you won't need to set aside chunks of time, and you won't need to be in a special place. For now, though, please keep a written account of your practice schedule.

Setting Up

To get the most out of your practice, it's important to make the right preparations:

1. You need to find some privacy. Please try to be undisturbed for a while. Turn off your beeper, your cell phone, your other phones, buzzers, and alarms.

2. I'd like you to have a timer, but I don't recommend the ones that scare you half to death. A gentle chirp, chime, or tone is preferable to those loud, startling kitchen timers.

3. Now choose a restful place. You can be on a bed, a chair, a reclining chair, a couch, or the floor. Set yourself up with pillows or cushions and be as comfortable as possible.

4. If anything you're wearing is tight, please take it off or loosen it: shoes, belt, tie, earrings, and so on. Are you wearing contact lenses? If it's possible to remove your contacts, please do so. It'll be easier for you to roll your eyes upward; you won't worry about the contacts getting lost.

Congratulations! You're about to empower yourself to make changes in your life and lifestyle. You'll be using your mind to control your body.

As you know, the hypnotic session consists of an induction and a suggestion. We'll write suggestions in Chapter 7; for now we'll practice going into hypnosis using an induction. Then we'll use a deepening exercise to help you achieve a greater benefit from hypnosis. In this practice session, there will be no formal hypnotic suggestions. You'll simply have the experience of feeling lightly hypnotized, and then you'll come out of hypnosis. Hypnosis with no suggestions does not solve a problem or eliminate a habit, it simply gives you the experience of being in a suggestible state. An induction, with no suggestions following, is called *neutral hypnosis*.

Hypnoscript

Neutral hypnosis is a relaxed hypnotic state with free-floating imagery, but no overt suggestions. It is the stage in the hypnotic process that comes after induction and before suggestions.

Beginning the Induction

Set your timer for 10 minutes. Now you will start your induction into the hypnotic state by choosing a spot to stare at. It can be anywhere in your surroundings. Perhaps your spot will be a place on your wall, a picture frame, a crack on the ceiling, or something outside the window.

Good. Let's begin:

1. Lean back and make yourself comfortable.

2. Stare at your chosen spot.

3. Take several good, deep breaths.

4. Tell yourself that your body is feeling warmer and warmer.

5. Tell yourself that your body is getting heavier and heavier.

6. Allow yourself to slowly drift off into a state of deep relaxation.

7. Feel how warm, how comfortable, how heavy your body is becoming.

8. You are at peace; you are at rest.

9. From now until the timer gently awakens you, you will concentrate on feeling rested and relaxed, calm and comfortable.

10. Keep staring at your spot; stare and stare and stare.

11. Your body is quiet.

12. Your hands and feet are particularly warm and heavy. They may feel a bit tingly.

13. Give yourself permission to feel the relaxation spread throughout your body.

14. You'll soon close your eyes. You may concentrate on whatever pleasant image pops into your mind, or you may prefer to keep your mind a blank.

15. Gently close your eyes, and keep them closed until the timer rings.

Focus On This _____

Coming out of hypnosis is referred to as re-alerting, reawakening, coming back to regular, waking up, and various other terms, none of which is precise. How can you wake up if you've never been asleep? How can you become re-alerted when hypnosis is actually an alert state? What term would you use for the process of coming out of hypnosis and returning to your pre-induction state?

When the timer rings, open your eyes and sit up. Slowly and gradually you can return your regular feelings to your body and to your mind. Take your time. When you are thoroughly back to regular, please continue reading.

Were You Hypnotized?

You just experienced a brief, light, relaxation exercise. If you are very hypnotizable, you felt the heaviness and warmth, and your hands or feet got tingly. If you are average in your hypnosis ability, you closed your eyes and were very relaxed. If you have low hypnotic talent, you could not keep your eyes closed and felt nothing happening to your body.

Awakening

Don't worry. Even if your timer malfunctions, you will awaken. You can't get stuck in hypnosis. Many, many, people do the exercise you just did without a timer and they all get up. In the very worst case, you might drift off to sleep for a few minutes and then awaken. Don't worry; you'll always come back. Focus your energy on getting into the hypnotic state, not getting out of it. That happens automatically.

Variations

The next time you do this, you may want to prepare a specific image in your mind to focus on when you are in relaxation mode. You can create a picture in your imagination and then concentrate on that picture. The following sections include suggestions you can use for your visualization.

A Staircase

See yourself on the bottom step of a staircase. It can be an old, plain staircase or a glamorous Las Vegas hotel staircase. It may be indoors or outside. It may be a staircase you use regularly or one from your imagination. See yourself slowly walking to the top. Tell yourself that when you reach the top you'll be deeply hypnotized. Tell yourself that you'll count as you walk up. Begin with number one when you're at the bottom step and continue to count until number five, when you'll be at the top step. Remain on top, feeling relaxed and content.

When the timer rings, begin to walk down. With each step you take, begin to return your regular feelings to your mind and your body. When you reach the bottom stair you'll be back to regular.

A Scene of Nature

Visualize a restful, calming, outdoor scene. It may be a place that's familiar to you, or it may be one you've dreamt about. In your mind's eye, when you're deeply relaxed and feeling warm and heavy, allow yourself to see this scene clearly. Count to yourself from one to five. With each number, let yourself see an additional detail. When you reach the number five, you'll be deeply engrossed and absorbed in the scene. When the timer rings, you'll slowly emerge and come back to regular.

Eye Movements

Some people go into an immediate trance when they give themselves this series of suggestions:

1. *Close my eyes.*

2. *With my eyelids shut, roll up my eyes.*

3. *Keeping my eyelids shut, roll down my eyes.*

4. *Feel relaxation as it spreads throughout my body.*

5. *Concentrate on an image in my mind's eye.*

Don't worry if you feel your eyelids fluttering. That's actually a good sign: It's a sign of being hypnotized.

Deepening

Deepening builds on your original experience and adds to it so that you feel more and more relaxed, rested, and hypnotized. When you are in a deepened state, and you add suggestions to the process, you have a richer hypnotic experience.

To deepen your experience while visualizing the staircase image, tell yourself that with each number you say while walking up the stairs you'll go deeper and deeper into the hypnotic state. When you reach number five, at the top of the staircase, you'll be deeply hypnotized. If you use the scene of nature image, engage all your senses to deepen your experience. Tell yourself that in addition to seeing five new details of the scene you also will hear some sounds, smell some aromas, and feel the weather. You will become deeply absorbed in this special scene.

Or simply use the sounds in your own environment to deepen your experience. Listen. What do you hear? Do you hear an air conditioner? A refrigerator? The occasional sound of an ice maker? A car honking? A dog barking? Is there music in the background? Use all the sounds in your environment to deepen your trance. Dr. Milton Erickson advocated the idea of incorporating whatever is around you into your induction. Tell yourself that each time you hear a particular noise or sound it will be a signal to go deeper and deeper into the hypnotic state.

Need More Proof?

Are you the type who can't believe you're in an altered state of consciousness? Do you want to feel that hypnosis transports you to another world? When you do either of the following two exercises, you'll have proof that you truly can use your mind to control your body.

Glued Fingers

When you're lying back, drifting into hypnosis, tell yourself ...

1. *I'll clasp my hands together, fingers intertwined.*

2. *With each breath I take, my fingers will feel more and more connected to each other.*

3. *It's as if there's glue on all my fingers.*

4. *My fingers will remain entwined until the timer rings.*

5. *It is impossible for my hands to separate now.*

And they will remain entwined. And when the timer rings you'll easily separate your hands.

Heavy Arm

When you're lying back, drifting into hypnosis, tell yourself …

1. *One arm will begin to feel heavy. I don't yet know which arm it will be.*

2. *That one arm will become so heavy, it will feel as if it is weighted down.*

3. *I'll actually make that arm feel even more heavy by imagining a heavy textbook being placed right on it.*

4. *Now, in my mind, I'll place a second book on top of the first.*

5. *My arm is so, so heavy. I cannot lift it, I cannot move it.*

6. *My arm will remain heavy until the timer rings. At that time it will be back to regular, and I'll easily lift it.*

> **In the Hypnotist's Office**
>
> Occasionally, I encounter clients who hate to relax and for whom the best hypnotic induction is an image full of action. I encourage those people to see themselves engaged in the activity of their choice. Then I add that they should see themselves repeating their activity—running miles, swimming laps, doing aerobics—in their mind's eye, over and over, and over and over, and … you get the picture.

Progressive Relaxation

Some people enjoy a progressive relaxation exercise as a prelude to their induction; others use it as an induction by itself. There are many progressive relaxation audiotapes on the market that you can try, too.

The idea of progressive relaxation is that each part of your body is invited to relax. To ensure a deep relaxation of all muscle groups, the muscles are first tensed and then relaxed.

In a typical progressive relaxation, you begin either at your head or your toes, mention each body part, and suggest a relaxation of each body part. For large muscle groups, tense your thighs, feel the tension, contract those muscles, and then say: *Relax my thighs, feel the relaxation, release those muscles … Feel the relaxation as it makes my body heavy and limp.*

Next, tense other muscles, one at a time—buttocks, stomach, arms, and so on. Now relax, one at a time, each of those muscle groups. Then proceed with the general relaxation of your entire body. Encourage yourself to feel floppy like a rag doll, heavier and heavier, more and more relaxed.

How relaxed are you? During progressive relaxation you'll feel quiet and slowed down. You'll be soothed and relaxed. While you're in this relaxed, hypnotic state, waiting for the timer to signal the end of your experience, you can assess the depth of your hypnosis. Visualize a ruler. See the numbers 1 through 12 on it. Let 1 represent your usual waking state; let 12 represent the deepest possible hypnotic state. Where are you? Which number immediately pops out at you? Each time you practice your self-hypnosis induction, gauge your depth of trance by using the ruler.

Practice, Practice, Practice

It's time to do your homework. It's time to practice your self-hypnosis. You will go into trance with ease and with pleasure.

Practice self-hypnosis today, tomorrow, and the next day, too. Remain in neutral hypnosis—no suggestions, yet. Use a variety of induction methods until you come upon the one that works best for you. When you find it, it will become your special path to hypnosis.

Before the Suggestions

Before you add a script of suggestions to your hypnosis routine, enjoy the neutral hypnosis state by thinking good thoughts about yourself and about others. Visualize yourself as you'd like to be. See yourself accomplishing what you want to accomplish. As you increase your talent for trance, you'll have a lifetime benefit. Bob Reese, former head trainer for the New York Jets, says, "If you can see it, then you can be it."

The Least You Need to Know

- You can use self-hypnosis in many situations.

- Self-hypnosis will help you accomplish your goals, by yourself, without having to pay for a hypnotist.

- Self-hypnosis consists of an induction and then a script of suggestions.

- There are a variety of inductions—you can choose the one you're most comfortable with.

- The more you practice going into hypnosis, the better your self-hypnosis results will be.

Giving Yourself Suggestions

In This Chapter

- Writing your hypnosis sentence
- Writing your hypnosis script
- Writing a hypnotic fairy tale
- Making a hypnosis audiotape

Now that you know how to put yourself into that delightful, restful trance state, what do you do next? You reach your goal! This chapter teaches you how to give yourself a suggestion that works. You'll learn to say just the right words at just the right time. You'll have a skill that will give you a benefit for the rest of your life.

Sentences, Scripts, and Stories

When you're hypnotized and ready to receive suggestions, your mind is eager to please. Whatever you say will be welcomed. After all, you're the one who's chosen the words. You know what you want.

You can give yourself suggestions by condensing your goal down to one, or maybe two, sentences. Or you can create a long script that covers every aspect of what you want to achieve. You can even come up with a story that is a metaphor for your situation. I explain each method to you.

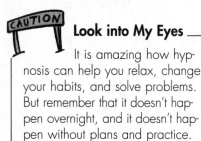

Look into My Eyes

It is amazing how hypnosis can help you relax, change your habits, and solve problems. But remember that it doesn't happen overnight, and it doesn't happen without plans and practice.

It would be wonderful if you could simply tell yourself that when you awaken from hypnosis you'll feel happy, all your problems or symptoms will be gone, you'll have a perpetually sunny, healthy attitude, and you'll easily accomplish everything you ever wanted to. Sorry, hypnosis is not magic. You have to plan your plan, and accomplish one step at a time.

Sentences

Vicki is chubby and wants to look glamorous and svelte at her June wedding. She's willing to practice self-hypnosis every day if it'll get her weight down. She knows how to use an induction to get into hypnosis, but she's uncertain about what to tell herself.

Of course, she'd be wise to consult Chapter 9 and select the suggestions that most apply to her. And she should also take the advice I offer in the following section about building suggestions.

How to Build a One-Sentence Suggestion

Suggestions come in all sizes, from lengthy scripts to just one sentence. Here's how to build a one-sentence suggestion:

1. Decide where you want to end up. (For Vicki: *18 pounds less.*)

2. Think of one thing you'd have to do differently—a new behavior—to achieve that goal. (For Vicki: *Cut out ice cream.*)

3. Think of two things you can do to make it easy for you to do that new behavior. (For Vicki: *Have fruit in the house; keep ice cream out of the house.*)

4. Write one sentence directing yourself to do the two things required in Step 3. (For Vicki: *I will buy fruit a few times a week; I will not buy ice cream.*)

5. Add the goal in Step 1 to your sentence in Step 4. (For Vicki: *I'll lose 18 pounds when I regularly buy fruit and do not buy ice cream.*)

6. Add a specific command to your sentence in Step 5. (For Vicki: *I'll lose 18 pounds when I regularly buy fruit and do not buy ice cream. Therefore I will buy fruit every Monday, Wednesday, and Friday, and I will not even pass the frozen-food section at the market.*)

7. After saying the sentence, while still hypnotized, visualize what you just said to yourself.

8. Add an awakening suggestion. For example, you might say, *"And now that I have absorbed the suggestions, I will return my mind and my body to regular. I will be back to regular by the time I reach the letter H, as I begin to recite the alphabet. A ... B ... C ... D ... E ... F ... G ... H. And now I can open my eyes and resume my ordinary life."*

In the Hypnotist's Office

Children learn self-hypnosis easily, but some kids hate to practice it. Lauren could control her bed-wetting when she hypnotized herself at bedtime, but her self-hypnosis skills decreased when she went for days without practicing. Finally, her mother hit upon a solution. Lauren would come to my office for the direct, authoritative suggestion to "have a strong desire to practice self-hypnosis every day, a few times a day." It worked! That suggestion lasted and Lauren controlled her bed-wetting by herself, using self-hypnosis.

Let's try this system again. Lucy is at the beginning of a pregnancy. She has what's unrealistically called morning sickness; she feels sick all day long. Lucy would benefit from reading Chapter 21, and she should also try this as well:

1. Decide where you want to end up. (For Lucy: *I want to end up feeling good, no nausea.*)

2. Pick one new behavior to achieve that goal. (For Lucy: *I have to keep my stomach full; hunger makes me much worse.*)

3. Decide on two things to make it easy. (For Lucy: *Keep crackers in the car and next to the bed; make sure there's always something ready to eat in the house.*)

4. Direct yourself to do what's required. (For Lucy: *When I leave the house in the morning, I'll take crackers into the car with me; every evening I'll prepare food for the next day; and when I go to bed, I'll take crackers with me.*)

5. Add your goal. (For Lucy: *I won't be nauseous when I take crackers out to the car with me in the morning, when I take them to bed with me at night, and when I have food prepared and available in the refrigerator.*)

6. Add a specific command. (For Lucy: *I will feel better when I have saltines in my briefcase in the morning, and keep a box next to my bed, too, and as soon as I finish dinner I'll cut up vegetables and dried fruit for tomorrow.*)

Focus On This

The difference between the almost-right word and the right word is really a large matter—it's the difference between the lightning bug and the lightning.

—Mark Twain

7. Visualize Step 6.

8. Of course, you will always add your reawakening suggestion to the end of all scripts.

Your Turn

Please try this for yourself now.

1. I want to end up (your goal):

_____

_____

2. Here's what I'll have to do differently to end up there (your new behavior):

_____

_____

_____

3. It'll be easier for me to do that if I (two things to make it easy):

_____

_____

_____

4. I must do these two things to easily accomplish Step 3:

_____

_____

_____

5. I will do (fill in whatever you've written for Step 4) to accomplish (fill in whatever you've written for Step 1):

_____

_____

_____

6. I will (add a specific command):

_____

_____

_____

7. After saying the above sentence to yourself, visualize Step 6.

8. Say that sentence once again.

9. Visualize that sentence once again

10. Add your reawakening suggestion to the end of your sentence.

Tell yourself that you are ready to return to your regular state and leave hypnosis for today. Allow it to be a gradual return.

Focus On This _____

During self-hypnosis you are your own guide, directing yourself to the place you want to get to. You're actually establishing a way for one part of yourself to communicate with another part of yourself. Some call it the conscious mind talking to the unconscious mind; others call it a left brain/right brain connection.

Experiment and decide whether saying the sentence once is sufficient. Some people say that repeating it two or three times makes a big difference for them.

You did it! You created a one- or two-sentence suggestion for yourself. Now how do you give yourself this suggestion when you're hypnotized? You can …

◆ Put it on an audiotape (more about tapes later in this chapter).

◆ Memorize it and tell it to yourself at the appropriate time. (This will work only if the sentence is short.)

◆ Put it on a piece of paper and read it.

You may wonder how you can read it if you're on your bed with your eyes closed in a deep hypnotic trance. Well, it can be done and I'll tell you how.

Eyes Open

After an interesting experience many years ago, I realized it was possible for a person to open his or her eyes during a trance, read the sentence, and then go right back into a trance. I was the guest hypnotist at a three-day conference for lawyers who wanted to experience hypnosis because some of their clients had been hypnotized by the police. It was my job to put the lawyers into a trance and then give them a suggestion. Easy, right? Not when I was dealing with 65 people who pride themselves on being adversarial. I couldn't get the group to agree on a suggestion. There was always an objection.

When many in the group agreed to *I'll easily fall asleep tonight*, one member was outraged. She said, "I have work with me; I need to work until well after midnight. I don't want to hear anything that will make me drowsy." When others wanted me to suggest *I'll eagerly look forward to tomorrow's meetings*, a few thought that would prejudice them

Look into My Eyes

Write your own sentences. Don't be influenced by someone else; you know the words that are meaningful to you. Don't worry if your sentences seem awkward; it's necessary for you alone to understand them, and you'll know exactly what they mean. Use your own words and your own expressions.

to favor tomorrow's topics over another day's topics. Most of the group enjoyed the process of debating and were prepared to discuss the options for hours. Some wanted to use arbitration techniques—all this, just to come up with a sentence for a hypnotic suggestion!

Eventually I figured out what to do. I taught them steps one through six (as I showed you earlier), and they each created a personalized suggestion. Then I asked them to write their suggestions on a piece of paper. (I told them to keep their glasses on during the process.) Then I hypnotized them, and when they were deep in trance I said:

- ◆ *You will open your eyes.*
- ◆ *You will see nothing but that piece of paper in your lap.*
- ◆ *You will read that sentence to yourself.*
- ◆ *You will read it again.*
- ◆ *You will close your eyes and think about that sentence.*
- ◆ *You will visualize yourself doing what that sentence tells you to do.*

Finally, they all agreed on something—this was a success!

You, too, can open your eyes while hypnotized, read your sentence, and then go right back to your trance state, absorbing the instructions in your sentence. All you need to do is plan ahead of time to do this during your self-hypnosis. You'll be pleased with the results. It's easy and it's fun.

Scripts

When you write a good narrative, it's full of detail and explains exactly what's going on. That's how a hypnosis script should be written, too. I'll help you write one, but you should also know that there are a number of books that you can pick up at bookstores that have hypnosis scripts. Most of them are good quality and cover many possible topics.

Your hypnosis script, which you use after your hypnotic induction, consists of ...

1. Stating the problem.

2. Stating the solution.

3. Seeing the solution as a series of steps.

4. Visualizing the series of steps, one at a time.

5. Describing details of the scene of success.

6. Reawakening.

This takes longer than simply giving yourself a one- or two-sentence suggestion. This gives you a chance to enjoy a full scene. Let's begin script writing by meeting Jay, who's a website designer about to lose his job.

He called last week to say he wants hypnosis to help him maintain his composure as his company gets bought out and he gets booted out. He's upset because he's put lots of effort into his job. But the buying company wants only the two key people to remain, and he's number four in the hierarchy. Also, he never imagined anyone would ever buy them out, so he did not make an investment in the company. Those who did will make money, even as they lose their jobs.

Jay is in another city, so I discourage him from flying in to see me and encourage him to use self-hypnosis. He does well with self-hypnosis after I give him some insight into what his problem really is.

> **Focus On This** _____
> Writing your own script gives you a chance to see yourself not only achieving your goal, but also experiencing new feelings, new attitudes, new behaviors, and new successes.

What's Your Problem?

Jay states his problem: "I put so much into this company, and I'm gonna end up in the street. How could they do this to me?" It seems that Jay's problem is his anger at the situation, not the fact that he'll be unemployed. He feels unappreciated and that seems to be most disturbing to him. So the first part of Jay's script will be about feeling unappreciated. He writes: "I need to be appreciated; I deserve to be appreciated, but no one at this place is acknowledging all my years of effort."

Steps to the Solution

Jay needs to find a way for his superiors to acknowledge his hard work. He writes: "My two bosses should say something to me that will make me feel better." These are the steps that Jay believes he should take:

1. I'll write a memo to each boss telling him about my major contributions to the company during all the years I've worked there.

2. I'll ask each of them to write me a letter of reference for future employers.

3. I'll ask them if they have any contacts for me.

Visualizing

Jay uses visualization to get from the idea of writing the memo to the reality of actually doing it. This is what he tells himself:

♦ *I can see myself writing that memo. I'll have to look through my old files and get records from the other office to get all my accomplishments.*

♦ *I can see myself walking into Walt's office and talking to him about a reference letter to my future new boss.*

♦ *I see myself stopping by Mac's desk, asking him for a reference letter, too.*

♦ *Now I'm asking Walt if he has any leads for me. I am speaking clearly and looking him right in the eye.*

♦ *I'm asking Mac to pass my phone number to some of his contacts.*

In the Hypnotist's Office

Clients who respond very well to hypnosis in my office may have limited success when they try to replicate everything we did. Self-hypnosis is not geared toward age regression or hallucinations. In a trance, Jessica could smell every smell of her college dorm while she was in my office; but when practicing at home, she could see her dorm room but could not create any of the smells. She accomplished what she wanted at home, anyway, which was to see herself studying for a lab test and reproduce that depth of concentration. Don't be disappointed if you're not able to engage all your senses during self-hypnosis. You can have successful self-hypnosis without necessarily hallucinating smells and sounds.

Details, Details

Your success is in the details. As you see the images and engage all your senses, you enhance your hypnosis experience. Jay's details are as follows:

◆ *I'm looking through all the files. What a pain. But I'm finding what I need—dates of my projects, revenue I generated, names of key clients.*

◆ *In Walt's office I see myself and I see the entire room. There's all that stuff on the walls. I hear the music his secretary always listens to and I hear the phone ringing.*

◆ *Mac's desk is a mess. I feel how warm it is, and I see the other desks from here. I hear the fax machine and all the people walking down the corridor outside.*

◆ *Boy, do I feel good. Just reading these two letters lets me know my work was not in vain. They really do know all that I've done for them. Look at these letters. I see myself reading them and feeling proud and happy. I'm not upset anymore.*

> **CAUTION**
>
> **Look into My Eyes**
>
> When you do self-hypnosis, remember that you must never take away any symptoms of pain, unless a physician has agreed that you should. You need your pain to diagnose what is wrong with you. If you take away the pain in your ankle, you'll never have a need to get an x-ray, and if your ankle is broken, you'll do permanent damage by walking on it.

Reawakening

The reawakening script has to do with the induction. Wherever you put yourself during the induction is where you begin your reawakening. For example, if you're on the top of a staircase, you say:

And now that my hypnosis is coming to an end, it's time for me to see myself at the top of the stairs. I'll count from five to one and with every number I say, I'll begin walking down. When I reach the number one, and when I reach the bottom step, I'll be ready to come back to regular.

Five ... four ... feeling less and less hypnotized ... three ... beginning to restore my ordinary feelings to my body ... two ... beginning to restore my ordinary feelings to my mind ... one.

And now that I've reached the bottom step, I can slowly begin to stretch out and open my eyes. At my own pace ... whenever I feel ready ... I will open my eyes and come back to my ordinary state. Hypnosis is over for today, but everything I've learned will stay with me. The benefit will last.

Self-hypnosis has the advantage of encouraging you to create rich imagery. You can expand your visualizations to embrace everything you want.

Your Turn

Please use the Script-Writing Worksheet that follows to begin writing your own script. You can use this format over and over, each time you wish to accomplish something under hypnosis. Begin with the brief, one- or two-sentence format, and have a good time. Remember, you're doing something wonderful for yourself.

Script-Writing Worksheet

1. Identify your problem.

   _____

   _____

2. Think of a solution.

   _____

   _____

3. What are the steps to take to get to your solution?

   a._____

   _____

   b._____

   _____

   c. _____

   _____

4. Visualize yourself taking those steps.

5. Describe the scene of your success.

   _____

   _____

   _____

   _____

   _____

6. Write your reawakening script.

_____

_____

_____

_____

Congratulations. You've completed a self-hypnosis script.

Stories

Your unconscious mind is really good at figuring out things. It can figure out things on a symbolic level because it's not as analytical as your conscious mind. When you're hypnotized and communicating with your unconscious mind, you can tell yourself a story. The story can have meanings on several levels. For example, literally, your story may be a story about building a house for yourself. But, metaphorically, your mind will understand that you're talking about building your life.

An easy way to begin creating your metaphoric story is by using transportation as the symbol. Planes soar and then land; cars speed or can run out of gas; if you're on a bike, you can whiz down the street or you can tumble off. A sled gives you a smooth ride, a boat can be smooth or choppy. You can get sick on a boat or you can enjoy the ride. When you end your trip, you can be at a new place, or you can return to the beginning. You can be met at your destination by anyone you'd like. And because this is a story, the person who meets you can be …

Focus On This _____

Metaphoric stories are the ultimate in indirect suggestions. Milton Erickson was the master of the metaphor and could quickly come up with just the right story for each client.

- Someone you know.

- Someone deceased.

- A figure representing a feeling.

- A person representing your future.

Another way to begin creating your personal metaphor is to use an existing fairy tale. Read some fairy tales and see which are particularly pertinent to your situation. What about some of the Disney stories? Which characters have personal meaning to you?

In the Hypnotist's Office

Good storytellers are geniuses of their craft. Herman Melville, author of *Moby Dick*, was such a vivid teller of tales that he once visited Mr. and Mrs. Nathaniel Hawthorne and told them a story about a fight he witnessed on a South Sea island. One of the warriors wreaked havoc using a heavy club. Striding about the room, Melville demonstrated the desperate drama of the battle. When Melville left, Hawthorne realized he'd left empty-handed and so they searched their home to find the club that he left behind. The next day he told them there was no club. His story was so vivid that Mr. And Mrs. Hawthorne each imagined they saw it!

A Metaphoric Story

When Ginny, a high school girl, came to my office, she complained that she didn't fit in anyplace. Her parents, older brother, and younger sister were athletic, outdoorsy, and always on the go. She preferred to stay indoors and read. In school she was not interested in the social scene but very interested in tutoring the students at the elementary school. Ginny's parents were on her case to join them in activities, her teachers wanted her to socialize more, and she was right—she didn't fit in.

I interviewed Ginny for awhile and determined that she was in excellent mental health. She had no problems, other than the fact that others had a problem with her. Her self-esteem was good, and she was generally happy when left alone. Here's the story I told Ginny:

There's a beautiful tree outside my window. It has a sturdy trunk and plentiful branches and limbs. And those leaves, oh, those leaves. Each one is delicate, and green, and smooth, and shiny. Some are more delicate than others. They're all of varying shades of green. Some have more of a yellow tinge to them. Others are a pretty dark green. A few are very smooth, others have patchy spots. Most of them are shiny, but a few of the leaves have dull spots.

It's a beautiful tree. Every leaf is important … and different from all the other leaves …. Some show their differences up front … others have to be turned over to see how they are less shiny … or more smooth.

One-of-a-kind leaves are particularly valued when trees get older … it's nice to see variations on older trees. Every leaf is exactly how it's supposed to be. Each leaf is just the size and shape it's supposed to be … Some leaves are clumped together and then they all look alike. Some leaves are by themselves and have distinct features.

When the leaves fall off for winter and I look out my window, I miss them. I look forward to their return in the spring.

When Ginny reawakened, we didn't talk about her session. I wanted the story to sink in without any interpretations. But, before leaving the office Ginny said, "It's true that I don't fit in, you know. But, it's not so bad. I can take it."

Have fun writing your story.

What About Tapes?

Hypnosis audiotapes are as good as the person who created them. Some are quite wonderful, and others leave a lot to be desired. Buy several, ask friends for recommendations, and you'll soon hit upon the right one for you. Or you can ask a hypnotist to make a tape specifically for you. If you contact me through my website, www. drroberta.com, I will help you.

Tapes are good if they have a relaxing induction, then give you the specific suggestions you want, and then guide you back to regular. When you evaluate tapes, pay attention to the voice, tempo, words, and style.

The voice that you consider soothing, someone else may consider boring. Do you want a voice to seem warm and intimate? Or far away and formal? Some people like a tempo with many pauses, others prefer to move along at a faster pace.

Words, of course, are most important. The right choice of words will feel comfortable to you. If you have to strain to figure out the meaning of something, or if a word is unfamiliar to you, the tape is for someone else, not you.

Style is important, too, because some hypnotists make tapes with direct suggestions and others with an indirect, permissive style. You'll respond best to the style that is consistent with your personality. Remember direct and indirect suggestions from Chapter 3?

Here are some examples of direct and indirect suggestions. Figure out which style is most appealing to you and form your statements in that manner.

Look into My Eyes

The only problem with audiotapes is the temptation to listen to them while driving. *Never, never* dare to use one in your car. Don't even listen in the car when you're a passenger, because the driver will hear and may respond accordingly.

Focus On This

When I lecture at universities and medical schools, I must remind myself to use a different voice and tone than when I am doing a hypnotic session. How did I figure out that a change in tone was necessary? I looked at the students in the lecture hall and many of them had their eyes closed and were nodding off.

Direct Suggestions	Indirect Suggestions
Close your eyes now	You may decide to close your eyes now or in a few moments
You can easily do well on the SATs	Many students find it easy to do well on the SATs
Lean back in the chair and make yourself comfortable	Many of my clients find it comforting to lean back in that chair
Please uncross your legs	Isn't it relaxing to uncross your legs?
Pay attention to my words	You don't have to think about listening to my words, your unconscious mind can do that all by itself

When you know which style you best respond to, please formulate your statements in that manner.

In the Hypnotist's Office

Here's an Ericksonian indirect suggestion: *It might be interesting to see if, when you close your eyes, you may be able to visualize a beach scene. I don't know exactly what your mind will see—maybe a bright sunny day, maybe a few clouds in the sky. Maybe you'll hear people laughing and playing, maybe you'll see people swimming. I wonder if you'll see yourself on the beach or in the water.* The direct suggestion equivalent is: *Close your eyes and visualize a beach scene.* Some people respond best to direct, authoritative statements, and others respond best to indirect, permissive statements. The best hypnotist knows how to offer both types of suggestions and spends enough time with you to determine which you are more likely to benefit from.

Making Your Own Tape

Trial and error will help you choose the right hypnosis tape. But, how about creating your own tape? You can do that by ...

- Scheduling a visit to a hypnotist and bringing your own tape and tape recorder.

- Writing your own induction, suggestions, and reawakening, and then recording them.

When you do your own recording, you first record the induction that you've selected. Then add your script. It may be a few sentences, a script, or a story. Then give yourself instructions to visualize yourself attaining your goal. Next record the reawakening. For the reawakening, remember to change your tone of voice and the pace of your speech. Start to get yourself ready to come back to regular.

If you want to use your tape at bedtime, then instead of reawakening, tell yourself: *Now it's time to sleep. This tape player shuts off automatically so I can drift off into a comfortable, good night's sleep. All the words I heard during hypnosis will help me tomorrow and every day. For now, I'll fall asleep and awaken at just the right time in the morning, feeling extremely refreshed and alert and replenished.*

The more you play your hypnosis tape, the more proficient you become at hypnosis. Your ability continues to improve with practice.

The Value of Self-Hypnosis

Self-hypnosis allows you the opportunity to act in your own best interest, to become your own best friend. This is the ultimate in self-cooperation and self-respect.

When you know self-hypnosis, you know how to …

- Prevent a habit from getting out of hand.
- Relax at will.
- Be oriented toward solutions, not problems.
- Feel comfortable seeing yourself succeed.

As much as I advocate self-hypnosis, I suggest you go to a hypnotist to know the feeling of a deep hypnotic state. Then when you do it on your own, you'll know if you've achieved the best possible depth.

 **Focus On This** _____

The best self-hypnosis comes after you've had the experience of deep hetero-hypnosis.

The Least You Need to Know

- You can write suggestions for your own good.
- Self-hypnosis suggestions can be brief and one sentence, or they can be long and involved.
- Audiotapes work. You can buy a ready-made tape or make your own.
- Self-hypnosis works best after you've already been hypnotized by a professional.

Part 3

The Healthy You

Do you want to kick a habit? Know someone who needs to quit smoking or stop overeating? Troubled by insomnia? Biting your nails?

Part 3 shows how hypnosis helps you get rid of an unwanted habit, stick to a diet, fall asleep promptly, and eradicate your phobias. Read case studies of actual clients who tried hypnosis for their addictions and are now clean and sober.

You'll learn how to hypnotize yourself into a new life of good habits by following a script that's already prepared for you in each chapter.

I CURED MY SMOKING HABIT WITH HYPNOSIS. NOW, I NEED SOMETHING TO STOP ME FROM CLUCKING LIKE A CHICKEN.

Chapter 8

You Are Feeling Sleepy

In This Chapter

- ◆ News from the sleep researchers
- ◆ Drifting off to sleep
- ◆ Your personal sleep prescription
- ◆ Banish nightmares with self-hypnosis

Sleep labs are popping up all over, yet more and more people cannot get a good night's sleep. Can you? Insomniacs of the world, you can benefit from the many recent discoveries in the area of sleep medicine. There are new ways to figure out why you're not sleeping and new ways for you to enjoy a good night's sleep. Hypnosis plays an important role in the treatment of sleep problems.

Read on and you'll soon be sleeping soundly—no, not because these pages will bore you to sleep, but because you can use the new information gleaned from sleep scientists as part of your hypnosis script. Pleasant dreams.

Why Can't You Sleep?

First, let's be sure you really have a sleep problem. Maybe you don't. Maybe you have *agrypniaphobia*. People with agrypniaphobia assume that

Hypnoscript _____

The severe fear of not being able to fall asleep is classified as a phobia. It's called **agrypniaphobia.**

they won't fall asleep, and get themselves so nervous about not falling asleep that their nervousness prevents them from drifting off promptly.

Maybe you have misinformation about the amount of sleep you need. Some people think they should be sleeping eight hours a night, and are upset that they sleep only for six. Everybody needs to sleep, but we each need different amounts of sleep. Where do you fit?

Percentage of Population	Sleep Needed
5	Less than 6 hours
10	More than 9 hours
85	Between 7½ and 8½ hours

Want to find out how much sleep you need?

Take a couple of weeks when you can risk awakening later than usual, maybe vacation time, and do this experiment:

1. Go to sleep the same time each night.

2. Do not set the alarm.

3. Sleep until you awaken naturally—until you have had enough sleep.

4. Keep a record of how many hours of sleep you get each night.

5. Note that the first week or so, you'll be catching up on missed sleep, so the number of hours you sleep that first week will be higher than during the second week.

Focus On This _____

Late-night talk show star Jay Leno is rumored to need to sleep only two or three hours a night. It's said that former British Prime Minister Margaret Thatcher requires only four hours of sleep.

6. Note the number of hours you sleep during the last five nights of this experiment. Divide by five.

7. This is it! You've determined exactly how many hours of sleep you need.

It's your responsibility to give your body what it requires.

Is It Insomnia?

Do you suffer from insomnia? Insomnia comes in different varieties. Which is yours?

- ◆ Cannot fall asleep?

- ◆ Cannot stay asleep?

- ◆ Awaken much too early?

Any one of these three categories qualifies you to call yourself an insomniac.

News from the Sleep Labs

Sleep medicine researchers study our biological clocks and come up with information we can use. Their science is called chronobiology, which is the study of our internal biological rhythms. Researchers' biggest contribution to insomnia sufferers is their discovery of the importance of *sleep hygiene*, the rules to follow in order to get a good night's sleep.

Sleep Hygiene

Did your mother tell you to go to sleep early? Did she insist that you shut off the light at bedtime? Scientists now say that Mother was right. They've come up with other habits, too, that facilitate sleep.

Follow these rules of sleep hygiene to get a good night's sleep:

- ◆ Go to bed at the same time every night.

- ◆ Awaken at the same time every morning.

- ◆ Stay away from caffeine.

- ◆ Relax before bed.

- ◆ Establish a bedtime ritual.

- ◆ Dim the lights, then shut them off.

Hypnoscript

The ways to develop good sleep habits, and eliminate habits that prevent or disrupt sleep, are called **sleep hygiene.**

Let's go over these sleep hygiene habits to understand why Mom was right all along.

Going to bed at the same time every night gets your brain accustomed to switching to sleep cycle at that time. Ditto for waking up at the same time every morning.

The stimulating effect of caffeine lasts for several hours in most people. For some very sensitive souls, it can last for up to 14 hours! In addition to being an ingredient in coffee, tea, and cola sodas, caffeine is found in chocolate and in some medications.

Watching the TV series *ER* is not conducive to sleep; neither is watching any other television show or movie that's full of action. Nor should you have an argument on the phone, or visit an exciting chat room, just before bedtime. The more stirred up you become, the harder it is to get to sleep. Give yourself wind-down time. Mom probably told you this, too.

Look into My Eyes

If you must go to sleep later than usual, or must sleep later than usual in the morning, perhaps on the weekend, never stretch beyond two hours. More than two hours of extra sleep throws your sleep schedule entirely out of sync.

What do the following behaviors have in common?

◆ Saying your prayers

◆ Brushing your teeth

◆ Kissing your honey good night

◆ Taking a warm bath

◆ Locking all the doors

◆ Setting the alarm

They are all well-known bedtime rituals. Perhaps when you were small, Dad read you a bedtime story, or you had milk and cookies in the kitchen with your sister. Bedtime rituals help your brain associate certain behaviors with sleep. Eventually, it becomes an automatic association, and as soon as you do your ritual behavior, your mind and body are ready to fall asleep.

Here is a chart on which you can record your sleep habits. Please keep a record of your sleep habits by entering the time each day that you perform the activities listed.

Activity	Time Sun.	Mon.	Tues.	Wed.	Thurs.	Fri.	Sat.
Get out of bed in A.M.	___	___	___	___	___	___	___
Last caffeine of day	___	___	___	___	___	___	___
Dim your lights	___	___	___	___	___	___	___
Begin bedtime routine	___	___	___	___	___	___	___
Have last alcohol drink	___	___	___	___	___	___	___
Turn off your lights	___	___	___	___	___	___	___
How much sleep did you get each night?	___	___	___	___	___	___	___

Use the preceding chart for one week, and then you'll know the behavior you need to change. You can change behavior with hypnosis.

Hypnosis to the Rescue

Hypnosis can help you observe proper sleep hygiene. You can learn new, specific behaviors that will help you get a good night's sleep.

Visualizations

When you get into bed tonight try one of these visualizations:

Rock-a-Bye Baby

1. Close your eyes and in your mind see yourself as a baby.

2. You are sitting on your mother's lap in a rocking chair.

3. She is slowly rocking.

4. She is holding you securely.

5. And she is gently rocking back and forth … gently, back and forth … back and forth … back and forth … You are safe and secure … in your mother's lap … gently rocking … back and forth … back and forth.

6. You are drifting off to sleep … gently to sleep.

7. Back and forth … back and forth … back and forth, drifting off to sleep … and gently rocking and rocking.

8. Continue watching yourself as you are rocked back and forth … back and forth … You are drifting off to sleep … to sleep … to sleep.

9. You are sleeping so peacefully, so comfortably.

Covered with Mud

1. See yourself on a small, private beach.

2. You are sitting on the shore watching the water.

3. You are absentmindedly coating your legs with mud.

4. And now you are covering the rest of your body with mud.

5. The mud is wet. The mud is heavy. See the mud on your arms and on your legs.

6. Your chest and stomach and back are covered with mud, too. Your body feels heavy from the weight of the mud.

7. The mud is weighing you down. You are heavier and heavier. Feel the heaviness as you sink deeper and deeper.

8. Your body is so heavy you cannot move.

9. The mud weighs you down. You lie still. You are calm.

10. You are cool. You are comfortable. Your body is so heavy you do not move … you do not open your eyes … your eyes close and you sleep … and you sleep … and you sleep.

11. Pleasant dreams and good night. You are sleeping so comfortably, so peacefully.

Focus On This

In *Cinderella*, Walt Disney said, "A dream is a wish your heart makes." Contrast that with psychiatrist William Dement's idea that "Dreaming permits each and every one of us to be quietly and safely insane every night of our lives."

Establishing a Bedtime Ritual

Please decide what you want to do to get yourself ready for bed. When it's all written out and you've done it for a few days, then it's time to go to a hypnotist with your script.

You'll be hypnotized to create the unconscious connection between your ritual and falling asleep. Or instead of going to a hypnotist you can read Chapters 6 and 7 and learn how to hypnotize yourself.

About your ritual: Choose the rock-a-bye-baby ritual, the covered-with-mud ritual, or develop your own. Be sure each individual ritual is something you're comfortable doing. Eva came to be hypnotized because of insomnia, and she and I decided to work on bedtime rituals. She chose the ritual of a nightly warm bath. Unfortunately, her apartment building shuts off the hot water at 11 P.M. on many nights, just at the time that she's getting home from work. (She works on Wall Street, and has very late hours.) She needed to come back for another session with a different hypnotic suggestion.

It is not necessary to get specific about the ritual in your script. When I hypnotize groups, where each person in the group has an individualized ritual, I simply say: *You will establish a sleep ritual. Shortly after you complete the ritual you will easily fall asleep.*

This works for most everyone in the audience.

Suggestions

Other hypnotic suggestions I offer insomnia clients are as follows:

◆ *You will fall asleep easily and stay asleep until morning, except for when you must awaken during the night. At that time you will find it easy to return to sleep as soon as your head hits the pillow.*

- *You will awaken from a good night's sleep feeling replenished and energetic.*

- *Moving your pillow in a particular way will promote sleep. Fold your pillow, or put your arm under it, or push it away from you. Whatever move you make can be a suggestion for sleep.*

- *You will ignore all extraneous noises, and sleep through unnecessary noises.*

If you are among the many who are bothered by their neighbor's sound system, the trucks passing on the highway, or the crying baby next door, consider earplugs.

Literally Speaking

When you're hypnotized you often take things literally; literalness is an aspect of the trance state. Note the phrase, "… when you *must* awaken during the night." If I suggest that you *must* stay in bed all night, you might refrain from leaving the bed even when you have to go to the bathroom.

In the next suggestion note the phrases, "extraneous noises" and "unnecessary noises." I do want you to awaken if the alarm rings, if the doorbell rings, or if a family member calls to you from another room in your home.

> **CAUTION**
>
> **Look into My Eyes**
>
> When you're hypnotized and your critical censor is inactive, you are likely to respond to all suggestions literally.

Imagery

This hypnotic script works very well with people who have trouble staying asleep all night. See if you can visualize it now:

In your mind's eye, please see yourself in your bedroom. Look around and see all the furniture, the windows, the floor. Look up at the ceiling … see the door, and see yourself on the bed. As I count from one to five, please see additional details of the room, the bed, and yourself. With each number I say, you will go deeper and deeper into the hypnotic state. One … two … three … four … five.

And now as you see yourself on the bed, ready to go to sleep, please see the clock in your room. Notice the time. It is your bedtime. Look at yourself. You are rested and relaxed. You are at peace … with yourself … with the universe. And now, please watch yourself as you fall asleep. Now you are sleeping, and your sleep gets deeper and deeper.

Focus On This

There are some clever new alarm clocks on the market these days. They don't wake you with sound, but with light instead. At a set time, a light bulb begins to dimly glow, and within about 10 minutes it reaches its maximum wattage. This goes along with the sleep experts and their ideas about light being a natural alarm clock.

And look at the clock again. You've been sleeping for one hour and you continue to sleep. A good, restful sleep. You are fast asleep. Look at the clock again … two hours have passed … you are sleeping soundly … now the clock tells you three hours … and continue to watch the clock and watch yourself sleeping … sleeping so restfully, so soundly. And the clock will show you that you are sleeping hour after hour after hour … and you will remain sleeping until it's the right time for you to get up.

I speak a bit more, and include suggestions to wake up in a good mood with plenty of energy. Then I count backward and invite the client to leave the bedroom and leave hypnosis and come back to regular.

Hypnosis for Nightmares

Do you have scary dreams? Do you have the same scary dream time and time again? Hypnosis can help you. You can hypnotize yourself to change your dream. Let's begin!

Think about your disturbing dream and figure out a way to introduce a new person into that dream. That new person will be your helper and your hero. Create a scene in your mind that has that new person change the outcome of the dream. Now the dream includes your hero/helper and has a comfortable, satisfying ending. You are no longer upset. You are no longer frightened. In fact, you are pleased with this new dream.

Close your eyes and rehearse the entire dream sequence. Notice that you are feeling good. This is not a nightmare anymore. This is a pleasant dream.

Please take out your timer and follow the induction procedure you established back in Chapter 6. Perhaps you'll concentrate on a particular spot on your wall, or maybe a special scene of nature, or possibly a staircase. You know your best way to become hypnotized.

As soon as you are in a hypnotic trance you will play your new dream in your mind. Do it once, do it twice. Then tell yourself …

◆ *My old nightmare is gone.*

◆ *This is my new dream.*

◆ *If I should ever again have a frightening dream I will immediately awaken.*

If you need to, you can write these three statements on a piece of paper and open your eyes during the hypnosis, after you've experienced your new dream, and simply read the statements. Then you'll close your eyes and resume your hypnotic state until the timer rings.

Congratulations. Your self-hypnosis has banished nightmares.

Creating Your Personalized Sleep Script

You can write instructions to yourself to fall asleep easily, stay asleep throughout the night, and awaken refreshed at just the right time in the morning.

Include your personalized bedtime ritual, giving yourself the suggestion that, as soon as you carry out that behavior, your body and your mind will be ready for sleep. Visualize yourself performing the ritual, and then watch yourself as you fall asleep.

Suggest that if your thoughts of tomorrow prevent you from sleeping you will write a full, prioritized "to-do" list for tomorrow. Prioritize by putting an A next to items that must be done, B next to items that you hope you will do, and C next to items that can wait.

Include the habits you need to reinforce: Dim the lights, write lists, and wind down. Mention the habits you want to eliminate: long naps, nighttime exercise, midnight pizzas, after-dinner drinks, and late-night cigarettes. Give reminders to yourself to slow down toward bedtime and refrain from late-night, aggravating conversations or violent movies.

When your script is written, you can hypnotize yourself by following the induction procedure in Chapter 6. Keep your script in your hand, and at one point during your self-hypnosis session, open your eyes and read it. Then return to hypnosis and enjoy yourself for awhile before opening your eyes again, this time to end your session and come back to ordinary.

For each item on the following list, decide if you should be eliminating that behavior or doing more of it. Please add your own items to this list. Then write a hypnotic script telling yourself to eliminate the habit or increase it. The script is for you only—a personalized sleep script.

> **CAUTION**
>
> **Look into My Eyes**
>
> Sleeping pills can have serious side effects; and so can some of the natural, herbal sleep remedies. Sleep hygiene and hypnosis can spare you the problems of putting sleep potions into your body.

Focus On This

Write all your thoughts and feelings for 15 minutes each night. When thoughts are on paper, they are no longer rattling around in your head keeping you awake.

Creating Your Personalized Sleep Script

Activity	More?	Less?
Watch stimulating TV	___	___
Drink tea	___	___
Take a one-hour nap	___	___
Do rituals	___	___
Smoke at bedtime	___	___
Drink cola after dinner	___	___
Eat heavy food before bed	___	___
Dim the lights	___	___
Calm down	___	___
Write a list for tomorrow	___	___
Write in your journal	___	___
Drink alcohol after dinner	___	___

Some people wish they could sleep like babies. But remember that babies wake up every few hours to eat, burp, and more. Instead, wish that you'll produce an effective hypnotic script to combat your insomnia. You can ask your hypnotist to make a tape of your session (more about hypnosis tapes in Chapter 7) so you can play it every night. Good luck!

The Least You Need to Know

- Observing sleep hygiene will bring on sleep.

- Being in a room with bright lights is equivalent to taking a stay-awake pill.

- Hypnosis works for sleep problems.

Chapter 9

You Don't Want Dessert

In This Chapter

- ◆ Which genes did you inherit?
- ◆ Changing your eating habits
- ◆ Thinking thin
- ◆ Creating your own food-control program

Do you want to gain weight? Go on a diet. Going on a diet means you will eventually go off the diet. Statistics show that going off a diet is the time of most rapid weight gain.

If dieting is bad, then what's good for losing weight? Changing behavior is good; changing habits is good. And that's where hypnosis comes in. Hypnosis can help you change your eating habits. You don't have to diet; you just have to stop a couple of your weight-gaining habits, and start a few weight-losing habits. Hypnosis works for weight loss—try it.

You and Your Genes

Are you lucky? Were you born with splendid genes?

Some people can eat all they want and maintain a perfect weight. Some people can eat all they want, become many, many pounds overweight, and not suffer at all. Their health remains excellent. If you were born lucky, this chapter is not for you.

If you've inherited genes for heart disease, hypertension (high blood pressure), or diabetes, however, you need this chapter.

Please note that I am purposely not defining the terms "fat," "obese," or "overweight." There's no need for you to label yourself. You have your standard; it may be your gray suit, or it may be a number on your scale. Maybe you have a fat closet, and wearing clothes from there more than twice a month is your signal to do something about your weight. Maybe you have a gorgeous outfit that fit you once, for 10 minutes, and now you hear it calling to you, so you're looking for a way to shed a few pounds. Maybe you weigh more than the charts say you should, but you're fit and healthy and have no "bad" genes associated with being overweight. Use common sense and check with your physician, no matter what your weight, just to be sure you're in good health.

There used to be a theory that fat people were emotionally weak or had psychological problems. That theory has been disproved, and now it's suspected that the opposite is true: Fat people are emotionally stronger than other folks. They endure so much ridicule and criticism, yet they don't give up. Many thin people confess that they would be reluctant to go out if they were obese, yet the overweight must put up with being called names, being told they're "sick in the head," insecure, sexually afraid—and they're accused of having a death wish, too. None of this is true.

The myth of the fat person suffering from poor self-esteem is just a myth.

Humans come in a variety of shapes and sizes. Yet, many people cannot accept that they or a family member may be genetically programmed to be larger than most others. I get many calls to my office from women who are so repulsed by fat that I could easily fill a group-counseling session called "Skinny Mothers Who Hate Their Fat Daughters."

Obesity is not an eating disorder. It is not a psychological disorder. Fat people do not have excessive oral urges. Fat people are not emotionally damaged. They are, however, genetically predetermined to be fat. They receive very strong "eat now" signals from their bodies. As they gain weight, glucose piles up in fat cells, and their predisposition to gaining weight increases.

This sounds grim, but weight loss *can* be accomplished. Genes confer the capacity and tendency to be fat, but your environment, particularly your eating habits, turn the tendency into a reality.

If you have a genetic handicap, you can adapt to it. It requires a conscious effort, but it can be done. You *can* counteract your inborn biological impulses.

Obesity should be treated as a chronic disease; there is no cure for it, but it can be managed. It is sometimes difficult to fight against nature in this way, but hypnosis makes it much easier. There are other ways to change your eating habits, but none of them is as appealing as hypnosis. Do you want to staple your stomach? Take pills that affect your central nervous system? Replace food with liquid drinks? Hypnosis uses words; other methods seem too risky.

The Skinny on Fat

Here are the facts you need to know about your weight:

- If you are overweight and are not genetically lucky, you must lose weight.
- To lose weight, you must eat less.
- Impulsive eating does not permit weight loss.
- Planning ahead, knowing in advance what you will eat at your next meal, helps you to eat less.

I will help you lose weight with a combination of hypnosis and behavior therapy. Please do not attempt to do this if you're suffering from an eating disorder such as anorexia or bulimia. Anorexia can be treated as a neurological medical condition, and bulimia is an eating disorder that responds well to medication. Please consult a physician for treatment of either of these diseases.

There are many ways to permanently change your eating habits. The easiest is to find a particular food program that appeals to you. Statistics show that people who follow a particular program—any program—fare better than people who simply decide to watch their weight. Take your time exploring your options. Your body is unique. The food program you choose to follow may not be the same as the program that appeals to your friend. Familiarize yourself with …

- Diet clubs.
- One-on-one nutrition/ diet counseling.
- Nutrition books.
- Weight-loss books.
- Weight-loss tapes.

 Focus On This

Americans spend $33 billion a year on weight-loss products and services, yet the percentage of Americans considered overweight increases annually!

When you choose your program, the challenge will be to stick to it. The evidence is in that those most likely to lose weight and keep it off …

◆ Continue with a program for at least 40 weeks.

◆ Are going to a wedding within a year—usually their child's.

◆ Had a health scare.

◆ Are recently widowed or divorced.

◆ Weigh in somewhere—doctor's office, weight-loss club—once a week.

◆ Include exercise in their program.

◆ Get a boost from a hypnotist, counselor, or therapist at regular intervals.

◆ Do their program with a buddy.

◆ Plan their menu in advance, every day.

Statistics show that the factors just listed are the best motivators for weight loss and are the best predictors of weight loss.

Focus On This

Check out the National Weight Loss Registry to read success stories. Members of the Registry have lost significant pounds and have kept their weight off for long periods of time.

Hypnoscript

Every person has an inborn control system, a **setpoint**, that attempts to maintain a particular amount of fat on the body.

You may have heard or read some misleading information. It has sometimes been said that a huge percentage of folks who lose weight will regain it. Please be informed that those statistics are from a few universities that have weight-loss research studies. The average person who loses weight does *not* enlist in a research study. The average person who loses weight is never asked by a national pollster how much weight was lost, kept off, or regained. Have you been polled? Do you know anyone who has been polled?

You *can* maintain your weight loss; many, many people do. In fact, some researchers say that if you can keep your weight down for three years you will have established a new *setpoint* and it will be easy to maintain your lower weight. Think of your setpoint as a thermostat that regulates your weight.

deciding to eat less, with no formal guidelines or program to follow, usually
t work. The most important things you can do to lose pounds and keep them
.

low a program.

your menus in advance.

boost from hypnosis.

, each of the above recommendations is possible. You can accomplish this,
time, and you can succeed.

its, Habits

fit from keeping a written record of your eating habits before you begin
Jotting down the foods and the quantities you eat, the time of day, and
helps you note your vulnerabilities.

she ate well and used good self-control at meals. She did. But when
er food log, she learned why her weight was creeping up. It was the
eating when not hungry, that did her in. The following three entries
d her.

ood Eaten	Quantity	Time	Place
tato chips	1 bag	8:30 P.M.	In front of TV
ly beans	3-oz. bag	4 P.M.	In car, driving home from work
els, eggs, se, etc.	Breakfast for three	11 A.M.	Sunday brunch café

The Mouth and Foot Painting Artists.

eating while watching television and while driving, and to stay
rom huge buffets at restaurant brunches. Margo's downfall is eating when she's
not hungry (in the car), and continuing to eat after her hunger is satiated (in restaurants). The hypnotic suggestions that will benefit Margo are as follows:

- *You will have no desire to eat while watching television.*
- *You will have no desire to eat while driving.*
- *You will eat only at mealtime.*
- *You will notice when you feel full during a meal.*
- *You will stop eating when you feel full.*

Luke was fine with food all week; it was the weekends that troubled him. His children spent weekends with him and he felt obliged to offer them sweetened cereals, cookies, and ice cream—you get the picture. I hypnotized him to buy only small quantities of junk foods; I trusted that his maturity would prevent him from fighting with his kids for the limited amount of sweets. Many clients request Luke's suggestions:

♦ *You will shop carefully and buy only foods on your program.*

♦ *When you shop for family members you will buy exact quantities—for them, not for you, too.*

In the Hypnotist's Office

Sarah's downfall was chocolate. I hypnotized her to be unable to buy chocolate at the supermarket, the candy store, or the chocolate specialty shop. After three good weeks on her program, Sarah guiltily confessed that during week number four she was desperate for chocolate, but the hypnotic suggestion was strong. She could not bring herself to go into a store and ask for chocolate. Sarah sent herself a Candygram!

Do you go to sleep with indigestion most nights? It's easy to overeat at night and difficult to eat heartily in the morning, especially on a workday. Scientists asked a group of men to eat their normal three meals a day for one month. Then half the group was asked to continue the same menu plan but reverse breakfast and dinner. After another month, the meat-in-the-morning guys all lost weight. The other group, who ate the same number of calories per day, stayed the same. No one is sure why this happened, but it did. Here are two more useful hypnotic suggestions for weight loss:

♦ *Eat lightly in the evening.*

♦ *Eat your heaviest meal in the morning.*

Abby cooks nutritious meals for herself and her family. She eats well, and then the trouble begins. She picks at the food in the serving platters. Before the dinner conversation is over, Abby has eaten the equivalent of another meal. Abby's hypnotic suggestions are:

♦ *Keep serving plates in the kitchen; do not bring them to the table.*

♦ *Cook realistic amounts of food to avoid leftovers.*

Bill told me he did the most damage to his waistline when he ate by the light of the refrigerator at night. Barbara told me she did her most damage when she cleared the table. On the way from the table to the garbage pail, she would gulp down whatever was left. Bill knew he wasn't hungry; the food just called to him. Barbara knew she wasn't hungry; the food was simply there, in her hands. They both benefited from the following suggestions:

- *You may not eat standing up.*

- *Once you get up from the dinner table, you will not eat again until breakfast.*

Please examine your eating habits. Use your food chart as a guide and figure out which of those habits you would like to change. Know your patterns and tendencies. Perhaps you would like to …

- Eliminate all junk food.

- Stop snacking while you are talking on the phone.

- Stop eating between meals.

- Stop eating in the bedroom.

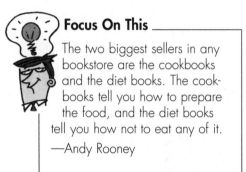

Focus On This

The two biggest sellers in any bookstore are the cookbooks and the diet books. The cookbooks tell you how to prepare the food, and the diet books tell you how not to eat any of it.

—Andy Rooney

We all have some food patterns that we'd prefer to keep secret. You know, the candy wrappers you hide, or the chocolate obsession, or the Chinese food for breakfast. Here's your chance to come clean. Identify the habit and you'll be on your way to getting rid of it.

Habit Pairs

Do you have certain behaviors that you associate with eating? Do you munch while you read? Do you open the refrigerator while you talk on the telephone? Do you keep a bowl of M&M's next to your computer?

Use your food list to discover your habit pairs. During hypnosis you can break the habit pair connection. A suggestion might be one of the following:

- *Visualize yourself talking on the telephone. Notice that you are not going toward the refrigerator. You are not thinking about food.*

- *From now on you will not use the phone in the kitchen. You will speak only from the bedroom phone.*

Eating When You Are Not Hungry

We know that fat people tend to get hunger signals very often. But many people, including fat people, eat when they are not hungry. Why? Sometimes, because the food is there and it looks good and smells good and tastes good.

Other times, because the food is there and what they really want is not there. Could this be you? Do you sometimes eat when you're not hungry, but you …

- Are bored and are looking for something to do?

- Are tired and too lazy to get ready for bed?

- Need some attention?

- Need some exercise but don't feel like getting out of the house?

- Need some love?

Warren solved his "eating when not hungry" problem by buying a dog. His dog is always ready to play, is full of affection, and insists that Warren walk him several times a day.

In the Hypnotist's Office

Overeating because of plentiful food was not always a problem in America. Toward the end of the Civil War, meat was an almost unobtainable luxury. For a special dinner party, Robert E. Lee's servant put out a serving plate with heaps of cabbage and one small piece of meat. The guests politely refused the meat and Lee looked forward to eating it the next day. When it was not served to him he complained, and the servant explained that the meat had been borrowed to impress the guests, and had now been returned.

Think Like a Thin Person

It's time to get started on your new program to control your food intake. Please start at the beginning of this chapter and identify all the hypnotic suggestions that seem appropriate for you. Write them on a separate sheet of paper. You will soon be adding to this list, and thus creating your personal weight-loss hypnotic suggestion script.

Then evaluate all the weight-loss programs you've investigated and decide which will be your number-one choice and which your second choice. (More about that second choice later.) Check with your physician before you begin your program to be sure that nothing in your health history makes the program unsuitable for you.

Make sure you have all the information you need about permitted foods, meetings, weigh-ins, and anything else that comes with your particular program.

If you can remember something you've done that was difficult, it'll help. What did you try and work very hard at? What are the challenges at which you've succeeded? How did you complete a troublesome task? What resources did you use? What did you say to yourself to keep on going? Sticking to your food program will be a challenge but it will not be nearly as difficult as previous challenges because this time you'll have the advantage of hypnosis. Hypnosis always helps.

To increase your motivation, create a list of positive and negative consequences of sticking to—or not sticking to—the program. First, let's look at Paul's list.

Paul's List: Consequences of Sticking to This Program

Positive	Negative
Will fit into my clothes	Will have to spend a fortune on a new wardrobe
My wife will stop nagging me	Will never have a quiet house—wife will not give up
Maybe will be able to stop	Might develop serious health problems—the blood pressure pills

Now please create your own list of consequences—positive and negative—of sticking to this program.

Keep your list. It's part of your hypnotic script. When you go to a hypnotist, you can use the positive consequences as part of an age-progression script. Remember age progression? It's the technique that allows you to see yourself years from now and have that future self-communicate with the person you are right now.

Focus On This _____

Ten years ago, 45 percent of Americans ate some sugar-free or low-fat foods. Today 92 percent of us include sugar-free or low-fat foods in our diets. Most of us weigh more now than we did then.

Getting with the Program

You will be eating according to the rules of your new food program. Hypnosis will help you follow that program one day at a time. Thin people automatically follow certain behaviors that help them to maintain their thinness. Hypnosis will help you adopt some of those behaviors.

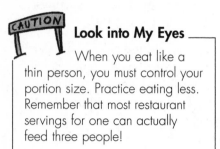

Portion Control

No matter which food program you choose, it will work best for you if you control the size of your portions. Len came to my office wondering why he was not losing weight. "I eat only healthful food," he whined. "How come I'm not thin?" The answer was obvious when I looked at his food chart. Looking at the next chart, you can see that Len's food choices were excellent; his portions were out of sight.

Food	Quantity
Chicken	1 whole, cut up
Apples	4
Bananas	3
Brown rice	2½ cups

In the end, calories do count. No matter how excellent your choices, you must watch your quantities.

Eating Like a Thin Person

Here are some thin-people eating habits. Adapt any or all of them to your food program, and incorporate your specific sentences into your hypnotic script:

- *Eat three meals a day with no food, except possibly vegetables, between meals.*

- *Drink plenty of water—between meals, before each meal, with meals, after each meal.*

- *Pause before you begin to eat. Enjoy the aromas and the colors of your food.*

- *Chew your food slowly.*

- *Put your utensil down after you put the food in your mouth. Do not pick up your utensil until your mouth is empty.*

- *Be on the lookout for a full feeling in your stomach.*

- *When you are aware of feeling full immediately stop eating.*

- *If a food doesn't taste good, don't eat it.*

- *Eat only while seated. Meals should last no less than 10 minutes, no more than 30 minutes. When your meal is finished, please leave the table.*

- *Substitute fresh fruit for fruit juices. If you must have some fruit juice, dilute it with several ounces of water or seltzer.*

My clients ask me to add some specific food suggestions. Here are the ones that work best:

- *Fried foods will not taste good.*

- *You will prefer skim milk to whole milk.*

- *You will prefer tuna packed in water.*

- *You will enjoy chicken without skin, potatoes without cream.*

The human body is quite remarkable in its ability to quickly become accustomed to new food habits. Often, four consecutive days is enough time to permanently adopt one or two new habits. Then, every four days, add another few and before you know it you're eating like a thin person.

In the Hypnotist's Office

Dr. Larry Deutsch, Canada's premier hypnotist/physician, encourages doctors to recognize that obesity is a complex, lifelong disease and not a cosmetic issue and not a moral issue. He encourages his overweight patients to use hypnosis to achieve *mind over platter*. Dr. Larry stresses four ideas in his hypnosis sessions: eat less, choose well, become active, and master stress without using food. Learn more at www.drlarry.com.

Your Personalized Weight-Loss Script

You probably have accumulated a full page of hypnotic suggestions. Here are four more I would like to offer you:

- *You need only follow your program one day at a time.*

- *There will always be enough food for you at your next meal. You will always have enough to eat.*

- *Be aware of everything you put into your mouth.*

- *You have permission to leave food on your plate.*

Add some suggestions that are specifically for you. Do you need help recognizing that you're sleepy, not hungry? Do you do best when you eat a large salad before dinner? Do you enjoy a diet soft drink as dessert? Individualize your script so that it's perfect for you.

You'll do very well on your program, and the hypnosis will help tremendously. What about when you reach a plateau? When the weight stops coming off? When you're feeling cranky about the program? That's when you go to your second-choice program. I think clients get bored—some after a few weeks, others after many months—and need some variety. When you assessed the food-control programs, there was one almost as good as the one you chose. Use that as a backup as an occasional variation.

Do-It-Yourself

If you decide to use self-hypnosis instead of going to a hypnotist to help you with food control, it will be a fine idea to begin today—right now, in fact. Get yourself into your special hypnosis place—take your timer with you. Choose your spot to stare at, or tune in to your visualization, as you learned in Chapter 6. Prepare three sentences to begin with. Three new eating habits or three sentences suggested in the last few pages are good starting places. Write the sentences on a paper and hold the paper on your lap while you proceed to go into your trance. When you are nicely hypnotized, tell yourself you may open your eyes, read your sentences, and then close your eyes and go right back into your deep trance state. While in the trance, visualize yourself carrying out the instructions of those three sentences.

Remain in your trance until your timer rings. When you emerge from hypnosis, you will have had lots of practice mentally carrying out your three new habits. Do this again in a day or two. After a week, write three different suggestions on a slip of paper and use them as your hypnotic script for about 10 days. Then go back to your original three sentences. At the end of a month, you will have many new eating habits. That is impressive; and you've done it all by yourself, for yourself.

Alternate Activities

Now that you'll be spending less time at the table, what will you do with your extra hours? To be sure that you don't hang out at the freezer, please have some noneating activities planned. I advise my clients to keep an activity list with them at all times— you never know when the urge to do "something" will strike, and you don't want that "something" to be eating.

Make a List

Here's a copy of Linda's activity list. Linda lost 50 pounds in 1 year, and has kept it off for 3 years and counting.

Linda's List of Alternative Activities

Outdoor Activities	Indoor Activities
Go to the mall	Do a crossword puzzle
Clean the yard	Do sit-ups
Walk around the block	Clean out the junk drawer
	Take a bath

Create your own list, and before you snack please do an activity chosen from that list. Chances are you'll quickly forget about food. Keep your list handy and refer to it regularly.

Distraction always helps because food cravings don't last too long, and moving around tends to diminish them.

What About Exercise?

It's a good idea to exercise for 20 minutes each day. On the days that you play tennis, go bike riding, take an aerobics class, or go the gym, you will easily fulfill this requirement. On other days, walk for 20 minutes; 10 minutes twice a day will suffice. You can write a sentence about exercise to add to your hypnosis script. Some sentences I use for my clients are …

- *You will have a great desire to walk up stairs and not use the elevator.*
- *You will be interested in participating in sports.*
- *Every morning you will decide what your exercise of the day will be.*
- *You will look for opportunities to walk rather than drive.*
- *You will enjoy going to the gym.*

Which of these exercise suggestions might motivate you? Please add it to your script.

Visualizations

While in your trance, see yourself, in your mind's eye, using self-control in dining situations. See yourself at a favorite restaurant asking the waiter to remove the bread basket. See yourself at a wedding, at a cocktail party, or at a business lunch and watch yourself as you eat carefully and slowly and stick to your program.

Visualize yourself at the supermarket. You are not galloping down the aisles loading up your wagon. Instead, you're following a shopping list and staying away from aisles that will get you into trouble.

Focus On This

Once when baseball great Yogi Berra ordered pizza, he was asked if he wanted it cut into four or eight slices. "Better make it four, I don't think I could eat eight," said Yogi.

See yourself at the weight you would like to be next month. Please be sure this is a realistic goal for one month. Remember Linda? She's the gal you just read about who got in the habit of cleaning out her junk drawer instead of eating. Maybe you were impressed with the fact that she lost 50 pounds. It is impressive. Did you note that it took her a year to lose those pounds? Well, it did. She lost 1 pound a week, never any more, even though she stuck to her program perfectly.

Now that you see yourself at a realistic weight for next month, please notice what you're wearing. Notice how proud you are of your accomplishment.

The Least You Need to Know

- Being overweight is a chronic problem that needs lifelong attention.

- Hypnosis can help you stick to a food program.

- You are supposed to stop eating when you feel full.

- Each evening plan your menu for the next day. Each day merely follow your plan.

- Slow and steady wins the race.

Chapter 10

A Trance a Day Keeps Cigarettes Away

In This Chapter

- The power of nicotine
- Self-medicating with cigarettes
- Cutting down on smoking
- Posthypnotic suggestions to quit smoking

Smoking used to be cool. Look at old movies and see the sexiest and hand-somest and most beautiful characters puffing away. Nowadays we know the dangers of nicotine, and we know how addictive cigarette smoking is. But ask high school students about their peers and they report that there are many, many smokers. Smoking *can* make you feel good. Unfortunately, it can also kill you. Read on if you want to stop smoking. Hypnosis can help you to quit.

You and Your Nicotine

Have you tried to stop smoking? Have you tried to stop with a patch? With gum? Cold turkey? The average ex-smoker stops on the seventh try, and 80 percent of those who stop do so because of a health problem.

The good news is that 30 million people in the United States *have* stopped smoking. In the late 1960s one half of the population smoked. Today, far, far fewer people smoke. *You* can join the millions who have stopped. It may not be easy (although it is for some), but it is doable.

Hypnoscript

In **addiction,** body chemistry changes and dependence on a drug becomes a biological need.

Are you a Sunday smoker? Are you a person who can smoke on the weekend and not even think about cigarettes during the week? Are you someone who can mooch a cigarette from a friend and then not smoke until the next time you see that friend?

Or are you an addicted smoker? Do you have a gene for *addiction?* Are you absolutely hooked on your cigarettes?

You know you are a nicotine addict when …

- You need your first cigarette before you get out of bed in the morning.

- You think of stopping and you don't know how you could do without that first cigarette.

- You smoke in the shower.

- You are unable to fly nonstop across the country.

- You smoke more than one pack a day—always, no matter what.

- You think of your cigarettes as your best friend.

- You, or a blood relative, has suffered from major depression.

- You smoke most of your cigarettes in the morning.

- You become desperate when deprived of your cigarettes.

- You continue to smoke even though you are ostracized and banished to garages, basements, backyards, and the outdoors in subzero weather.

If you are not addicted it will be extremely easy to stop smoking. Hypnosis works particularly well if smoking is simply a bad habit and nothing more. You'll know that is your situation if you …

- Use cigarettes as a reassuring ritual, something to do with your hands when you're socially uncomfortable.

- Use smoking as an interval activity, something to do when you're making the transition from one task to another.

If you are an addicted smoker, you can stop smoking by using the power of your mind to control your body. That's what hypnosis is all about. Sometimes you may need additional help, too, in the form of an antidepressant (as discussed soon). You will be able to stop smoking, no matter how addicted you are. Remember, there are 30 million ex-smokers in the United States and that number increases daily.

My friend Rona is a fastidious woman, always well-dressed and meticulously groomed. Years ago, on one of her first attempts to stop smoking, I was walking in the mall with her on her second day of no cigarettes. Suddenly, finicky, immaculate Rona dug her hand into the sand-filled urn outside Macy's. She frantically searched and then came up with what she was desperately looking for—a stranger's lipstick-stained, saliva-covered, cigarette stub. Nicotine addiction is real.

Throughout the centuries, in all cultures, people have found ways to get nicotine into their bloodstreams. In the eighteenth century, they got their nicotine through the nose—they used snuff. In the nineteenth century, they got their nicotine through the mouth by chewing tobacco. In the twentieth century, nicotine enters the bloodstream by way of the lungs, by smoking cigarettes.

> **CAUTION**
>
> **Look into My Eyes**
>
> Forty-five million Americans smoke cigarettes, and 440,000 will die prematurely because of the effects of their smoking habit.

Self-Medication

You're not stupid. You wouldn't be smoking if it did nothing for you. Somehow you've figured out that nicotine helps you feel better. You are actually self-medicating by smoking.

For some people, smoking cigarettes makes it easier to perform tasks because it improves concentration, the ability to focus, and alertness. It also improves memory.

> **In the Hypnotist's Office**
>
> Years ago smokers were everywhere and smoking was permitted everywhere. People didn't go into their garages or basements to sneak a cigarette, and all public places had ashtrays. Not so, anymore. Dr. C. came for hypnosis to stop smoking. He is the president of a university, and whenever he flies to fundraisers or to meetings, he is embarrassed when he must remind the travel agent to break up his trip into 2½-hour segments. That's the longest time he can be without a cigarette.

Smoking cigarettes can change your mood. It can calm you down from hyperactivity and it can bring you up from depression. Smoking can relieve boredom and it can give you courage.

Focus On This

Dr. Alexander Glassman of Columbia University, one of the most prominent scientists studying nicotine addiction, believes that "cigarette smoking is strongly associated with depression." People who tend to get depressed are often the very same people who get hooked on cigarette smoking.

Too bad it can kill you.

Smoking is unique in that it provides rapid delivery of nicotine to your bloodstream and your brain, and it permits you to control the amount you get. How do you get that control? By puffing your unique way:

- Short puffs give you a low dosage of nicotine that works as an antidepressant by arousing and stimulating you.

- Deep drags give you a high dosage of nicotine that works as an anti-anxiety drug, calming and sedating you.

If you smoke one pack a day, you take 70,000 puffs a year; each one is a hit of pleasure.

Nicotine is your self-administered drug—no prescription needed—and you can give yourself precisely the right amount. Yes, it can help you control symptoms of depression, anxiety, and social phobia. But these are real diseases and they should be treated with real pharmaceutical medications—medications that won't kill you.

Have you attempted to lower your nicotine intake by changing to a cigarette with less tar, or by smoking a lighter, milder brand? What happened? Smokers in a scientific study published in the *New England Journal of Medicine* switched brands, but then inhaled more deeply, took more puffs, and smoked more cigarettes. Thus, they kept up their optimal level of nicotine, the dosage of medication that they needed. Smoking is the leading cause of preventable death in America.

Focus On This

Each day more than 3,000 American teenagers start smoking. At least 3.1 million adolescents are current smokers.

Teens become dependent on nicotine as quickly as adults and find it just as difficult to quit. The tobacco industry spends over $5.2 billion a year on advertising to convince people they should take up smoking.

If you were born with a tendency toward depression and then sometime in life tried a cigarette and it took away your depression, you can be helped. Before you stop smoking, go to your doctor and get a prescription for an antidepressant drug. Cigarettes have deadly side effects, antidepressants do not. After you're stabilized on your medication, you won't need your nicotine any more. You'll be a Sunday smoker who can stop with ease.

Two chemicals in your brain help you feel good:

◆ Dopamine gives you the capacity to be joyful and to experience pleasure.

◆ Norepinephrine gives you energy and helps you concentrate.

Nicotine influences the production of both of these chemicals. When you started smoking, way back when, you probably tried a few puffs along with some friends. Those friends who had sufficient dopamine and norepinephrine did not get any kicks from cigarettes and never got hooked.

Getting Ready to Quit

You're on the right road—the road to becoming an ex-smoker. You'll succeed and feel very proud of yourself. Remember, you're not alone—there are 30 million ex-smokers.

All you need to do is follow these easy steps:

1. Decide when you will stop and choose a quit date. Your birthday? Anniversary? Next Monday? January 1?

2. Go to your doctor for medication if you or a close member of your family have depression.

3. Tell everyone you know about your quit date. Peer pressure will help you.

4. Postpone lighting your first cigarette of the day by one hour.

5. Forbid yourself to smoke in the car or on the street.

6. Limit yourself to smoking in only one part or one room of your home.

7. Smoke only half of each cigarette. When you're ready for your next one, light up the remaining half.

8. Don't empty your ashtrays. See and smell your mess.

9. Take your last cigarette of the day an hour or two before usual.

 **Focus On This** _____

Today there are prescription drugs that restore the healthy chemical balance of your brain; you don't have to rely on nicotine.

Remember that it's easier to quit now than it's ever been, because there are not only fewer public places you can smoke in, you also have hypnosis to help you.

Gradually Cutting Down

You may decide to limit your cigarettes to 10 or fewer each day. To accomplish this, have only that number available. That means you clear out your pockets, your desk drawers, your hidden stash in the car. Also tell family and friends not to listen to you if you ask for a smoke.

Cut down gradually by deciding in advance when and where you will have your precious allotted cigarettes. A hypnotist can help you stick to this plan. I recommend this plan for just a few days, though. After that, complete withdrawal, also known as cold turkey, works best.

Tracking Your Smoking

A few days before your quit date, keep a smoking chart on which you enter all the cigarettes you smoke and some other important information.

Here are excerpts from Mike's chart. Keeping this record helped him understand the role that coffee played in his cigarette smoking.

Mike's Daily Smoking Record

Day	Time	Place	Activity	Feeling
Monday	8:30 A.M.	Kitchen	Drinking coffee	Tired
	11 A.M.	Desk	Drinking coffee	Overwhelmed

Mike discovered a *habit* pair. His cigarette smoking is a *habit* that is paired in his mind with drinking coffee.

Each time you light up a cigarette, please answer the following four questions:

Hypnoscript

A **habit** is a learned response to a stimulus. Some smokers respond to the smell of smoke with the desire for a cigarette.

1. What time is it?

2. Where are you?

3. What are you feeling?

4. What are you doing?

Create a chart to record your own daily smoking record. It should look something like the following chart.

My Daily Smoking Record

Day	Time	Place	Activity	Feeling
___	___	_____	_____	_____
___	___	_____	_____	_____
___	___	_____	_____	_____
___	___	_____	_____	_____
___	___	_____	_____	_____
___	___	_____	_____	_____

The more you know about your smoking habits, the easier it will be for you to cut down. Study your chart and figure out your own smoking behavior.

Cold Turkey

The day comes when you must stop smoking. So gather all your smoking paraphernalia. You know what I mean: ashtrays, lighters, matches, that full pack of cigarettes, the pack with a few cigarettes left inside, and an empty carton if you still have it. Anything else? Search your pockets, desk drawers, old briefcase, and car glove compartment. Where else have you stashed a pack? Please get it.

Dispose of all this stuff. Not in the trash basket under your desk and not in the kitchen garbage. Please get rid of these items somewhere outside of your house and office. Then brush your teeth and feel your mouth being cleansed. This is the feeling of purity that you want. This feeling will stay with you, and no one will ever again equate kissing you with kissing an ashtray.

Calculate how much money you'll save in one month by not buying cigarettes. Then decide how to spend that money. In one month, buy something totally indulgent just for yourself. It's your reward. Decide on the next gift to yourself six months from now. What will you buy? Think about it, fantasize about it, get a picture of it and hang it on your wall. Another reward for you, for not smoking.

Distractions

Cravings come and go. Distract yourself with something to do, and while you are busy your craving may leave you. The most popular distractions that smokers use are …

- ◆ Drinking water.
- ◆ Going for a walk.

- Exercising.

- Going online.

- Knitting, needlepoint, sewing.

- Woodworking, model building.

- Tinkering with the car.

- Snacking.

Notice that most of the above activities give you something to do with your hands, give you something to put into your mouth, or get you moving. I don't recommend snacking as a distracting activity. If you must snack, though, then when you're hypnotized specify the exact foods you'll permit yourself to eat.

Think about the distractions you'll use and list them on the following blank lines. Practice, even before your quit date, distracting yourself with each activity on your list. By the time you quit you'll know which ones work best for you.

Before giving in to a craving, I will distract myself by …

1. _____.

2. _____.

3. _____.

4. _____.

Have a busy day planned for your quit date. Plan to be with friends who are non-smokers and plan to be in places where smoking is prohibited. Go bowling, ride your bike, take a hike—just keep moving.

Stay away from your habit pairs. Any person, place, food, or behavior that you associate with smoking must be avoided for the first few days of your new smoke-free life. Skip the bar or restaurant that you hang out in every Thursday night if you usually sit with a bunch of smokers. Don't drive home along the route that you usually follow, if you always pause on Simpson Street to light up. Don't drink coffee from your green mug if that's the one your brain will pair with having a cigarette.

Have your list of distractions on hand, as well as a list of people you can count on for support. Ex-smokers are your best supporters now.

The Patch

In addition to hypnosis you can use the nicotine patch, which has been available since 1992, to gradually decrease the amount of nicotine you use. It eases withdrawal by slowly releasing nicotine into your bloodstream. The nicotine travels from the patch, through your skin, and into your body. One size does not fit all. Patches come in different strengths, depending upon your body weight, the health of your heart, and the number of cigarettes per day you are accustomed to smoking. More than half the people who use patches stop smoking in a few months. The patch helps you taper your craving for nicotine.

In the Hypnotist's Office

I like to think that I am innovative when I use hypnosis to help someone give up smoking. But according to Dr. Mel Gravitz, in the 1840s a Massachusetts physician, Dr. J. W. Robbins, had a patient addicted to snuff. Using hypnosis and posthypnotic suggestions for amnesia of the hypnosis session, Dr. Robbins said, "The attachment to tobacco in its various shapes has been entirely destroyed, though the patient, a medical student, knew nothing of the cause of it while in the ordinary state." Is there nothing new under the sun?

After you address your physical addiction to nicotine, you can then use hypnosis for your psychological addiction. If you still feel a need for cigarettes as a social aid, as something to keep in your hand, and as a way to feel more self-confident, hypnosis will help you.

Acupuncture

Another adjunct to hypnosis is acupuncture. There are reports of patients who reduce their cravings for cigarettes and reduce withdrawal symptoms, particularly nervousness, after acupuncture sessions. During the session the acupuncturist places special acupuncture needles in the earlobes (this doesn't hurt), a point that somehow affects the smoker's craving.

Like hypnosis, nobody really knows how acupuncture works, but we do know that it does work for some smokers.

Focus On This

Mark Twain had no patience for friends who made a big fuss about giving up smoking. He always claimed it was easy to quit: "I've done it a hundred times," he boasted.

Aversion

Aversion techniques are also helpful in addition to hypnosis. Did you ever see 45 cigarette butts crammed into a water-filled jar? It's enough to make you sick. And that's the idea. Aversive techniques are aimed at making you so repulsed by smoking that you will be unable to light up another one. Such techniques include watching movies of lung cancer operations, seeing a video of an emphysema patient gasping for breath, and exhaling onto a clean white handkerchief. When the black debris appears on the white fabric, you see the contamination that your body receives with every puff you take.

If you tried the patch, acupuncture, aversive activities, and gradual cutting down, and you are still smoking, you are ready to use hypnosis—the method you should have tried first, not last!

Your Plan

Regardless of your method of stopping, studies about smoking cessation all agree that you must have a plan. A written plan is best. It should include …

- ◆ Your list of distracting activities.
- ◆ Your list of supportive people.
- ◆ A list of things to do, because you will now have more time on your hands.
- ◆ A list of behaviors to eliminate because they are paired with smoking.

Here's how Hank decided to defeat his cravings.

Hank's Plan

Distracting Activities	Supportive People	Time Fillers	Habits
Play the guitar sports	Mom	Organize my workshop	Don't read the page on the living room couch
Lift free weights	Next-door neighbor	Sign on to the Internet	Don't play cards at Sid's house
Walk around the block	My boss	Go to the gym	Don't sit on the recliner while watching TV in the den

Please note that after Hank is smoke free for a week or so he will be able to resume his old habits. His unconscious mind will no longer associate those behaviors with smoking.

Writing a Script Just for You

Are you an interval smoker? Do you use cigarettes to fill the interval between one activity and another? Do cigarettes help you make the transition from one place to another—perhaps the car to the office? From one task to another—perhaps cleaning the living room to reading a book? Is smoking a reassuring ritual for you? Does a cigarette in your fingers give you self-confidence in a social situation? Be sure you think about and understand how you use cigarettes and what they do for you.

The majority of ex-smokers who slip up and return to smoking do so after they have mooched a cigarette. Do you have friends who are smokers? Do co-workers smoke? Do members of your family smoke? You will instruct all smokers you know never to give you a cigarette.

Now it's time to write your script. Get plenty of sheets of paper and create your script by including items from each of your lists of ...

- ◆ Distractions.
- ◆ Supportive people.
- ◆ Time fillers.
- ◆ Habit pairs.

Other suggestions to add might be ...

- ◆ *You will drink water to get rid of a craving.*
- ◆ *You will call your brother on those rare occasions when you might think of lighting up.*
- ◆ *You will start your new crafts project immediately.*
- ◆ *Whenever you see Joe smoking, you will feel sorry for him, because he still smokes, and proud of yourself, because you are an ex-smoker.*

In the Hypnotist's Office

The addiction to cigarettes is so strong that we all know people who willingly continue to smoke, even though they are already suffering from some physical disability caused by their cigarette addiction. Last month I got an urgent call from a physician. The doctor wanted Mrs. T. to have an appointment for smoking cessation set up before she was discharged from the hospital. The doctor had found Mrs. T. smoking while she was on oxygen, through the incision in her throat!

Other suggestions to add include …

+ *You can never have "just one" cigarette.*

+ *You will have no desire, no urge for a cigarette.*

+ *You will be unable to put a cigarette in your mouth.*

+ *You will be unable to buy a pack or a carton of cigarettes.*

+ *You will find it easy to do without cigarettes.*

+ *You will notice and appreciate the fresh smell of your hair, your clothes, your home, and your car.*

+ *Smokers are losers; you are a winner.*

+ *At times of emotional stress you will find ways to deal with your feelings without picking up a cigarette.*

Ask the hypnotist to encourage you to visualize yourself in many situations without a cigarette. In each place that you see yourself without a cigarette, notice how proud you are, how good you are feeling.

An age-progression technique can work here. An older you, perhaps 10 years from now, will speak to the current you, thanking you for stopping smoking.

Focus On This

While hypnotized you might want the hypnotist to remind you of the health benefits of quitting smoking, the money you will be saving, and the people who will have a new respect for you.

Sometimes I suggest that a client visualize a deceased relative or a religious figure. That person then speaks to my client, usually a brief but right-on-target bit of advice about smoking.

When you and your hypnotist create just the right script, you'll have an easy time stopping your cigarette habit. Hypnosis can change your attitude so you do not need to use willpower. Hypnosis alone will do the trick.

Do-It-Yourself

You know how to hypnotize yourself. Simply go to your special place and visualize your special scene—the one you established back in Chapter 6. When you are ready to set your timer and begin your induction, give yourself the following instructions:

+ *I cannot touch a cigarette.*

+ *I cannot put a cigarette near my mouth.*

+ *I will gag if a cigarette is in my mouth.*

Repeat these instructions several times. Write them if necessary. When you hypnotize yourself, you may use these instructions as your only script or you may add them to your full list of hypnotic suggestions. Say them, visualize them, and say them again. You will become an ex-smoker.

The Least You Need to Know

- ◆ Nicotine is an extremely powerful drug.
- ◆ Sometimes smokers self-medicate by smoking and need a prescription drug to quit.
- ◆ It is possible to give up cigarettes.
- ◆ Hypnosis can make it easy for you to stop.

Hypnosis to Stop Drinking and Drugging

In This Chapter

- People in trouble with drugs and alcohol
- Getting out of trouble
- Hypnosis to stop your drugging
- Hypnosis to stop your drinking
- Preventing addiction

We all know the dangers of too much alcohol and too much pill-popping. We also know how difficult it is to get drinkers and users to consent to enter treatment. When they finally do enter a treatment program, there's a strong likelihood that they won't stay, or that, once out, they'll relapse.

Hypnosis can help. If you're troubled with a substance-abuse problem, hypnosis can change your attitude so that you will want to get help. Hypnosis can help you comply with the program of your choice. Read on and you'll be amazed at these success stories.

Fred and Carol, Anthony and Tina

Fred, Carol, Anthony, and Tina are typical substance-abuse clients. It's been years since I first met them, and they each were treated with different hypnotic techniques. When you go to a hypnotist, be sure you get a method that is right for you. Each of these four clients had different personality styles and different needs. Thus, they responded best to individualized scripts.

Today they are still drug- and alcohol-free. I know they're drug- and drink-free because I speak to them once a year. They were each given the posthypnotic suggestion to check in with me on their anniversary date—the date they became sober. I use their hypnosis sessions as the models for clients who come to my office for help with drinking or drug problems.

Fred

Fred is a carpenter who enjoys his job, particularly when the project is outdoors. He's a hunter and fisherman and has a country house as well as a city apartment. Fred grew up with his mom, dad, and two older sisters. No one in his family had a problem with alcohol. Possibly one or both of his parents may have a gene for addiction but it was never apparent because neither of them ever drank—not socially, not at formal dinners, not even a beer. Alcohol did not appeal to them. But it did appeal to their son.

> **Look into My Eyes**
>
> Excessive alcohol consumption is responsible for more than 100,000 deaths every year in the United States.

Fred says he had his first drink of alcohol in sixth grade at a party. "I'll never forget the feeling," he recalls. "I finally felt normal. Just a few minutes after that drink I knew I could be like anybody else. I considered myself a regular kid from that day on." When he came to my office he was in his mid-20s. His fiancée was concerned about marrying him because of his excessive drinking. He wanted to marry her but he wanted to continue his feelings of normalcy.

I know the value of Alcoholics Anonymous (AA) and every drinker I previously treated had agreed to be hypnotized and given the suggestion that they'd attend meetings. (Twelve-step programs work for all addictions, not just alcoholism.) I hoped to persuade Fred to join AA, too, but he would not hear of it. We talked, and he told me that he never drinks in his country home, yet always drinks after work in a variety of bars in the city or at his apartment. Fred cut down on his drinking after our first session and stopped drinking after six hypnosis sessions. The useful suggestions were as follows:

Session One

- *You are as good as anyone else.*

- *You are a good worker and a good fiancé.*

- *You will not drink anywhere but the bars.*

- *There will be no liquor in your apartment. Any time you are tempted to violate this agreement, you will take the two-hour drive to your country house where you know you'll be safe from temptation.*

Session Two

- *You are as good as anyone else.*

- *You are a man of your word.*

- *You'll notice traits about yourself that you admire.*

- *You will continue to drink only in bars, and only Monday through Thursday evenings. You will drive to your country house if you are tempted to violate this agreement.*

Session Three

- *You are a competent, capable man.*

- *You will continue your after-work drinking, but you will be satisfied with fewer drinks.*

- *You will leave the bars earlier than usual and be happy to do so.*

- *You will be proud of yourself.*

Session Four

- *You are a strong man capable of accomplishing a major life change.*

- *Each evening at the bar, you will notice things you do not like about the environment. You will be happy to leave.*

Session Five

- *You don't need to drink anymore.*

- *You will order less alcohol, more soda.*

- *Walking into a bar will feel uncomfortable. Coming home will feel extremely warm and inviting.*

- *You will know where and when AA meetings are held in your neighborhood and you'll know you can always go there.*

Focus On This _____

There is treatment available for you if you are chemically dependent and motivated to stop. On the Internet, drop into any search engine the terms, "chemical dependency," "addiction," "rehabilitation," "substance abuse," or "drug treatment," and you will find plenty of options.

Session Six

◆ *You have no interest in alcohol.*

◆ *Drinking alcohol will make you feel sick.*

◆ *You will be unwilling to go into a bar.*

◆ *Not drinking will make you proud.*

◆ *You'll enjoy working on new projects in your country home. You'll plan these projects after work, at home in the city.*

◆ *You'll know if and when AA will be useful to you.*

These hypnotic interventions worked for Fred. He keeps in touch every year and so far, so good.

Carol

Carol is a 36-year-old mother of two who began smoking pot while in college and never gave up her daily habit, except during her pregnancies. I explained to her that regular pot smokers often use marijuana to regulate their moods. They are actually self-medicating, and if placed on the right prescription drug, will do just fine. Carol wasn't interested in that idea. She was concerned that her children were getting old enough to know what she was doing and she wanted to stop her addiction immediately.

Carol confessed to moodiness that only pot could take away. In conversation, she spoke about her interest in music, particularly the folk songs of the 1960s. Carol gave up her pot habit after two hypnosis sessions. Here are the suggestions that worked for Carol:

Session One

◆ *You will surround yourself with music—at home, in the car, and at work.*

◆ *You will become aware of the songs that change your mood.*

◆ *Every time you smoke pot you will remember that you are a mother of two precious children.*

◆ *You want to protect your children.*

Session Two

- *Music is your new tranquilizer and mood stabilizer.*

- *Smoking pot is extremely unappealing to you.*

- *You will forget to smoke most days this week.*

- *You will have no interest in buying more illegal drugs when your supply runs out.*

Carol and I did talk about attending a 12-step program and she agreed to get information about meetings in her area. To date, she's not gone and she's maintained her drug-free status. She says she will go to a meeting if the desire or even the thought of pot returns.

Anthony

Anthony is a tough guy from the Bronx who has been arrested because of possession of drugs. He was once in a gang but now, at age 31, would like to get rid of his drug addiction. Our conversation revealed his feelings of shame. He knows he has disappointed his mother who still prays for him; she has not given up hope that he will change. Anthony's family is religious, and he attended parochial school. Anthony stopped using after one session, but I persuaded him to come in for a session once a month for six months. Anthony's suggestions follow.

Focus On This

Hypnosis can teach you how to create feelings of well-being. The good feelings you once got from alcohol or drugs can be yours again by hypnotically pairing those feelings with music, or prayer, or almost any activity or behavior you can come up with.

Session One

- *You are finished with your old ways.*

- *A new group is waiting for you. They are people just like you.*

- *You will eagerly go to your first 12-step meeting.*

- *You will go to meetings daily.*

Session Two

- *You will continue to follow the 12-step procedures.*

- *You will eagerly choose your sponsor.*

- *You will enjoy your sobriety.*

Session Three

- *You will ask your mother for the honor of escorting her to church next week.*

- *You will begin a personal relationship with a forgiving God.*

- *You will think about your future in a realistic, mature way and plan for the next part of your life.*

Anthony's continuing monthly sessions reinforced the suggestions to comply with the 12-step program and congratulated him for his attention to his mother and his religion.

Tina

Tina is a middle-aged nurse who has had a prescription-drug habit for years. She was not interested in getting off her drugs; she liked them. But, new policies at her hospital made it impossible for her to continue pilfering pills. She said she was desperate to eliminate her need for the drugs. I said she was too physiologically dependent upon the drugs to think about abruptly stopping. I advised a *detoxification* program and then *rehab*. She wasn't sure about that but agreed to four hypnosis sessions. Here are the suggestions that worked for Tina.

Session One

- *There is a place that will take good care of you.*

- *You no longer have to be a criminal.*

- *You deserve to have experts wean you off your pills.*

- *You can recover and lead a normal, law-abiding life.*

- *It will feel so good to lead an honest, open life.*

- *You won't need the pills after you get proper care.*

Hypnoscript

Detoxification is a hospital-based program that maintains your physical health while gradually withdrawing you from a drug, under medical supervision. **Rehab,** or rehabilitation, is the program that teaches you how to live without that drug.

Tina called after the first session to announce that she was leaving for a three-month drug-treatment program and did not need the rest of the four sessions she originally agreed to.

Your hypnotist should know how to build on your strengths when asking you to give up something that has been important to you. I based my suggestions to Fred, Carol, Anthony, and Tina on the following information:

- **Fred** drank to feel normal. He did not drink all weekend. The outdoor activities he did at his country home probably helped him feel equal to others. He needed evidence of his competence and he needed to stay away from bars, the only other places where he felt good.

- **Carol** was able to stop smoking during pregnancy, because her unborn children were her motivation. Her children can continue to motivate her, and she needed something to call her own that would put her in a good mood—music filled that bill.

- **Anthony** needed a ganglike sense of belonging. Alcoholics Anonymous provides that. He also needed someone to follow. His gang leader could be supplanted by his AA sponsor. Anthony's spiritual and religious needs were apparent when he discussed his mother, so encouraging him to escort her to church would provide him the opportunity to benefit both from church and from his mother's attention.

Look into My Eyes

Beer commercials are known to trigger episodes of drinking. If commercials are responsible for your binges, please watch television with the remote in your hand. Beer is the nation's fourth most popular beverage. Soft drinks, coffee, and milk are the first three.

- **Tina** had a state license and was motivated to protect it. She needed reassurance that all was not lost and that there was a facility and a program that could handle her.

Triggers

When you walk into a bar you want to drink. When you hang out with druggies you want to drug. It is the hypnotist's job to get you away from the situation that propels you to do something you really don't want to do anymore.

What are your triggers for drinking or drugging? The usual triggers are ...

- **People.** Someone who is what your mother called a bad influence

- **Places.** Environments that encourage the kind of behavior that you want to stop doing

- **Feelings.** Emotions that you prefer not to handle, so you bury them under drugs or alcohol

Figure out what your triggers are and arrive at your hypnosis session with a list of people, places, and feelings that encourage you to continue your addiction. Your hypnotist can tell you to stay away from those people and places and can suggest ways for you to cope with the feelings you don't want.

An interesting method for getting rid of feelings while hypnotized is as follows:

1. Visualize a balloon.

2. Feel that unwanted feeling.

3. See that unwanted feeling as a geometric shape.

4. Insert the shape into the opening of the balloon.

5. Release the balloon.

6. Watch your feelings fly away.

Please use the "My Triggers" chart to identify your triggers.

My Triggers

People	Places	Feelings

Hypnotic Techniques for Substance Abusers

You know you are suffering from substance abuse if you continue your pattern of use even though it gets you into trouble. Several hypnotic techniques are useful in treating this condition, and I find the use of audiotapes, age regression, and age progression particularly helpful.

Audiotapes

If you have a good talent for hypnosis you might be as fortunate as a young lady in Ohio who at age 29, with a husband who was a drug dealer, two children, and a daily drug habit herself, gave up cocaine after listening to a hypnosis tape every day, twice a day, for six months. Dr. Roger Page of Ohio State University kept track of her for six years and she remained drug-free. Amazingly, the tape she listened to was not a "stop drugs" tape. It was a hypnosis tape for weight loss! She said that when it put her into a hypnotic trance she substituted the word "cocaine" for the word "food" and soon enough it ended her nightmare.

Some clients are reassured if they take home a tape of their hypnosis session. They play it any time they feel their resistance waning. (Read more about hypnosis tapes in Chapter 6.)

Age Regression

As you remember from Chapter 4, your hypnotist can *age regress* you. In your mind, you can return to the time and place you had your first encounter with the substance that you are now abusing. In the hypnotic state you can change the outcome of the situation and pursue different options.

If I were to do an age regression with Fred, I would have him clearly see himself at that sixth-grade party. But, after he takes the drink I would suggest that he feels sick, gets yelled at by some adults, makes a fool of himself, and decides never to drink again. Then I would ask him to visualize himself at the same party talking to friends while drinking soft drinks. I would have him notice that he feels comfortable and is socializing with ease.

Focus On This _____

In 1994, $20 billion of tax-payer money went to Medicare for inpatient hospitalization and treatment of substance abuse and addiction-related illnesses. Nearly 14 million adult Americans have alcohol-abuse problems. Alcohol abuse is involved in half the homicides in America.

Look into My Eyes _____

During a typical year in the United States, there are 90 million (!) visits to hospital emergency rooms because of over-doses and other drug-related problems.

Sometimes I age regress clients to the time of their worst hangover or overdose. I encourage images of the hospital, jail, or worse. Then I give the posthypnotic suggestion that if they are ever tempted to indulge, they will immediately re-experience these bodily sensations and emotional feelings.

Age Progression

Clients can see themselves in the future, at events where they have the opportunity to drink—a family celebration, a business lunch, a friend's wedding, or on an airplane—and so, with hypnotic suggestions, they can also see themselves refusing the drink, preferring water.

Prepare yourself for future events. Think about next week and next month. Actually take out your calendar. Where and when will you meet temptation? Please list each upcoming event and then practice, in hypnosis, visualizing yourself at the occasion without indulging.

Hard Drugs

How do you know you are addicted? When you have a compulsive need for a habit-forming substance that you know is harming you, you are addicted.

Health professionals prefer to use the terms "substance dependence" and "substance abuse." First comes substance abuse—using a substance that gets you into trouble at home, at work, in school, or with the law, and persisting at using it even though it causes serious problems in your life. Then comes *substance dependence*, which means that you can't get off this substance even though you are trying, and you want to end the trouble it's causing you. Instead you spend a lot of time trying to obtain this substance and then recovering from its effects on you, and to make matters worse, you need it in larger amounts as time goes by.

Hypnoscript

Substance dependence is an out-of-control pattern of substance use. The user is unsuccessful at stopping, spends a lot of time, energy, or money to get the substance, and needs more and more of it.

In substance dependence you develop a tolerance for the substance. A smoker might have choked on his first cigarette and could smoke a second only after waiting one hour, and even then got dizzy. Years later that smoker might need 20 cigarettes a day to feel good. That is tolerance. Drinkers, too, may remember when one drink was sufficient; years later a few six-packs may not do the trick.

Certain drugs are more addictive than others. The World Health Organization defines addictive drugs as those that produce, in the great majority of users, an irresistible need for that drug, an increased *tolerance* to its effects, and a physical dependence so that when it is stopped there are severe symptoms.

In the course of a year, I may see clients with addictions to amphetamines (uppers, stimulants, diet pills, speed), marijuana, cocaine, sedatives (sleeping pills, tranquilizers), heroin or other opiates (Codeine, Demerol), and lately I've seen some youngsters addicted to sniffing glue and other solvents. I do not hypnotize any of them to help them get off their drug until I first speak to their physicians. It's possible that they are physically dependent upon the drug and, whereas hypnosis can take care of the psychological dependence on it, it cannot address the physical dependence. That must be done under medical supervision, usually in a hospital.

Drug use changes your body chemistry so that your brain no longer remembers how to manufacture certain chemicals that you need. In an experiment where mice were offered a choice of cocaine or food, those who were already exposed to the cocaine chose the cocaine over the food. The physical addiction for the drug was so strong that the mice ate cocaine until they died, never stopping to eat food or drink water—both of which were available.

When you are finally off drugs, please find a program that will give you the emotional support you need. Most rehabilitation centers have out-patient treatment programs that are run by substance-abuse counselors. Many mental health centers have psychotherapists who specialize in the treatment of recovering addicts. When you start using drugs, you stop growing emotionally and psychologically. Your emotional age may be decades younger than your chronological age. It wasn't noticeable when you were stoned all the time, but now people will expect you to function in the world of responsible behavior.

I tell my clients that they used to "shoot up and throw up" but now they must "suit up and show up."

Look into My Eyes

Many drugs need to be withdrawn under medical supervision, and a good hypnotic suggestion that gets the client to stop using could kill that client. Be sure your hypnotist knows which drugs need medical support for withdrawal.

Hypnoscript

When you need more and more of a substance to get its desired effect, you have developed **tolerance**. Your body can become less responsive to a drug because of repeated use.

The Power of Alcohol

At some time in their lives, as many as 90 percent of adults in the United States have had a drink. Of those, 60 percent of the men and 30 percent of the women will have had a hangover. Most learn from the experience. It is suspected that those who repeat their mistakes or do not at first suffer any adverse effects may be biologically predisposed to develop alcoholism.

You know you are drunk when you have any of these symptoms following a drinking episode and not caused by any medical problem:

- Slurred speech

- Unsteady gait

- Crossed eyes

- Trouble paying attention to anything around you

- May be in a stupor or a coma

- Impaired judgment

- Behavior that is socially inappropriate

Alcoholics cannot drink like other people. They are unable to stop at one or two drinks; their body chemistry makes them crave more and more alcohol once they begin drinking. Sadly, alcoholics often have the delusion they can control their drinking, even though they have plenty of evidence to the contrary. During hypnosis I remind my alcoholic clients that they have a progressive illness and their genes will not permit them to control it.

Alcoholics cannot be social drinkers. "Just one drink" is a myth. Alcoholics like to make deals with themselves such as …

- I'll never drink when I'm alone.

- I'll drink only when I'm alone.

- I won't drink until after 6 P.M.

- I'll drink at parties, only.

> **In the Hypnotist's Office**
>
> I playfully ask my alcoholic clients to rate their addictions according to the following scale: Imagine you are in your favorite bar and a fly lands in your drink. If you order another drink, you're a moderate drinker; if you shoo away the fly and then gulp down the drink, you're a serious drinker; if you pick up the fly, smack it around, and demand it "spit that out right now," you know you are in big trouble.

The deals never work—once an alcoholic, always an alcoholic. The risk of taking just one drink is far too high.

One hypnotist did such a good job keeping his client Jack away from alcohol that when Jack went to the chiropractor for a massage, he smelled the alcohol in the office and promptly left!

Higher Powers and Powerful Hires: AA and Hypnosis

Ask yourself what you would do with your time, your energy, and your money if you were not drinking or drugging. It's important to know where you would go, who you would be with, and what your goals would be. That's why the structure of AA or any other 12-step program is useful. It provides …

- ◆ Meetings at specified times.
- ◆ Immediate fellowship.
- ◆ Goals (steps) to work toward.
- ◆ Role models who have been in your position.

Some drinkers have strong addiction needs. I like them to transfer their addiction from alcohol to AA. With hypnosis they become compulsive about going to meetings and the rooms serve as the friendly barlike atmosphere. Everyone is sober at AA, and there are usually some role models at meetings who demonstrate that it's possible to get high on life.

Alcoholics Anonymous teaches the value of surrendering to a Higher Power to help overcome alcoholism. I teach my clients to also surrender to the "Powerful Hire," the hypnotist they have engaged to help them control their addiction.

I include some slogans from AA in my hypnotic script for substance abusers. I tell them they need only follow the program one day at a time, and I urge them not to complicate their lives and instead KISS: Keep It Simple, Stupid. I remind them that if they take a drink, that drink will take them right back where they started.

In the Hypnotist's Office
I was trying to get Alan to see that his drinking problem was about to get him fired. He had already lost his wife and kids because of his alcoholism. He was insisting that AA was too spiritual for him; he didn't want any religious awakenings. He said, "The only flashes of light I'm comfortable with are the ones from the police car chasing me down the highway." He got fired and then straightened out.

People who've attended 12-step meetings often hear warnings about the feelings that can bring on a relapse. You can benefit from this information by asking your hypnotist to include the following warning in your script:

*You might slip up if you are **h**ungry, **a**ngry, **l**onely, or **t**ired. You will remember the acronym HALT and immediately attend to any of these feelings when they come up.*

During hypnosis I suggest to drinkers that they not drink alcohol between sessions or meetings, but that they can still drink like a fish—water, that is. And if they agree beforehand, I encourage them to go to as many meetings as possible. Finally, it's always a good idea for them to have role models—that's one value of attending meetings.

In the Hypnotist's Office

When I hypnotize an addicted person to enthusiastically go to a 12-step program, the results are impressive. Alcoholics Anonymous has no requirement for membership other than a desire to stop drinking. According to their last survey, the majority of members are between 31 and 50 years old, with an average age of 44. There are more men than women, but among those under age 30, 40 percent are women. Forty percent of AA members are married, professionals account for the largest occupational group, and 45 percent of members have been sober for more than 5 years.

Hypnosis for Addiction Prevention

Most substance abusers get into big trouble before they finally quit. It is necessary for intervention to begin early, in the form of education. In a poll of teachers and students, both were asked what it is that teenagers worry about most. Teachers thought teenagers worried most about their parents and family problems. But teens said they worried most about drugs. Both groups were then asked if their school was free of drugs. The majority of teachers said "yes." The majority of students said "no." (Half of the high school students said they could buy pot in their school.)

We spend taxpayers' money on drug treatment programs, law-enforcement programs, and jails and hospitals for drug abusers. Hypnosis could be a low-cost, highly effective adjunct to our efforts. Hypnosis can help in training children to …

- Resist negative influences.
- Become more assertive.
- Understand that "users are losers."

An interesting way to accomplish this is through the use of role-playing. Heather's parents worried about her because her best friend in junior high had fallen in with a bad crowd, and Heather was torn between loyalty to her friend and loyalty to her family's values. Her parents asked me to help strengthen her to resist her friend's influence.

Heather and I spent the first session chatting and building rapport. During the second session we role-played. I was her friend using the power of persuasion to convince her to come with me to a party. Heather tried to offer excuses but stammered, hesitated, and finally shrugged her shoulders and agreed to join me.

Then I hypnotized Heather and asked her to visualize herself as strong and powerful. In her mind's eye she was able to refuse her friend's invitation. While she was hypnotized, I did an age progression, where she saw herself as a happy, successful, drug-free high school student. At our third and final session, we again tried the role-play situation. With no additional hypnosis, Heather was able to clearly refuse my invitation and get me to shut up.

Focus On This

A child who reaches age 21 without smoking, abusing alcohol, or using drugs, is virtually certain never to do so.

—Joseph A. Califano Jr., President of the National Center on Addiction and Substance Abuse at Columbia University

Hypnosis is a most underutilized intervention.

Do-It-Yourself

Here's a way for you to strengthen yourself to resist temptation. Think of a person who is a bad influence on you. You know who I mean. The one your mother would never approve of. The one who encourages you to drink or drug. Now picture that person clearly in your mind. Now picture yourself talking to that person. You are trying to resist temptation but your so-called friend is encouraging you to enjoy yourself with recreational drugs or drink.

Now's the time to utilize your hypnosis skills. Grab your timer, go to your favorite place for hypnosis, and visualize your best hypnosis induction scene. Remember your induction instructions from back in Chapter 6? Use them now.

When you're in your hypnotic trance, you will see yourself talking to your "friend." You will listen closely and hear your friend trying to persuade you to do something you know is wrong. Watch yourself in this scene. You are becoming stronger and stronger. With every word this person utters, your resolve becomes more and more intense. You are stronger. Your friend no longer has influence over you. You are adamant in your position. Listen to yourself speak. You are definite. You are positive. You are firm. You are staying away from addictive substances and you are staying away from this friend. Watch yourself as you say good-bye to this person. You are stubborn. You are unyielding. You are right.

Congratulations. When you emerge from your hypnotic state you will be able to replicate this scenario in real life.

The Least You Need to Know

- ◆ Substance abuse is a major health problem and social problem.

- ◆ Hypnosis can be useful in prevention and in recovery.

- ◆ Hypnosis should not be your only intervention; your hypnotist should work along with other appropriate medical professionals.

Chapter 12

Nail-Biting and Other Nasty Habits

In This Chapter

- ◆ All about bad habits

- ◆ Are you a worrier?

- ◆ Pulling out your hair

- ◆ Biting your nails

- ◆ Mastering your habits using hypnosis

Are you a perfect passenger? When you sit in the front seat of the car and someone else is driving, do you always have your feet on the floor of the car? Or do you have the habit of placing your foot on an imaginary brake whenever the car needs to be stopped? We all have habits—some bad, some worse—that seem to stay with us no matter how hard we try to get rid of them.

You can erase a bad habit or trade in an ugly old habit for a bright new one by using hypnosis. Hypnosis makes it easy to change your behavior.

If you're one of my clients, you're probably coming to see me because you'd like hypnosis to help you get rid of your nail-biting, phobia, or worry habit. These are the most common nonaddictive habits that folks look to hypnosis to solve.

Habits, Habits, Habits

Some of your *habits* are wonderful. You probably don't even think about it, but whenever someone greets you, you respond with a cheery "Hello!" That's a good habit. When you bend down to put on your sneakers and take each end of the shoelace into your fingers, you don't think about what you're doing. Your fingers automatically twist and maneuver to create a knot and a bow. Tying shoes is a complicated habit. When you were a toddler you couldn't do it; a few years later you could, but with lots of effort. Today it is an automatic behavior—a habit.

Hypnoscript

A **habit** is a behavior pattern acquired by frequent repetition.

Remember the time that you felt just awful. Your head was pounding, your throat was sore, your bones ached, and you hoped you'd make it home before collapsing from the flu. Just before you got to your door, your neighbor greeted you. "Hi, how are you?" she innocently asked. You, staggering, replied, "Fine, thank you." That's your habit kicking in.

The wonderful and terrible thing about a habit is that the more you do it, the easier it becomes to do it. You no longer have to think about tying your shoes—that's wonderful. You automatically light a cigarette when you pick up your cup of coffee—that's terrible. After you've repeated a series of actions, one after the other, your brain knows how to go there. And it does go there, over and over.

Agatha Christie wrote, "Curious thing, habits. People themselves never knew they had them." Life is more hopeful when you acknowledge your habits and understand that you can control your behavior and change your habits.

When my children were small they used to drop everything and dash outside whenever they heard the bells of the ice-cream truck. One evening as we were concluding a family birthday celebration by stuffing ourselves with slice after slice of a yummy chocolate ice-cream cake, the familiar jingle could be heard through the window. Without missing a beat, the kids each pushed away from the table and ran. When behavior is propelled by habit it may no longer be serving any purpose. What are you doing out of habit, not out of need?

Focus On This

Thoughts lead to acts, acts lead to habits, habits lead to character.

—Ezra Taft Benson, U.S. statesman

The Worry Habit

Most of us have plenty to worry about but we don't let our worries interfere with our living. We are able to cope. Some people develop the habit of worrying to the extent that joy is removed from their lives. Tension doesn't go away. Sometimes this is because of an inborn tendency toward anxiety. Other times it is because of a bad habit.

The worry habit is easy to create. What do you worry about? While you're growing up, you worry about your face (pimples), your parents, your teacher, your friends; then you reach an age where you worry about earning money, finding a job, finding a mate, and having children. Before long you're worrying about keeping your money, keeping your job, keeping your mate, and finding your children. As you get older you're back to worrying about your face (wrinkles), your parents—and the worry cycle never seems to stop.

In the Hypnotist's Office

Joan answered an ad for a bookkeeper in a hypnotherapist's office. The doctor offered her the job and said, "It will be your responsibility to do my worrying for me." Joan was puzzled. The doctor explained, "I worry about my patients; I don't want to worry about money, too." Joan understood and then asked about her salary. "Eighty thousand dollars a year, to start," said the doctor. "Wow! That's an amazing salary for a bookkeeper. How can this small office afford to pay me so much money?" asked Joan. The doctor replied, "You can start today. That's your first worry."

Hypnosis can help you stop worrying. You can stop your worry habits by paying attention to the behaviors and thoughts that lead up to your worries. After you identify those specific actions and ideas, hypnotic suggestions can intervene. Are you worried about paying your bills? What starts the worrying? For Sherman the worry habit takes this route:

1. It's almost the sixteenth of the month; that's when my mortgage payment is due.

2. I don't have enough in the checking account to cover it.

3. The bank will repossess the house.

4. My family will be homeless.

5. I am a poor provider.

6. I am so worried. It's almost the sixteenth of the month.

Sherman is forgetful. He forgets that "almost the sixteenth" is not the same as "the sixteenth." Every month he goes through the same mental torture. Every month he worries and worries about paying the mortgage even though on the fourteenth of the month he gets a monthly check from his basement tenant. Every month he pays his mortgage exactly on time. He has never paid a late penalty, which is more than many nonworriers can claim. Sherman has a behavior pattern that is based upon monthly repetition of the same thoughts. Hypnosis can break his worry pattern.

He may have begun this pattern of thoughts years ago, when money was scarce, or he may have begun this pattern because it is the only one he knows.

Did you grow up in a home with a worrier? If that's all you know, then you can't expect to behave any other way. New behavior needs to be learned. Who will teach it to you if everyone in your environment perpetuates the old ways, the old responses, the worry ways?

If every month of every year of his childhood and adolescence Sherman saw a parent panic because it was almost mortgage day, and if there is no intervention to teach him another way to respond to the approaching date, then that worry behavior will persist.

Sherman eradicated his monthly mortgage dread with one session of hypnosis. He wrote his own script. He asked me to give him the following suggestions:

- *You will not think about your mortgage payment until the day it is to be mailed in.*

- *On that date you will write a check and mail it.*

- *In the rare circumstance that your checking account does not have enough to cover the check, you will borrow money from your pension fund and put it into your checking account.*

- *You will always have enough money to pay your mortgage.*

Sherman grew up with worriers and his mind easily goes down those worry paths so clearly etched in his brain. Hypnosis has helped him create new pathways—pathways of optimism and ease.

Your Worry Pathway

What do you worry about? Try breaking down your worry into successive thoughts. What is your first thought? Then your next? Where does that lead you? This is your worry pathway.

Answer the following questions to trace your worry pathway.

1. My first worry thought is:

   _____

2. My next worry thought is:

   _____

3. I am led to the following worry thought:

   _____

4. Now I am really worried about:

   _____

5. Next worry thought:

   _____

6. Next worry thought:

   _____

7. Next worry thought:

   _____

It always takes you around in a circle; as you continue writing, you'll find yourself repeating the first item on your list when you get to number 5, 6, or 7. Now, look at each item individually. Come up with an answer or solution or opposing idea to just one of the worries on your pathway.

Fill in the following list to eliminate your worries.

Worry #	Possible Solution, Answer, or Opposing Idea
1.	_____
2.	_____
3.	_____
4.	_____

Then, answer another and complete your chart. You'll have clear sentences that you can take to your hypnotist or use when you practice self-hypnosis. (See Chapters 6 and 7 for self-hypnosis instructions.) Hearing and visualizing the responses to your worry list will help you to overcome your worry habit.

The Phobia Habit

People who are likely to develop *phobias* are also likely to be good hypnotic subjects. Scientists haven't yet figured out why this is so. Some guess that very suggestible people, the ones who have lots of talent for hypnosis, are suggestible enough to believe many horror stories that others would disregard. If you have a phobia, you're in luck because hypnosis will work very well.

Hypnoscript

A persistent illogical fear of a thing or specific situation is called a **phobia.**

Focus On This

Sometimes when the hypnotist is very skilled and experienced, regression works. Hypnotist Paul Gustafson regressed a client who was terrified of thunder. When the client saw himself at a young age, he saw his mother shrieking when it thundered. Gustafson hypnotized him to think of his mother's response as a distant, out-of-date memory that could no longer influence him. It worked!

The phobias I treat most often are fear of flying, fear of dogs, and fear of heights. There is no limit to the fears that people have.

Phobias begin to take over your life. A young woman I recently treated was afraid of dogs. She first stopped walking down certain streets, then stopped going to work, then stayed indoors—all this in an effort to avoid seeing a dog. If you're afraid of dogs and go to moderate lengths to avoid them, and you lead a normal life, you do not have a phobia. The phobic person becomes extremely inconvenienced and limited because of fear.

When I attended an out-of-town weekend conference last month, I sat next to a physician who had traveled 2,000 miles for the meeting. I was puzzled to see him rush away after the Saturday-evening lecture. Sunday morning he explained that his fear of elevators made it impossible for him to stay at the hotel. Instead, he had to call the Chamber of Commerce to locate someone with a ground-level room to rent for the weekend.

Most phobias have some truth to them, and your hypnotist must respect that truth. You should not be dreadfully afraid of dogs to the point where you stop your life. But the hypnotist should not tell you to embrace all dogs. Some caution is necessary with some dogs. The words of the hypnotist are very important. You don't want to be told to give up your fear of heights, and then find yourself dangling, fearlessly, from a rooftop. Carefully plan your script with your hypnotist.

In the Hypnotist's Office

Gloria said, "For 20 years my husband and I flew around the world, but last year I became extremely frightened, certain our flight would end in disaster. Dr. Temes suggested hypnosis. I was skeptical, 'I'm too strong-willed,' I protested, 'it will never work on me.' After an hour-and-a-half session I knew I was right. 'See, it didn't work,' I insisted, 'I feel the same as before I walked in.' Dr. Temes smiled serenely. I left, convinced nothing had been accomplished. Two days later my husband and I flew to London, then Paris and Venice. I was calm and relaxed. My husband said, 'How nice to land without gashes on my arms from your nails digging into me.' Perhaps hypnosis works, after all."

Phobia hypnosis always includes suggestions for visualizing the feared situation, beginning in gradual increments. A dog-phobic client would be encouraged, over several sessions, to visualize a sweet, small dog contained inside a pen. The person then imagines herself looking at the dog:

- From the window of a car, across the street.
- From outside the car, still across the street.
- From a few yards away.
- From up against the pen.

And then she is instructed to visualize the dog on a leash and then gradually see herself walking toward the dog, eventually petting it. This may take several sessions. In addition to visualizations the dog-phobic person is given hypnotic suggestions such as these:

- *There are sweet, nice dogs and not-so-nice dogs. You can easily tell the difference between the two.*
- *You will be wary of certain dogs.*
- *You will be fond of other dogs.*
- *Lovable dogs will make you smile. You'll enjoy playing with them.*

Hypnosis must change the pathway in your mind to eliminate a phobia. The client is instructed to go from seeing a dog and feeling panic and fear to seeing a dog and feeling self-control and then delight. Self-mastery is an important part of the phobia cure.

Remember the age-regression technique? It's a useful hypnotic method for phobia elimination. I regress the client to an age before the phobia began. At that point we recall the first time the phobia appeared, and then go back to a few moments before it appeared. The client re-experiences that unafraid response, and visualizes responding like that whenever that situation comes up, until the present day. Recalling the first time the phobia appeared gives the client the opportunity to then re-create the situation in a positive light; this time there is no phobia.

Hair-Pulling

Compulsive hair-pulling is not just a habit, which is bad enough, but it is a neurological disorder. It is treated with medication and/or hypnosis. Most clients first try hypnosis because there are no side effects. There are almost 9 million people in the United States who have the uncontrollable urge to pull out their hair. For some, it is the hair on their heads, for others it is eyelashes, eyebrows, or arm or leg hairs. The average age of onset of this condition is 12½ years old.

A letter to Ann Landers' column about compulsive hair-pulling resulted in 12,000 requests for information! It is thought that 25 to 35 percent of the wig buyers in this country have *trichotillomania*—that's the name of this hair-pulling disorder. In Greek, *thri* means hair, *tillein* means to pull, and *mania* is a frenzy of activity. There is usually noticeable hair loss, perhaps an empty patch on a certain place on the scalp. The many clients I've treated who have trichotillomania are always wishing they could stop it, but all their attempts fail. It is a compulsive disorder over which they have no control—until they try hypnosis, that is.

Hypnoscript

Trichotillomania is a term coined by a French dermatologist in 1889 to describe the irresistible urge to pull out one's own hair.

My most useful suggestions for hair-pullers is to prohibit them from plucking hairs, encourage them to treat their body gently, and tell them that their hair will feel terrible to the touch. During hypnosis I inform them that they will hate to touch their hair except for grooming purposes.

In the Hypnotist's Office

Yvette was a successful business owner whose employees didn't know that her fashionable brunette wig hid a large bald spot caused by Yvette pulling out her hair. Sometimes the urge was so strong that Yvette would leave her office and have a cab drive her around the block a few times so she could remove her wig and pull. Afterward, she'd return to work calm. A good hypnotic subject, Yvette eliminated the need to pull her hair in three sessions. Her wig is long gone, but she does have one complaint: Some gray hairs are coming in and she wants to pull them out. No matter how hard she tries she cannot get her fingers to pull!

Nail-Biting

Ed is a trial lawyer who makes a good impression in court. He's large, handsome, and kind of tough looking—except for his hands. His nails are bitten down to the cuticles, his fingertips are often bloody, and he is ashamed of his hands. He's concerned that the jury may take him less seriously when they notice that he's a nail-biter.

Some people erroneously believe that if you take away one habit another will replace it. That's a rare occurrence, but it did happen to Ed. After one session he proudly reported that he'd stopped biting his nails, but sadly admitted that he was tugging on his tie. That's when I gave him my red-pen suggestions:

- *Whenever you see a red pen, hold a red pen, use a red pen, or know that a red pen is in your pocket or your briefcase it will satisfy you.*

- *The red pen will keep you calm.*

- *You will find it easy to accomplish your task when the red pen is near you.*

- *All the words of this session will be accessible to you when you have the red pen with you.*

Remember, I special-order my red pens and buy them in bulk. Clients who need them leave the office with their pockets full.

The nail-biting script that worked well for Ed emphasized his need to protect his hands and his desire to present an image of strength. I offered this prohibition and visualization: *Whenever you lift your hand toward your mouth, for the purpose of nail-biting, one hand will lower the other.*

While in a trance, Ed spent several minutes watching himself attempting to bite his nails with no success. His other hand would immediately come between his fingertips and his mouth, and push his hand back down.

Literally Speaking

Your hypnotist needs to clearly and specifically state the exact suggestion because you tend to interpret statements literally while you are in hypnosis. If I had told the hair-puller that she would never be able to touch her hair, she might have had trouble shampooing it. If I'd told Ed he could never put his fingers near his mouth, how would he have eaten, or brushed his teeth?

In the Hypnotist's Office
David Hilbert, a world-renowned mathematician, was famous for his theorems in geometry, and for his absentmindedness. One evening, while he and his wife were entertaining some guests, his wife whispered to him that his shirt had a stain on it. She suggested he slip upstairs and change it. When he didn't return for 15 minutes, Mrs. Hilbert went up to see what was wrong. David Hilbert was asleep in his bed! It was his habit to take off his shirt, then the rest of his clothes, and then go to sleep. Habits are hard to eradicate; hypnosis helps in the eradication process.

Do-It-Yourself

Do you bite your nails? Want to quit? Visualize yourself under many circumstances, circumstances where you usually do your nail-biting. Maybe in bed, maybe while driving, perhaps when you're alone in the house, or while you're watching TV or reading. Clearly see yourself biting your nails, and then see yourself refraining from biting. Allow one hand to stop the other from reaching your mouth.

Put yourself into a hypnotic trance according to the guidelines you learned in Chapter 6. Then, watching yourself in many circumstances—outdoors, indoors, by yourself, with others, in your bedroom, or in your car—notice that one hand lowers the other. Tell yourself that one hand will lower the other anytime you are tempted to bite your nails or cuticles. Watch yourself as you clearly see one hand lowering the other.

More Habits

I'll always remember Dr. Wilson as the loud dentist. He wanted to change his life-long habit of speaking loudly. Dr. Wilson has been married for 25 years and, as an anniversary present for his wife, wants to speak softly. She has complained about his abrasive voice for 26 years. He claims that every morning he awakens with the intention of modulating his tones, but by 10 A.M. he's back to his old ways. I know that our one session worked because some weeks later I received a bouquet of flowers from Mrs. Wilson!

Emily came to my office to be hypnotized to break a habit that she hated but could not get rid of: She neglects to close the kitchen cabinet doors and drawers, and by the end of the day most are wide open. Here's a case where I was not specific enough in the suggestion. Emily called to tell me she was doing fine in her kitchen, but when she visited her boyfriend's mother's home she boldly entered that kitchen and began closing all doors—with the mother in the midst of cooking!

I hypnotized a family member, who prefers to remain anonymous, to put her keys in the jar on the shelf in the kitchen as soon as she walks into the house. I hypnotized a neighbor to remember to lock her back door every night. I hypnotize myself, regularly, to drive within the speed limit—even when the roads are empty, even when I'm in a hurry, and even when there's no police car in sight.

> **CAUTION**
>
> **Look into My Eyes**
>
> Human minds need to be communicated with and then convinced and motivated to do what comes naturally to most other species, which is to take proper care of themselves.

Developing the Exercise Habit

So many clients want to be motivated to exercise that I've developed two different strategies, and use them both on the assumption that if one doesn't get them exercising the other will.

Indirect Suggestions

You remember indirect suggestions: They're the sentences that hint at a future course of action, with no trace of authority or forcefulness. Some indirect suggestions for exercising are …

- *You are in charge of your body.*
- *You are sincerely interested in taking care of yourself.*
- *Please do a good job of protecting your body.*
- *Some people go to a gym, others prefer to work out at home.*
- *It's fun to play tennis, to swim, or to be in a regular softball game.*
- *Many people exercise in the morning, before they start their day.*
- *I wonder when you will enjoy exercising. Will it be mornings? Will it be in the evening?*
- *You are a smart person. You know how to make good decisions.*

Dr. Milton Erickson, the famed psychiatrist/hypnotist, used suggestions like these. Rather than give authoritative suggestions, he offered his clients food for thought. He believed that indirect suggestions stimulate ideas and memories. He had confidence that sooner or later the client would take the appropriate action.

Habit Pair

A more direct approach is pairing exercise with an activity that the client already engages in. When I'm interviewing exercise clients I ask, during our initial conversation, if they brush their teeth every morning. When they say "yes" I know I can proceed with the following suggestions for exercise:

◆ *Every morning, while brushing your teeth, you will think about your exercise plan for that day.*

Focus On This

Excess on occasion is exhilarating. It prevents moderation from acquiring the deadening effect of a habit.

—W. Somerset Maugham

◆ *Some days you will be thinking about your aerobics class; other days you'll think about taking a walk, going bowling, or going out dancing.*

◆ *Before you finish brushing your teeth, your exercise plan for the day will be very clear. You will know where and when you will exercise.*

◆ *When you put away your toothbrush you will notice how motivated you are to exercise, how you are already looking forward to that time of day.*

Writing Your Personal Habit Script

Which of your habits do you want to get rid of? Which good habit do you want to develop? Use the following worksheets to get started. The first worksheet will help you get rid of a bad habit.

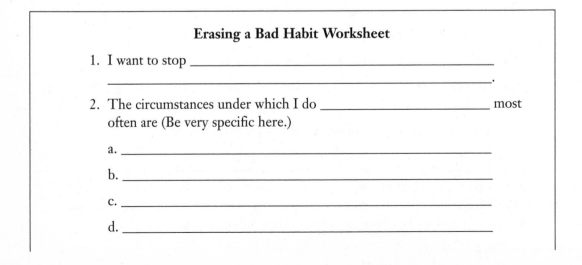

Erasing a Bad Habit Worksheet

1. I want to stop _____
   _____.

2. The circumstances under which I do _____ most often are (Be very specific here.)

   a. _____

   b. _____

   c. _____

   d. _____

3. Every time I think about doing _____, I will
   immediately think about _____ instead.

4. Every time I am about to do _____, I will
   immediately do _____ instead.

5. The first time I ever experienced _____ was in the
   following situation: _____

6. Here are the details about that situation: _____

   _____

7. I can visualize that incident occurring in a different way.

8. I can see it happening in a way where I do not begin doing

   _____.

9. I feel proud when I see myself _____.

10. I am capable of getting rid of my bad habit.

To develop a good habit, use this worksheet.

Developing a Good Habit Worksheet

1. I want to develop a new, good habit. I will begin to _____
   _____.

2. I can see myself doing _____ under
   the following circumstances:

   _____

   _____

3. Whenever I do _____
   it will be my reminder to myself to do _____

   _____.

The wonderful benefit of curing yourself of a phobia or bad habit is that your mind gets practice in making you a better person and you get practice in taking control of your life.

Self-mastery is the goal, hypnosis just the tool.

The Least You Need to Know

- ◆ We all have good and bad habits.
- ◆ Habits can be eradicated with hypnosis.
- ◆ Hypnosis can help you develop new habits, too.
- ◆ Phobias can be cured with hypnosis.

Part 4

The New You

Hypnosis can go with you—to school, to work, to the playing field—even to the bedroom! Yes, hypnotic suggestions can improve your sex life, and your social life, too.

Learn how to use hypnosis to stay calm before and during tests and while at work. Interviews and public speaking assignments will be easy for you. You'll read about professional athletes and their experiences with hypnosis, and you can use the same techniques for your athletic activities.

Parents, hypnosis can help children write better, play soccer better, and cooperate in the pediatrician's office—among many other things. Hypnosis can make parenting a whole lot easier.

Chapter 13

Learning to Spell While Under the Spell

In This Chapter

- ◆ Knowing your learning style
- ◆ Staying calm before and during your test
- ◆ Speaking up in class
- ◆ Talking to the authorities

Bookstores, the Internet, workshops, college classes, graduate schools, audiotapes, movies, video recordings, lectures, seminars, study abroad, symposiums—there's no end to your opportunity to learn. Hypnosis can help you learn new information, retain it, recall it, and use it.

This is not your parents' world; this is the world of the twenty-first century where you're expected to acquire information, enjoy several careers, and be sharp and productive throughout your lifetime. Age is not an excuse; both nursery schools and senior residences are computer friendly. Let hypnosis help you learn better and smarter.

How Do You Learn?

Dave looked at my unassembled exercise bike, never consulted the instructions, and put it together in no time. He's a good driver, too, and knows how to get from here to there and back again with no trouble. Dave is energetic and thinks best and learns best while he is on the move. He does not do well when he's required to read or to listen to someone explain something to him. He's not good at sitting still, either.

Karen could put the bike together after watching Dave do it. She's really good at learning from descriptions and diagrams. She remembers whatever she sees; she never forgets a face. When she watched Dave assemble the bike she was not at all bothered by the loud drill, but she was disturbed when the dog came frolicking in. Movement distracts her, noise does not.

Lewis listened while Dave explained what he was doing. Lewis asked questions and concentrated after each answer. He learned from the back-and-forth dialogue, and discussed each part as it was attached to the bike frame. He always remembers names—of bike parts or of people. He was distracted, though, by the drill, but not by the dog.

I could have put my bike together myself, but, first of all, these family members were right there, and second, I would have had to first read the directions and take notes, in my own words, on the whole procedure.

We all have different learning styles. A teacher standing in front of a classroom dispensing pearls of wisdom won't convey lasting information to me, unless I can take notes. If Karen can't doodle, and Dave can't move, and Lewis can't speak, none of us will benefit from the great teacher.

Focus On This

It's good to know your learning style because there is an explosion of learning in our country today. Sooner or later, you're going to be asked to learn one thing or another. Almost every college now has some students old enough to be the grandparents of other students!

When you know your learning style, you can put hypnosis to work for you. Do you learn best by ...

- Listening and discussing?
- Writing?
- Watching?
- Doing?

If you're not sure about figuring this out, ask your mother.

If you prefer to be an active, involved learner, but you are told to sit still and listen to a lecture, hypnosis can help you by using a time-distortion technique.

If you prefer to watch a demonstration but are told instead to read, you can use hypnosis to help your imagination convert the words to pictures.

If you prefer to listen and then ask questions, but you are told to watch a film instead, hypnosis can help you create an inner dialogue.

According to Harvard professor Dr. Howard Gardner in his multiple intelligence theory, children are one of the following types of learners:

- A linguistic learner (excels at words)

- A logical learner (excels at numbers)

- A spatial learner (excels at visualizing)

- A musical learner (excels at music)

- A kinesthetic learner (excels at physical activity)

- An interpersonal learner (excels at relationships)

- An intrapersonal learner (excels at working alone)

Which type of learner are you?

In the Hypnotist's Office

Howard Gardner, a professor at Harvard University, developed the theory of multiple intelligences—the MI theory, as it is called. He says that every child has a best way of learning and it is the teacher's responsibility to use that way to reach that child. No more long lectures for a child who needs to move around, no more films for a child who learns best with words. Dr. Gardner categorizes children by their learning styles.

Hypnotic Suggestions for Your Learning Style

Your hypnotist should create suggestions specifically for your learning style. In this section you'll read about three people, each with a unique learning style. Their hypnotic suggestions were tailored to suit them; your suggestions should be tailored to suit you.

The Kinesthetic Learner

If you are an active learner and are forced to sit in a large, stuffy lecture hall listening to a long-winded professor drone on and on, you can use hypnosis to make the time pass quickly and to create some interesting hallucinations.

Miriam is on the girl's basketball team. She's bright and energetic and has trouble in her world history class. After about 15 minutes she reaches her "sitting still" limit, but it's a 2-hour lecture. During hypnosis I asked Miriam to visualize herself in that classroom, and then I gave her the following hypnotic suggestions:

Look into My Eyes

Former president of Harvard University, Derek Bok, was aware of the sacrifices that parents make to send their children to prestigious universities. He said, "If you think education is expensive, try ignorance."

◆ *While paying attention to the instructor, you will ever so slightly move your right leg back and forth. After each movement your body will feel as if you walked for one minute. After the equivalent of a 10-minute walk, you will stop moving your leg and be ready to absorb the teacher's information.*

◆ *As you listen to the instructor her voice will seem exceptionally pleasant to you. You will become so interested in the material she is presenting that you will lose track of time; in fact, time will fly by.*

Miriam comes in for a session at the beginning of each school term and we devise strategies for the semester. Last time I saw her she told me how she embarrassed herself when leaving a lecture hall. Amid all the groggy, bored students shuffling out of the room, Miriam exclaimed, "Wow, over so soon?"

The Visual Learner

Mr. Daniels came to my office because at age 20 he still has no driver's license. He says he's a good driver and has passed his road test. The written test is his problem. He is a visual person, so I gave him the following suggestion: *As you read each question you will automatically see the words change into a picture in your mind. Studying the picture in your mind, you will quickly know the right answer.*

The Linguistic Learner

Bob and Vera consulted me before their son's wedding. Bob Jr. was marrying into a family of dancers. During the wedding celebration Bob and Vera would be asked to join the bride's family, in the center of the dance floor, in front of all the guests, for a special wedding dance. The bride's family sent a videotape showing the dance steps. Vera watched the tape and soon caught on. Bob was another story. "I learn with words, not pictures," he moaned, just days before the wedding. Here's the hypnotic suggestion that worked for Bob: *As you watch the video you will quickly and naturally tell yourself what you see. The words you say will easily guide you.*

Tests

"I like school. I understand what I'm supposed to. But I just can't take those tests. If there were no tests I'd be fine." Is this you talking? Hypnosis can help you to …

◆ Study efficiently.

◆ Stay calm before the test.

◆ Remember everything you need to know during the test.

◆ Stay calm during the test.

Studying

Hypnosis can help you to remember everything you learn. The catch is: You must first learn. Arrange your studying circumstances according to your learning style and you will learn more material in less time. You know what to do: Take a walk, draw a diagram, talk about the subject, listen to music, study with a buddy, write lots of notes, or barricade yourself in your room. Use whatever method works for you and your individual learning style.

Prepare your studying environment. Assemble your supplies and decide ahead of time if you should unplug the phone, turn off the TV, turn on some music, prepare some food, or do whatever you need to do to make your environment conducive to studying. Do you learn best in a chair, on the floor, or on your bed? When you're all set give yourself a realistic time frame to learn a portion of the material and then schedule a break. Actually write on a piece of paper your study times and your break times.

Now you are ready. Either with the help of a hypnotist or by using self-hypnosis, which you've practiced in Chapters 6 and 7, simply receive the suggestion that *You will follow your study schedule.*

It's really that easy!

When you finish your studying give yourself a test. Pretend you're the teacher and ask yourself questions to test your knowledge of the material. Answer orally, in writing, or in diagrams, depending upon your style. (Don't sing, even if you are musical; don't dance, even if you are physical.)

Focus On This

New material sinks into your brain better when (1) it is repeated and (2) you are motivated to learn it. Every day you see many license plates without really noticing their letters and numbers. But if there were a reward for spotting certain numeric combinations, you would be motivated to pay attention to every passing car. Think of a high mark as your reward for studying.

Staying Calm

You've studied, you've tested yourself, and now you're ready for the big test. Are you nervous? Will you be able to fall asleep easily the night before? Will you be able to eat in the morning? When you enter the test area, will you feel confident or clutched?

Some students know the material and study well, yet do poorly on tests because of test anxiety. You can exempt yourself from that group of students. Let hypnosis rescue you. Here are the suggestions I use for students with test anxiety:

- *You will have one final piece of paper on which you've written (or drawn) a few pieces of information that remind you how much you know and how well-prepared you are.*

- *You will fall asleep easily, knowing this piece of paper is nearby.*

- *When you awaken in the morning you will easily memorize everything on your paper.*

- *Your feeling of self-confidence grows every minute.*

- *You know everything you need to know.*

- *You will be calm and organized on your way to the test.*

- *You will look forward to beginning the test.*

- *As soon as the test begins you will notice how alert, yet comfortable, you've become.*

- *Your memory is excellent. You can recall everything you need to know.*

- *The correct answers easily make themselves known to you.*

- *You will work in an organized fashion, answering one question at a time.*

- *You will express yourself clearly so that anyone marking your paper will know just what you wish to communicate.*

- *When you complete the test you will check your answers once and then leave happy.*

- *You are proud because you tried your best.*

These suggestions work well with all ages and stages—the junior in high school, the college senior, the medical school student, and the scared-to-death grandma returning to get her diploma.

A group of medical students was taught self-hypnosis as a coping skill to reduce distress during their first year of medical school. Another group in the same class was taught relaxation techniques, but not actual hypnosis. At the end of the semester every student filled out a questionnaire and it was determined that the hypnosis group …

- Experienced less anxiety throughout the semester.

- Felt stressed less often.

- Slept better than the other group.

Hypnosis often has the side effect of helping you fall asleep quickly and easily.

A group of doctors consulted a hypnotist at their hospital. Each of the doctors was considered knowledgeable, yet each had flunked the fellowship exam in a specialty area. They all were interested in becoming hypnotized before they had to retake the test; they were certain it was test anxiety that caused their failure.

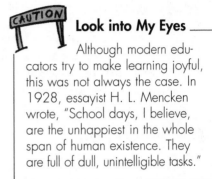

Look into My Eyes

Although modern educators try to make learning joyful, this was not always the case. In 1928, essayist H. L. Mencken wrote, "School days, I believe, are the unhappiest in the whole span of human existence. They are full of dull, unintelligible tasks."

The hypnotist used the Stein "clenched fist" technique, and it did the trick for most of the docs. I'll give you the steps for this technique next, in detail, so you can use it on yourself. If you're nervous before tests, this is for you!

1. Prior to the induction, practice clenching your fists, right and left.

2. Enter a hypnotic trance.

3. Recall a situation where you were confident and relaxed, and make a fist with your right hand.

4. Hear the suggestion that whenever you close that hand into a fist you will re-experience all those good feelings.

5. Repeat Step 3.

6. Remember the anxiety and self-doubt that sometimes occur when you take a test.

7. Put all those negative feelings into your left hand. Make a fist with your left hand.

8. Repeat Step 3 and make that fist tight and strong.

9. Squeeze your strong, confident fist into your weak left hand. Force your right fist into your left palm.

10. Self-doubt and anxiety have been displaced by self-confidence and relaxation.

11. This feeling about test situations will be permanent.

Focus On This

If you are easily distracted while taking a test, try the rubber-band trick. Place a rubber band around your wrist and whenever you notice your mind wandering, snap yourself back to reality.

If you need any encouragement right before or during the test, all you need to do is put your right fist into your left hand and you will be as comfortable as you are right now.

Classmates

Some people can speak to their peers and to authority figures easily. Communication comes easily to them and they have no problem speaking their minds. Alas, many otherwise mature, strong, healthy, stable folks—both children and adults—have lots of trouble speaking up when they're not with their families or closest friends.

Who Took the Grater?

Mrs. Winters is in cooking school. For years, everyone who tasted her food had been telling her she ought to be cooking professionally. Finally, in her 50s, she's about to graduate from culinary school. In fact, she has just one class left and that is why she's in my office. Pastry is her problem.

Mrs. Winters actually bakes just fine and the goodies she brings me when she comes for a session are scrumptious. It's her fellow students who trouble her. Mrs. Winters has never learned to speak up. All the students use their own equipment, and she happens to have some amazing pieces that she picked up on a trip to Paris some years ago. Last week, during a test, she was unable to find her stainless steel precision grater and had to use someone else's. Then she saw hers—on Joe's table.

You or I would have yelled, or taken it from Joe, or done something—anything. Not Mrs. Winters. She was stunned and horrified, but she stayed mute. Her problem is she is unable to speak up for herself in class. In this instance, she thought she might be mistaken—maybe that wasn't her grater after all. She thought she might be considered rude; maybe she shouldn't say anything to Joe at all. In general, she believes if she speaks up people will look at her and maybe it's not right to make a scene. On account of this, she risks not graduating, all because she is unable to speak up in class.

Mrs. Winters needed several sessions of hypnosis. In the first session I gave her suggestions that she is as good as anyone else in the class and is entitled to succeed. In the second session we role-played, asking Joe for that which is hers. In the last session I helped her to visualize herself employed as a chef.

If you have trouble speaking up in class, you'll benefit from the suggestion: *You are equal to everyone in the class. This is a class of peers.*

If you have trouble asking for something from a particular classmate, consider role-playing. Have your hypnotist play that other person. When I played Joe, I made some nasty comments that at first upset Mrs. Winters. With practice she learned to say them right back to me. For example, playing Joe, I said:

- *Who do you think you are, you and your ritzy stuff?*

- *Keep your hands off this; I'm using it.*

- *Calm down, lady, don't get all bent out of shape.*

During hypnosis Mrs. Winters practiced responding. She rehearsed her answers. When she finally confronted Joe in class he was nicer than I was in the office so she had an easier time. She did have to be firm, though, and clearly articulate a sentence we had practiced: *This is mine. Never take it again.*

We had to practice this many times because she kept adding a phrase or two to the end of the sentence making it: "Never take it again, okay?" Or, "Never take it again, if it's not too much trouble." We succeeded, she graduated, and I receive occasional pastry delights.

Stop That Teasing!

Ronald is a sixth-grader who gets teased in school, and the teachers seem powerless to stop it. His parents brought him to me in the mistaken hope that I could teach him to hypnotize other kids to be nice to him!

I explained that hypnosis is about personal mastery and control of the self, not others. They agreed to try one session of hypnosis. Ronald benefited from the hypnotic suggestions:

- *When kids say things to you, you will not respond. You will act as if you don't hear them and you'll continue doing whatever you are doing.*

- *Every time you succeed in ignoring them you will feel proud of yourself.*

- *You will have the courage to talk to some of the kids in your class. You will look around and notice that one or two of them might make a good friend.*

 Focus On This _____

Harold Taylor, who at age 30 became president of Sarah Lawrence College, said, "The whole educational system has become one massive quiz program, with the prizes going to the most enterprising, most repulsively well-informed person—the man with his hand up first." Hypnosis can help the timid or less-assertive child to claim the attention he or she needs and deserves in the classroom.

Occasionally there are teachers who cruelly criticize, and there are school programs that are unfit for kids. Yet even in those circumstances, the majority of students are capable of enduring. It's that sensitive minority who can use a boost from hypnosis.

Hypnosis can make school more palatable by giving a student some protection from harshness, from boredom, or from whatever it is that the student finds unbearable. Sometimes I just use common sense when devising suggestions.

The Unspeakable

Kelly's parents brought her to my office because, although she was perfectly fine at home, all through the grades her teachers have complained that she does not participate in class. In fact, Kelly has what is called *selective mutism.* She speaks only under certain circumstances. Her parents had taken her for years of psychotherapy, which helped her feel better about herself but did nothing about her school silence. This condition is very responsive to hypnosis.

Hypnoscript

Children who have normal language skills but refuse to utter a sound except when with certain people, usually their closest family, suffer from **selective mutism.** It is a type of extreme shyness that persists for years.

This is an interesting condition just recently categorized by psychiatrists as a mental disorder, and it can be successfully treated with hypnosis. Kelly, like others with this condition, uses gestures when in school. It took three sessions for Kelly to reach her goal, which was to speak like all the other kids in her fifth-grade class.

Focus On This

Your hypnotist can take a negative situation and put a positive spin on it. You can change from a person who is the victim of a disease to one who is in control of him- or herself. This can happen during the interview, even before any formal hypnotic induction has taken place.

In Kelly's first session, she and I chat, or, more precisely, I chat and Kelly nods. I talk about what it must feel like to be different than everyone else, how much fun she has at home playing and speaking with her sister and parents, and how much she likes the one friend she does speak to. She speaks to Robin but only when they're at Kelly's house. She doesn't speak in Robin's house and she doesn't speak to Robin in school. I tell Kelly that she is a very strong girl; I don't know too many people who could refrain from speaking. I congratulate her on her persistence.

Kelly enters a light trance and I ask her to visualize herself in school. I create situations where the teacher asks a question and no one but Kelly knows the answer. I compliment her on keeping silent, even though she would have been given extra credit for knowing the correct answer. In her mind, she maintains the image of herself in the classroom, while I ask her to imagine that her power of speech is suddenly taken away and it is impossible for her to speak up in class—it is no longer under her control. I ask her to feel the feelings she would have if she knew all the answers but could never say them.

Then I ask her to return, in her mind, to her regular state, where she could speak but chooses not to. We go through many scenarios with Kelly never speaking up, sometimes by choice, sometimes because she has no speech.

I end the first session by having her visualize a new child admitted to class—a girl who does not speak in public. I ask her to investigate her feelings about that new girl. I encourage Kelly to enjoy the hypnotic experience before it ends, and I tell her to look forward to the next session.

At no time do I give Kelly the suggestion to speak: Not to me, not to her teacher, not to her school friends. When the change in habit occurs it will be long lasting if it comes from her and not from me or anyone else.

Two weeks later, at her second session, Kelly's mom reports a difference in Kelly's behavior around the house. She says she is more open, makes better eye contact, and communicates more. She also reports that Robin mentioned that Kelly spoke to her in school on a few different occasions.

Kelly is eager to get started, but first I talk about Robin and ask Kelly to imagine Robin not speaking in school, so that the two of them have to communicate in gestures. She laughs. When she's hypnotized, I ask Kelly to notice that new, silent girl hanging out with Robin. Then I ask her to replace the image of that girl with herself, but a speaking version of herself. It takes some time, because hallucinations are not always easy to create. She nods when she can finally hear herself speak to Robin in the classroom.

> **CAUTION**
>
> **Look into My Eyes**
>
> Remember, your hypnotist must have patience. If you have had a problem for years, it's okay if it takes you an extra 15 minutes during the session to visualize what you need to do. Sometimes, slowly is the only way to go.

Next I ask her to select three children in the class and, in her mind, hear herself speak to those three children about homework, a test, or the new girl. It takes more than 10 minutes for Kelly to finally nod her head, indicating that she did speak to all three of them. I congratulate her, acknowledging the great effort it must have taken to give up her silent position.

Kelly's posthypnotic suggestions are …

♦ *Now that you know you can speak to those three kids and Robin, please be very careful. Don't speak to anyone else in school. It will be too shocking for the class if you just suddenly start chattering.*

♦ *You now know that sometimes you could participate in class discussions, but I think it would be too shocking for the teacher. You're best off speaking to her privately or when at least some of the students are not around.*

♦ *You have great determination. If you determine that you want to speak in public that's okay with me, but please don't talk during lunch. The kids will be too shocked. The entire cafeteria will be stunned. Please continue being silent at lunchtime.*

Before session number three, which is scheduled for one month later, Kelly's mom calls. The teacher contacted her to report that Kelly was chatting away, participating in class, and socializing with a few of the girls.

On the designated day, I hear Kelly walk into the waiting room and greet Jeanne, my secretary. When Kelly sees me she smiles and says a shy, "Hi." We start the session and I'm hoping for some introspection on her part, but there is none. I'm curious, and wonder aloud how her life is different now, but Kelly simply replies, "I talk." I ask her if the image of the new girl was what got her going. (I suspect it was. Preadolescent girls will do anything to hold on to their friends and will compete for friendships.) She shrugs and says, "I dunno." So much for the profound wisdom I thought I'd hear from the silent child who finally spoke.

For our last hypnosis session I encourage Kelly to stay in the hypnotic state as long as she needs to visualize herself having the ability to speak all through the school day, and then in several out-of-school circumstances. Our work is done and her selective mutism is gone.

Talking to Teachers

Authority figures sometimes bring out the baby in us. Some students become paralyzed with fear at the thought of speaking to a teacher, dean, or principal. Others become frightened when they need to question an authority figure, as in: "Why did you take off 10 points for this answer?" or, "May I hand in my paper on Tuesday instead of Monday?" or, "I think you made a mistake and forgot to go over yesterday's assignment."

Children brought up to fear authority figures grow up to be adults who fear authority figures. It's a good idea to differentiate between *respect*, which is appropriate, and *fear*, which usually is not appropriate. I've had parents in my office who are not able to go to bat for their child because they are intimidated by the child's teacher and by the whole idea of opposing a teacher. It's possible to have a respectful difference of opinion and communicate your (or your child's) side of the story without having an out-and-out confrontation.

A useful hypnotic technique that helps develop the ability to easily speak to an authority figure is role-playing. Sometimes role-playing, without hypnosis, works well, but most people achieve better results while under hypnosis. Here are two different ways to role-play speaking up to an authority. Try both ways.

Hypnoscript

Respect is the high regard and consideration we may have for a person. **Fear** is a feeling of alarm and anxiety that is brought on because there is an expectation of danger.

Role-Play 1

The Scene: You (or your child) bought a great new shirt at The Gap. You wear it for the first time today and notice the pocket is ripped. It apparently came that way and you didn't notice it in the store. You want to exchange this shirt for another. You go back to the store, stand in the customer service line, and wait your turn.

Manager: *Why are you bringing this back?*

You: *Look at the pocket. It's ripped.*

Manager: *What do you want?*

You: *I want to get the same shirt again, but one with no rip.*

Manager: *I'll get it for you, no problem.*

That's a perfect exchange.

Role-Play 2

The Scene: Now, let's say you are at a different store, a neighborhood shop where the owner had a hard day and is grouchy, cranky, and overworked.

Owner: *Why are you bringing this back?*

You: *The pocket is ripped.*

Owner: *That's not my fault. No money back. You probably ripped it yourself.*

You: *Sir, I did not rip it.*

Owner: *How do you expect me to make a living if you rip things and bring them back?*

You: *Please permit me to take another one of these shirts in exchange for this one. Thank you.*

Practice the second type of exchange while hypnotized. It increases assertiveness skills by giving you practice in …

- Saying one polite sentence ("Sir, I did not rip it") and not becoming flustered, angry, or defensive.

- Having a solution ready ("Please permit me to exchange it") so that it becomes easy for the other person to do what you want.

Use your ability to hypnotize yourself now. Just go to the place where you successfully enjoy a hypnotic induction and quickly and easily guide yourself into hypnosis. When you are hypnotized, simply visualize yourself saying one polite sentence and then offering one solution. You can do this. It's easy. Just follow the scene in your mind. Say one polite sentence. Good. Now say a sentence that gives a solution to your problem. Good.

Success in school, as in life, depends upon relationship skills as much as it depends upon learning skills. Fortunately, both types of skills are amenable to hypnosis.

The Least You Need to Know

- We all have different learning styles. Identifying your style will help you succeed.

- Some smart people do poorly on tests because of test anxiety. Hypnosis can cure test anxiety.

- Communicating with classmates and teachers is a necessary skill for school success. It can be learned. Hypnosis always helps.

Chapter 14

Wide-Eyed at Work

In This Chapter

- How to get and keep that job
- Speaking up at work
- Enjoying yourself at work
- Getting along with your colleagues

Do you work because you have to work? Or do you work because you love to work? Life is fabulous when you can't wait to get up in the morning to go to work, you enjoy a productive day, and then return home fulfilled and looking forward to tomorrow.

It can happen to you, with a little help from hypnosis. A slight change in attitude, a simple change in behavior, and you, too, can say, "I can't believe I get paid to have such a good time." This is not a new idea. In the Bible, Ecclesiastes 3:22, we are told: "There is nothing better for a man than to rejoice in his work."

Getting the Job

To have a good time at your job you need to get the job that is right for you. You must know yourself—your skills, aptitudes, preferences, and personality style:

- Do you like to be the leader or the follower?

- Are you at your best working indoors or outside?

- Do you do best by yourself or as part of a group?

- Do you like to plan and organize, or do you prefer to execute someone else's ideas?

- Do you want to have friends and the opportunity for socializing at your job, or do you want to do your work and go home?

- Do you prefer a job with diverse tasks or one with predictable work each day?

- Is working at home good for you, or do you work to get away from home?

- Are rigid working hours best for your schedule or is flexibility important to you?

- Can you start at a low salary, with promise of more in the future?

Please ask yourself all these questions before you apply for a position. Don't try to fit yourself into a place that is wrong for you. Every company has a corporate culture, every office has a feeling to it. That culture and those feelings won't change and you can't make them change. Find a job situation that is compatible with your needs.

If you're working in a large company and are not happy in your job, talk to the folks in Human Resources. Let them know what you're looking for. If you're a valued employee, they'll want to keep you and may accommodate your needs in a different department.

Before your interview arm yourself with information, whether you're interviewing with your current company or with a new one. Find out everything you can about the position, and know why you are the right person for it. Before the interview do some role-playing. Have someone—friend, family member, hypnotist—ask you the following questions:

- Why do you want this job?

- What particular skills are you bringing to the position?

- Why are you leaving the job you're at now?

- Where do you see yourself two years from now?

- What are your strongest points?

- What are your weaknesses? How will you compensate for them at this job?

Practice answering these questions. Ask yourself some other questions, too. Answer all questions with certainty and clarity, and with a smile. No gestures, no throat clearing, no "you know what I mean" comments. This is a dress rehearsal. Please don't tell any jokes during your interview, and don't belittle anyone—not even that previous boss who didn't appreciate you and didn't know how to run a company.

When you rehearse your answers pay attention to the words you use. Instead of using phrases like "I did" or "I was," use words that show activity—words like "analyzing," "teaching," "writing," "organizing," "planning," and "coordinating." The latter group of words is dynamic as opposed to the former phrases, which are static. It's to your benefit to be associated with energetic and powerful words.

Tape record your practice sessions and role-playing sessions. Play back the tape and learn from it. Improve on any weak spots and then tape your answers again.

Use self-hypnosis (see Chapters 6 and 7) to put yourself into a light trance and then visualize yourself doing the following:

1. Walking into the interview

2. Making eye contact

3. Shaking hands

4. Speaking clearly

5. Answering all questions

6. Maintaining your composure

Then give yourself the hypnotic suggestions: *I will be calm before the interview, during the interview, and after the interview; and I will get the job if I am suited for it.*

Hypnosis will help you stay calm and focused during your interview. It's important to remain calm after the interview, too, because urgent phone calls from prospective employees are not welcome. It is appropriate, though, to send a letter to the interviewer thanking that person for his or her time and interest.

Rather than performing self-hypnosis, go to a hypnotherapist if you tend to say either of these negative remarks:

- I'll never get the job.

- Nobody is going to hire me.

◆ I'm too _____. (Fill in the blank with whatever word you use to put yourself down.)

◆ I don't deserve a high-paying job.

I suggest you go to a hypnotherapist and not do it yourself if these are your issues, because you might need some psychotherapy along with the hypnotic suggestions.

A hypnotist or a hypnotherapist can help you with your self-confidence. But neither one is a magician. If there is some validity to your negative ideas, this is the time to make changes in your life. Be honest about who you are and what you can do. You're better off admitting what you don't know because then someone will teach it to you or tell you how to learn it yourself. If you pretend to know everything, you'll learn nothing.

There's a story about just such a pretender who furnished a gorgeous office and on his first day, when he still had no clients, a man wandered into the reception area. Trying to impress the man, Mr. Hotshot picked up the phone and loudly talked about deals and mergers and acquisitions. When he finally hung up he asked his guest, "May I help you?" "Yes," the man replied, "I'm here to hook up your phone."

In the Hypnotist's Office

Mark came to my office requesting hypnosis for self-confidence. He said that his lack of self-confidence prevented him from being promoted; his co-workers all were moved up at the last evaluation. Mark wanted his quietness and his "nerdy ways" (his words) to be replaced by self-assertion and the ability to socialize with his office mates. Before I proceeded with hypnosis I asked to see his evaluation. It said nothing about his behavior and personal style, and everything about his frequent lateness, his reluctance to learn how to use new equipment, and his slowness at completing assigned tasks. Mark's lack of self-esteem was well founded; in the work environment he had nothing to be confident about.

Keeping the Job

Hypnosis can help you get to work on time and be open to learning new procedures at work. Hypnotherapy can help you figure out why you're unwilling to hand things in on time, and hypnotic suggestions can help you change your ways.

If you're working in the right job, in the right company, and your work is not up to par, the usual reason is that you were not trained properly and lack specific skills. Your supervisor is not a mind reader. You must learn how to ask for skills training and any other help that will improve your job performance. Hypnosis can help by teaching you assertiveness skills.

To help clients become appropriately assertive in the workplace I spend at least one session with them figuring out exactly what needs to be communicated. We do some role-playing, too. At the next session I use the following hypnotic suggestions to encourage employees to speak up:

◆ *You will know exactly what to say.*

◆ *You will know precisely who to say it to.*

Are you the boss? The manager? The CEO? CFO? COO? Your employees won't care how much you know until they know how much you care. Become aware of your employees' jobs and have an idea of what their workdays are like. According to the U.S. Department of Labor, of all the reasons why people quit their jobs, the most common reason is that they feel unappreciated.

Don, the owner of a small manufacturing company, was so out of touch with his employees that one evening one of his young executives found him standing helplessly in front of a shredder with a piece of paper in his hand. "Can you help me?" Don asked. "I don't know how to make this thing work and my secretary is gone for the day."

"No problem," said the young executive as he turned the machine on, inserted the paper, and pressed the start button.

"Thank you. Thank you," said Don, "I need only one copy."

Hypnosis can build up your empathic qualities. Those are the qualities that will bring out the best in your employees. When you can feel the feelings that your employees are feeling, you are no longer adversaries, but are on the same team. During hypnosis you can be instructed to look at your workers from a new viewpoint and see them as struggling to please you. That helps you show appreciation, which then motivates them to do a better job.

Also, set a good example. *Modeling* behavior and attitude is an excellent way to encourage your employees to do their best. Years ago, when I was a counselor at a summer camp, the owner of the camp, a well-known educator and psychiatrist, used to patrol the grounds, stooping to pick up litter. By the second week of camp all of us college students got the hang of it and we constantly were bending over to pick up another Hershey's wrapper or piece of string blown away from the lariat project in the arts-and-crafts shack. By the third week of the summer our campers simply stopped littering, and they'd immediately chase after any fly-away items. No one ever said a word about litter, trash, or the like.

Carl wanted courage to confront his boss who constantly yells and curses. We worked on just one sentence: "Please don't speak to me in that manner."

Carl seemed prepared to say those words without any boost from hypnosis, and he did. He called me a few days later to announce that his boss was stunned, and said, "I yell at everybody. Can't you take it?" When Carl said no, he couldn't stand it any more, the boss agreed to stop yelling, and so far has kept his word. Direct communication can be simple and effective.

Public Speaking

Politicians and salespeople want hypnosis to help them remain "up" while speaking. People in the helping professions usually want to calm "down" with hypnosis. Everybody wants some help with public speaking.

The most effective hypnosis scripts I've used for speaking up at meetings and making presentations are as follows:

Script 1

Please visualize yourself sitting at a conference table. There are several other people there, too. They are looking at you; waiting for you to speak. Please see yourself. You like the way you look. You seem self-assured. You are calm. Now please watch yourself as you begin to speak. You are communicating with precision. You are expressing yourself clearly. Listen to yourself presenting your ideas. You are a winner. Throughout this presentation, you are calm and in total control of yourself.

Script 2

Visualize yourself getting ready to address a large audience. Please see yourself as you are walking toward the stage. Notice that you are walking with ease. You feel secure. You are comfortable. You are well prepared. You know your subject matter thoroughly; you've done your homework. As you walk onto the stage you begin to feel extremely pleased. You are happy to have this opportunity to address the audience. Watch yourself and listen to yourself as you speak. You are saying everything that needs to be said. You are a fine speaker. Calm, relaxed. You are enjoying yourself. You continue to communicate easily and sincerely. You speak clearly. You are thinking about the subject, not about you. Your presentation is all that matters right now. As you look into the audience you realize that everyone is receptive to your ideas. You are an excellent pubic speaker: calm, cool, collected, and interesting, too.

Script 3

From now on it will be easy for you to relate to an audience. You will enjoy public speaking. You are a good public speaker. You present your ideas clearly. You are never nervous. Instead, you are calm and well organized. And you have a good time. You are an excellent public speaker. You will look forward to more opportunities to share your ideas with others, more opportunities to speak in public.

Precise communication occurs when you know your material and you also know your audience. To help my clients keep this in mind, I tell them about the man who calls home to speak to his wife and is told by the housekeeper that she's in the bedroom, with a male visitor.

"Who is he?" asks the frantic husband.

"Her usual Tuesday-morning friend," replies the housekeeper.

"Oh, no. How long has this been going on?" he asks.

"About six months on Tuesdays; Thursday's friend has only been coming around for a few weeks."

"I can't accept this. Do you know where I keep my gun?"

"Yes, sir, I do."

"Go get it, enter the bedroom, and aim and fire at both of them."

"Are you sure, sir?"

"Yes, I'll hold on while you do this, then come back to the phone."

After some minutes, breathlessly, the housekeeper returns: "It's done, what do you want me to do with the gun?"

"Go to the backyard and drop it in the pool," he answers.

"Pool? There is no pool."

"Wha'? Is this 769-4 …?"

Enjoying Yourself at Work

Are you shy? Shyness is very different from lack of confidence. Although it is possible for you to have both traits, that is most unusual. Some people are shy, some have no confidence, a few have both characteristics, and most people have neither one. Shyness is an inborn trait that you can work with and overcome, if you want to. Many shy people accept themselves as shy and have no problem with their timid ways. In fact, being reserved is a most civilized way to behave. Sometimes, though, shyness may prevent you from asking for what you need.

To help yourself become more assertive at work, you might want to hypnotize yourself now. Simply go to your hypnosis place and use a wonderful induction. Perhaps it will be the staircase induction today. Whichever induction you choose will be just fine. When you are hypnotized, give yourself the suggestion that tomorrow you will …

- *Say hello to at least one person.*

- *Smile and nod to at least one person.*

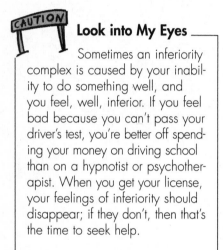

Look into My Eyes

Sometimes an inferiority complex is caused by your inability to do something well, and you feel, well, inferior. If you feel bad because you can't pass your driver's test, you're better off spending your money on driving school than on a hypnotist or psychotherapist. When you get your license, your feelings of inferiority should disappear; if they don't, then that's the time to seek help.

You can hypnotize yourself every day to accomplish these two social skills. Then next week, get ready to hypnotize yourself to add some more suggestions to help you overcome shyness. Those suggestions are …

- *Compliment someone on anything you find positive about him or her.*

- *Every day ask a stranger for the correct time.*

- *Once a week ask a stranger for directions.*

The second time you do a task is always easier than the first time you tried. Hypnotize yourself to do the five commands I've just given you, and after a few months you'll be a natural.

Do you lack self-confidence? Your confidence level can rise and fall depending upon your environment. Learning new skills raises your self-confidence. Hypnosis can help with skill learning. Use hypnosis to help you motivate yourself to take classes, do your assignments, and learn, learn, learn. Work hard at everything you do and you'll earn your self-confidence.

Writer's Block

Raymond is the author of a couple of books and now has a contract to write another. Lately, whenever he sits at his computer his mind blanks and he can't seem to begin the flow of words. His literary agent is angry, his publisher is panicky, and he, in desperation, is in my office hoping I can get him to write.

I spoke to Raymond to confirm that his goal is realistic—he does have the knowledge and talent to write the new book. Because he is a literary sort, I wrote a script that was *metaphoric*. It's a tale that Raymond could listen to on the level of a story and also on a symbolic level. Before I began, I helped him deepen his hypnotic state so that he was very absorbed in his trance. Then I gave him the suggestion that he'll enjoy the tale I tell and be curious about it. He will think about it while in trance, and all during the week at home, too. When he thinks about it, he'll be interested in understanding it in many ways, some of which will have special meaning to him.

Hypnoscript

A **metaphor** is an implied comparison between two unlike things that surprisingly do have something in common.

I told Raymond a story about my garden. I spoke slowly, in a quiet voice, often pausing between words and always pausing between sentences. I said:

I don't know much about plants or grasses or flowers. I was born in the Bronx and nature was not part of my childhood …. Now, though, I want to have a beautiful garden. I am not Martha Stewart and I don't know names of flowers, and I don't know the exact formula to follow to get certain results … but I do know what looks beautiful … so I garden using my own silly method …. I plant everything I can, and weed out later [long pause].

I get them all in the dirt … the pansies and the tiger lilies, the impatiens and the begonias …. I choose red flowers and yellow flowers; some blues and some violets …. I plant an assortment of wildflowers from a seed packet, and I plant white flowers and I plant pink flowers …. Sometimes I think I don't know what in the world I am doing … but, my lawn is not empty anymore. It's not blank …. It is full of life and color [long pause].

When everything comes up, when all the flowers bloom, I decide what is beautiful just where it is and what may have to be transplanted …. Some flowers are moved to one side, others to the other side … some stay right where they are [long pause].

Two times in the past I planted gardens that blossomed and bloomed and bore fruit for me …. Now I will begin my third garden …. It, too, will bloom. I'm not sure what to plant first so I'll throw a bunch of seeds over here, some seeds over there …. I'll plant some potted flowers on one side, and a tub of blue flowers … I don't know what they're called … on the other side [long pause].

Look into My Eyes

Do not become a hypnotist if you are looking for praise, recognition, or appreciation. When you do a really good job with your clients, they develop self-confidence and feel certain that their accomplishments have nothing to do with you!

Each day I look at my garden, make some changes, and then add something to it. It is mine … my creation, my effort. I take care of it. I water it. I weed out whatever doesn't belong …. Every day I do something in my garden.

Raymond remained in trance when I finished reading that script, and did not open his eyes for many minutes. He finally awakened, said nothing, and prepared to leave the office. He never again called or came in, but I've heard from his agent, who is an occasional client, that his third book is almost completed. Something unblocked him. Was it hypnosis? We'll never know.

Dancer's Droop

Patti dances with a ballet troupe and has studied for years with Madame. Madame is a harsh taskmaster who tolerates no funny business, no slacking off. She often reprimands Patti for poor posture, and has threatened to terminate her lessons if Patti continues "drooping." Patti believes that she's standing exactly the way she's supposed to and can't understand why Madame is making such a big deal. When Patti calls me for an appointment she's angry at Madame, but worried because her dance contract may not be renewed if she's dropped by Madame.

Patti arrives early and I am shocked to see her slumping in the waiting room chair. When she walks into my office she looks more like a rag doll than a dancer. Patti does have poor carriage and she's not trying to straighten up. She asks for hypnosis to control her anger at Madame. She mentions nothing about her posture. My original idea was to hypnotize her to stand up straight, but that doesn't seem to be on her mind now.

Instead of direct suggestions, I ask Patti if she'd like some hypnosis to clarify what's going on with her. She agrees and I instruct her in ideomotor signaling. (Do you remember that pinkie wiggle from Chapter 4, where a subtle finger movement actually means something to the client and the hypnotist? Here is another example of its interesting usefulness.) Patti will answer my questions by moving her fingers. After the induction, she's in a very light trance because she's not particularly talented at hypnosis. I begin speaking:

RT: *So many things are on your mind these days. You have conflicts with Madame, maybe you have conflicts with yourself. I don't know, but you know.*

P: (Signals yes.)

RT: *You might like to take this opportunity to figure out what you really want. Deep down, you know what you need and you know who you are. Deep down, you know how you really feel about Madame and about the ballet troupe. Give yourself some time to say the truth to yourself.*

P: (Silence for several minutes.)

RT: *Is it okay with you if I ask you some questions now?*

P: (Signals no.)

(I remain silent. Patti appears to be struggling with some thoughts. She's frowning, moving her head, now lifting her left heel. Several minutes pass.)

RT: *How about now?*

P: (Signals yes.)

RT: *Now that you've had a good talk with yourself and perhaps with another person or two, you may be interested in ....* (I stop in mid-sentence because Patti looks like she's trying to say something.) *Please allow your regular speech to express whatever needs to be said now.*

P: (Slowly and softly.) *Stop dancing. Can't tell girls in troupe. Career finished.*

RT: *It seems like you're thinking of giving up your dance career for a while.*

P: (Signals no.) *Not a while.*

RT: *I get it now; you are going to change careers.*

P: *Yes, I am.*

RT: *You are a courageous woman. You've admitted the truth to yourself. We can discuss this further in trance or when you awaken. Would you like to continue in trance?*

P: *No, get up.*

Patti opens her eyes and is back to her regular state in a minute or less.

P: *We have a lot to discuss.*

RT: *We still have some time left.*

Focus On This

Nothing is really work unless you would rather be doing something else.

—James Matthew Barrie, Scottish writer

P: *Sorry, I don't mean you and me. I mean my husband and me. You see, he never thought the dancer's life was good for our marriage and now I kind of agree with him. I want to have a baby. Most of the girls I dance with don't have husbands or boyfriends so they don't feel the conflict I feel. I know what's bothering me. I thought I was angry at Madame, but I was just using her to make it easy for me to leave.*

RT: *I wish you well and hope you and your husband have good talks and make good babies. I wonder if you could explain something to me before you leave. While you were hypnotized you were lifting your left heel. What was that all about?*

P: *I was taking off my toe shoes and trying on sneakers and then a pair of sandals. It was a relief to get rid of the toe shoes and I really did get rid of them—I threw them out the window.*

With that, Patti got up to leave. She had perfect posture and looked like a dancer! Patti used her one session of hypnotherapy to gain the strength to end her career. I thought she'd benefit from a couple of sessions to talk about her options for the future, and the repercussions of her decision. But she apparently has good communication with her husband—and they can talk for free!

Getting Along with Your Co-Workers

If you believe in yourself and your values, you'll become a more valuable employee, particularly if you foster the same self-confidence in your co-workers. Use hypnosis to remind yourself of all that you believe in.

Here is a script of hypnotic suggestions to help you get along at work. Use these as self-hypnosis:

- *I will treat everyone, no matter their job, with respect.*

- *I will be helpful to others, sharing information gladly.*

- *When I listen, I will give people my full attention.*

- *I will tell the truth to others and to myself.*

Focus On This

Outstanding leaders go out of their way to boost the self-esteem of their personnel. If people believe in themselves, it's amazing what they can accomplish.

—Sam Walton, founder of Wal-Mart

Focus On This

If you are called to be a street sweeper, sweep streets even as Michelangelo painted, or Beethoven composed music, or Shakespeare wrote poetry. Sweep streets so well that all the hosts of Heaven and Earth will pause to say, "Here lived a great street sweeper who did his job well."

—Martin Luther King Jr.

How about the people you work with? Are you having a hard time getting along with some of them? There's always someone who's a jerk and another person who's a know-it-all, and of course, there's the office trouble-maker. Offices are like families and people play out their accustomed roles. Here's the most important fact you need to know about getting along with the people at work: They don't mean to harm you.

If someone you work with has a criticism about your work it's important that you talk about it and learn from that criticism. But if someone you work with is petty about your personal life, please don't take affront. Those kinds of comments, while directed at you, are probably not really meant for you. Maybe you remind Marty of his older sister and he's hated her for years; maybe you remind Lloyd of the teacher who wounded him with criticism.

Don't take everything in the workplace to heart. People will say and do things that offend you. If you ignore them or look at it as inevitable it will soon be beyond you. If you take it personally it will stay with you and harm you. Go to a hypnotist or use self-hypnosis to understand that they don't mean to harm you.

Analyze, don't personalize. Put your energy into understanding why someone is saying something to you, rather than into reacting to it.

The Least You Need to Know

- Rehearse before your interview.
- Do a good job by concentrating on the job, not on yourself.
- Hypnosis can help you overcome specific job-related problems.
- Be kind to the people you work with.
- Don't take petty office politics seriously.

Chapter 15

Having Fun Automatically

In This Chapter

- Why you need close friends
- How to feel comfortable with new people
- Maintaining relationships
- Enjoying yourself in social situations

Imagine living in a community where everybody knows your name. The TV show *Cheers* was very popular in the 1980s, and continues to draw a large audience in reruns. Why? Because it creates a world where people get together, casually, and become a fellowship of caring folks.

Scientists are just beginning to understand the value of close friendships, but you probably knew it when you were a child. What happened? Did you get sidetracked? In this chapter, hypnosis will help you get back your ability to be warm and attached. You'll overcome your personal obstacles to close connections.

Friendships

How isolated are you? Do you walk home from work and pass neighbor after neighbor sitting on the front porch, inquiring how your day was, giving you news about Gus in the hospital, Maggie's pregnancy, and the toy store's two-for-one sale? Or do you drive straight into your house using the electric garage door opener, thereby avoiding any possibility of neighborly contact?

People used to participate in community activities; today you can get your Sunday sermon online! We used to need each other—remember borrowing that proverbial cup of sugar? We are still linked to one another, but more often it's by coaxial cable.

When I was growing up, my grandparents lived around the corner and caught up with family news by dropping in. I catch up with my grandchildren's news by logging on! When I was bringing up my children I gathered with other baby-carriage moms (as we called ourselves) to gab and gripe. Today when I want to chat with one of those very same women, we compare calendars, squeeze in exactly one hour, usually four weeks hence, and enter it into a Palm Pilot.

And we call this progress.

Making Friends

How do you make friends? Do you struggle when you meet new people, wondering what to say and how to say it? Some people are easily sociable and some are not. Your natural way of responding today is similar to the way it was when you were born.

Your *temperament* determines how you perceive the world and your place in it. Some babies cling to Mama and others crawl away. Some youngsters run off to the first day of kindergarten, barely saying good-bye to their parents, and others have stomach-aches and great difficulty separating from parents.

Hypnoscript _____

The aspect of your personality that has to do with the way you generally respond to experiences and react to situations is your **temperament**.

People vary in their need for social contact and in their need to be alone. Please respect your basic temperament. The most important factor in determining whether someone will be your friend is physical proximity. You are likely to become friends with a neighbor, a co-worker, someone in your music class, or the person who stands next to you every week in the Laundromat.

After physical proximity creates the possibility of a friendship, the stages of making a friend begin:

1. **Awareness.** This is the time when you realize this person might be a potential friend and although you know nothing about him or her, you begin saying hello.

2. **Surface contact.** This is the stage when you begin speaking about superficial topics (the weather, an item in the news) while you are doing something else (the laundry, taking a walk, playing the violin).

3. **Mutuality.** This is the phase when you each speak about yourselves and acknowledge your common interests and ideas.

Focus On This _____

Experts say that parents can help their children overcome a predisposition to shyness by providing a supportive home environment that recognizes fearfulness and encourages children to do things at their own pace and rate of readiness.

Shy people often have trouble going from awareness to surface contact. Hypnosis can help by reminding you to focus on the other person, not on yourself.

When Mark came to my office he was upset because he had no social life. Mark was thrilled when his boss offered him the chance to move to New York, but within three months of the move his job description was changed. Now Mark works from home. There are days, he complains, when he doesn't even get dressed. Sitting in front of the computer and doing his job has become his entire life. To meet people, men and women, he will have to venture out. He will need to engage in an activity and then look for physical proximity. He was overwhelmed at the idea and began thinking that maybe it was okay to be isolated and limit his socialization to a couple of people who live on his block, but with whom he does not have any deep connection.

Here's the hypnosis script I gave him during his first session:

Please listen carefully while I tell you that you will find it easy to be sociable. You'll be surprised to notice that you're actually looking forward to social situations. You will look forward to social situations. You will enjoy talking to others. And when you are with others you will pay attention to what they are saying. You have good listening skills. You will enjoy relating to other people. And when you are with others you will pay attention to them. It will be easy for you to think of the other person ... to be interested in the other person ... to care about the other person.

The next week Mark returned. Usually, to better help clients, I make an audiotape of their sessions. That way they can save their money and experience hypnosis on their own. Mark, though, wanted to come back to the office. He was hungry for the human contact. During the second session I gave him the following hypnotic suggestions:

- *You will find it easy to engage in conversation.*

- *You will ask questions to draw out the other person.*

- *You may notice something about the other person that deserves a compliment.*

- *It will be easy for you to compliment the other person.*

- *Making conversation and giving praise will come naturally to you.*

Mark was making progress but wanted more direction. In his third hypnosis session I said:

- *When you are talking, you'll speak clearly.*

- *You will want to make eye contact.*

- *You are a good communicator. Your voice is clear. Your words are well chosen.*

- *You will remember that a social situation is a give-and-take situation.*

- *You will listen attentively while the other person speaks.*

- *When it is your turn to speak you will be generous. You will give information about yourself.*

In the Hypnotist's Office

When FDR was president of the United States, he did not like the polite small talk at White House social functions. He thought the guests were so in awe of their environment that they paid no attention to what was said to them. To prove his point he would sometimes amuse himself by greeting smiling guests with the words, "I murdered my grandmother this morning." He was right—no one listened closely enough to realize he was not making polite small talk. Finally, one day there was a guest who did pay attention. The guest gasped and then tried to cover his horror by responding diplomatically, "She must have had it coming to her."

For Mark's final session we did just a few minutes of hypnosis and spent most of the time talking about friendships—what they mean and how they occur. The hypnosis we did was simply to reinforce the suggestion: *It will be easy for you to be sociable.*

Mark and I talked about the few people he had begun to greet and hesitantly converse with. I explained that after the mutual sharing of information and getting to know one another, the next stage in building a friendship is knowing the new friend's role in your life. Friendships tend to be based upon utility, ego support, and stimulation.

When Mark moved to New York he left his friends and family back in Texas. But he quickly met Dave, who told him where to shop, where to get a good hamburger, and who the best dentist in town was. Dave and Mark have little in common, but they live on the same street; this is a utility friendship. Also on Mark's street is Mario, who reminds Mark of his brother back home. Mario calls to find out how Mark is getting along, encourages him when life looks gloomy, and congratulates him when things are going well. This is an ego-support friendship. Then there's Rob who is not particularly supportive, doesn't have a clue about neighborhood shops or services, but works in publishing, just like Mark, and is a telecommuter just like Mark. That is, he works from home. New ideas and experiences often come from stimulating friends like Rob.

When you want to begin a new friendship, think about ways that you can be useful, supportive, or stimulating to that person. It's often necessary for shy people to be hypnotized to stop thinking about themselves. Their preoccupation with themselves makes them nervous and unable to form a relationship.

> **CAUTION**
>
> **Look into My Eyes**
>
> It's been said that solitude is an interesting place to visit, but a terrible place to live. Create a life where you have the option of friendships when you want them.

Do you know the difference between being alone and being lonely? Many people are in relationships, even marriages and close friendships, where the lack of emotional communication is so apparent that they are extremely lonely. Other people live and work by themselves yet never feel lonely. Your relationship with yourself and your inborn needs determine how much intimacy you require. Figure out what you need by recalling when you are most happy. In a crowd? In a one-on-one relationship? By yourself? Then go for it.

Here is a useful hypnotic script to help at the beginning of a friendship:

Every day you notice a pleasing little something about yourself that you weren't aware of before. What you see adds to your self-confidence. You are comfortable with yourself.

You are confident about yourself. During a social encounter you have no interest in thinking about yourself. You are busy focusing on the other person. All your energy will go toward the other person. You will be concerned about the other person. You will really listen when the other person speaks. Your warmth will be obvious. You will have a good time while chatting. You are okay just the way you are.

Keeping Friends

It's difficult to keep up friendships. But, some people manage to have lots of friends and somehow those friendships last. Do you have any lifelong friends? You're more likely to if you returned to settle in your hometown. Have you heard about friends who have annual reunions? Do you know anyone like Lenny, who has been in a poker game with the same people for the last 16 years? Or do you know anyone like Sheila who goes shopping for summer clothes every June with her college roommate? Sheila is 50 years old.

These examples are all friendships that are maintained by *rituals*—a certain time of year, a certain activity. Whether it's a weekly card game or a monthly garden club meeting, when you weave social contact into your schedule, you maintain friendships.

Do you have friendships you wish to maintain? Think about establishing daily, weekly, monthly, or annual rituals. You might want to e-mail a certain friend every day, go to religious services with another every weekend, meet yet another friend for lunch once each month, and plan an annual vacation with another friend.

Hypnoscript _____

A **ritual** is a way of marking an occasion by a prescribed repeated series of actions.

Think of particular family members, friends, and neighbors to include in your plan and invite them to participate in your selected rituals or activities. At the conclusion of that encounter suggest doing it again at regular intervals.

Rituals such as these can continue for a lifetime and maintain friendships forever.

Social Situations

Social situations range from going to a restaurant with one or two friends to attending a gala event for hundreds. You may be more relaxed in one kind of situation but not in another. Some people prefer the intimacy of a small group; others like the superficial socializing at a large gathering.

Try to figure out the social environment in which you do best. Some people thrive in a dance club, others in a university club. Some are at their best in a bowling alley, others out on a boat. Some prefer a classroom, others a boardroom, still others a poolroom. Put yourself in the atmosphere that brings out the best in you.

Intimate Gatherings

When you are preparing to be with just a few people, it's a good idea to hypnotize yourself (see Chapters 6 and 7 to learn about self-hypnosis) and read the following suggestions:

- *It will be easy for me to give compliments and to ask questions.*

- *I will be thinking about the others and not about myself.*

- *I will assume the others are shy and I will try to make them feel comfortable.*

Preparing in advance, with hypnosis, will make a big difference. You'll actually enjoy yourself!

Large Crowds

To shine at a social occasion where you will be one of many, please hypnotize yourself and visualize the upcoming event. Notice everything about the scene in your mind. Use your senses and smell the aromas, hear the sounds, see everything all around you, feel the weather (or the temperature indoors), and become totally involved in that scene in your mind. Then tell yourself …

- *I am feeling comfortable and calm.*

- *I am self-confident.*

- *I smile, I have poise, I am at ease.*

Listen to yourself as you speak to others. You are speaking in a positive way—no complaining, no criticizing.

Tell yourself …

- *I have something to offer. My opinions count.*

- *I am enthusiastic.*

- *I am concentrating on the task at hand, which is socializing.*

- *I am thinking about the people around me, not about myself.*

- *No one is here to examine me. No one is interested in judging me.*

- *My words, my comments, are well received.*

Practice some of these hypnotic suggestions when you're doing casual, everyday activities, and you'll see the difference they make. You'll know then how powerful hypnosis will be when you're going somewhere special or planning for a new experience.

The more you concentrate on helping others, the less you'll be involved with yourself. Volunteering to help anyone, anywhere, is a good experience in focusing on the other person. When you play down your importance in favor of the other person or the activity you are doing, you play up your ability to be relaxed and at ease.

Focus On This

Do you work out at a gym? That's a great place to practice your social skills. You can speak to someone, practice making conversation, and then when you've had enough just start huffing and puffing and the other person will move away, assuming you're too winded to speak.

Serious Shyness

Bonita came to my office complaining that the other mothers in her son's school think she's aloof or indifferent. She is terribly ashamed, she said, because she doesn't feel cold or distant at all. She feels terrified. She said, "I am always self-conscious. It's too much of an ordeal for me to say 'hi' to someone, no less engage in conversation. I tremble a lot. I'm a big disappointment to my husband but I just can't help myself."

Bonita tries to avoid any situation where she'll have to speak; she is certain she'll make a fool of herself. She knows her fear is excessive, she tells herself it is unreasonable, and yet it persists. She knows the truth, which is that she never has made a public spectacle of herself.

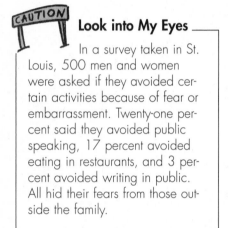

Look into My Eyes

In a survey taken in St. Louis, 500 men and women were asked if they avoided certain activities because of fear or embarrassment. Twenty-one percent said they avoided public speaking, 17 percent avoided eating in restaurants, and 3 percent avoided writing in public. All hid their fears from those outside the family.

Bonita explains, "I think everyone else is perfect. They are competent and I am a loser. I'm sure everyone notices my hands sweating so I try to keep my hands behind my back and that makes me look very strange."

During the hour in my office Bonita made no eye contact with me, spoke so softly I could barely hear her, and apologized for talking too much (she wasn't), for arriving late (she didn't), for complaining about "nothing" (she wasn't), and for taking up space in my driveway (that's what it's there for).

Bonita confessed that she drove to my office, although she lives in walking distance, because she's afraid of facing oncoming pedestrians. At one point during our interview I asked her what she was thinking of. She replied, "I probably didn't smile enough when you introduced yourself, and I don't know if I'm supposed to look at you and for how long I should keep my eyes on you when I do."

Bonita suffers from social phobia. It is a real disorder, classified as an anxiety disorder, and there are several variations to it, including being afraid to eat in public and being afraid to make a telephone call. I had a client who was afraid to drive for fear her car would break down and then she'd have to talk to a tow-truck driver. Her fear was not only of speaking to the stranger (the tow-truck driver) but of having others watch her while she did so. Her assumption was that she would say or do something to embarrass herself.

Eye contact is a major problem for all social phobics, as is the pervasive fear of acting like a fool.

Bonita embarrasses easily and suffers from *erythrophobia*, the fear of blushing. She will avoid most any public circumstance to escape the possibility of someone noticing her turn red. Like Bonita, most social phobics are perceived as being snobby, not as being scared to death.

Social phobia responds to several different treatments. Medication is very successful and psychiatrists know just what to prescribe. Behavior therapy works, too. Hypnosis is often the last resort, and yet the results are impressive.

Bonita's hypnosis sessions deal with the fears that all people who suffer from social phobia have:

+ Fear of speaking to strangers

+ Fear of speaking to authority figures

+ Fear of being humiliated in public

+ Fear of being criticized

+ Fear of being watched while doing a task

Hypnoscript

Erythrophobia is the fear of blushing. The tendency to blush runs in families, but babies are exempt from it, and it's usually not until childhood that blushing begins.

We also deal with her physical symptoms:

+ Blushing

+ Trembling

+ Perspiring

+ Resounding, rapid heartbeat

The hypnosis treatment is spread over several months. That way she has time to get accustomed to her gradually changing behavior. I hypnotize her to go into a fairly deep trance, and then ask her to visualize herself in certain situations. Eventually Bonita is able, in her mind, to see herself asking other moms in the community when the next parent-teacher conference will be held. We worked for well over an hour to accomplish this; it was extremely difficult for her to see herself approaching someone and initiating conversation.

At the end of the session Bonita was exhausted. It was very hard work. With one exception the entire time was spent on visualization. The only hypnotic suggestion I gave her, at the end, was that she would be able to accomplish in real life that which she visualized: *You will find it possible to speak to other moms and when necessary to ask them for information or exchange information with them.*

In subsequent visualizations Bonita saw herself …

- Asking her aerobics instructor if she is entitled to a credit for missed classes.

- Finally attending an aerobics class.

- Eating at the snack bar in the health club.

I wanted to "immunize" Bonita from the criticism she so feared. In her mind I asked her to see herself in class exercising to the music. When the teacher instructs everyone to turn to the right, I ask Bonita to see herself inadvertently turn to the left. She is deeply hypnotized and says:

Bonita: *No, no, I can't.* (She shakes her head and she frowns.)

RT: *Everyone in the class is turning right. You are having fun. You are enjoying the exercise. You are making a common mistake. You are turning to the left. Please watch as you do that.*

Bonita: *I see myself falling to the floor. I am so embarrassed. I can't go on.*

RT: *Look around you, from your spot on the floor. No one is paying attention to you. They're all focused on themselves. In fact, if you look closely, you'll see a couple of the people in the class are doing the steps all wrong. Look and spot that while you stay on the floor.*

Bonita: (Long pause.) *Well, maybe one woman is a little off. Another is winded so she's stopped. But everyone else is keeping up and doing everything right.*

RT: *Please watch yourself stand up and get right back in to the rhythm. Join in now.*

Bonita: (Nods, smiles.)

Focus On This

Psychologist Richard Heimberg says that "Social phobia is shyness gone wild. It cuts people off from the good things of life—social interaction, love."

We repeat this five times. Each time Bonita sees herself doing something that is potentially embarrassing, and each time she survives. It becomes easier with practice.

Many actors and actresses suffer from painful shyness and originally went into the theater to help overcome their fright. How does acting help? It takes the spotlight off you and puts it on someone else—the character you're portraying.

Bonita and others with social phobia can take a cue from show business. They can learn to act "as if." Acting "as if" means that when Bonita enters the snack bar she acts as if she loves eating in public. She concentrates on playing that role, which deflects her attention from herself. Acting "as if" is a way to fake it until you make it. This is a useful strategy for everyone, not only shy folks. You can incorporate an act-as-if statement into your personal hypnosis script for socializing.

Eventually, acting "as if" begins a habit and it becomes your preferred mode of behavior.

Hypnotic Suggestions to Enjoy Socializing

In addition to the suggestions throughout this chapter, you will benefit if your hypnotist reads you the following script or if you hypnotize yourself according to the directions in Chapter 6 and read the following script to yourself:

- *You have what it takes to socialize and to succeed at socializing. Please visualize yourself in a particular social situation. Perhaps you are with someone you just met, someone you do not know well, at all.*

- *Notice how relaxed you are. Socializing is easy for you.*

- *Look at your face—you're enjoying yourself. You are listening carefully and then when it is your turn to speak watch what you do …. You speak with ease and confidence.*

- *You are listened to. You are respected. You are admired. You are understood. Congratulations, you're a social person.*

- *Now you may leave that social scene and put yourself, in your mind's eye, in your home. You are anticipating a social event. You've just dressed for it. Soon you'll be on your way. You are looking forward to this event.*

- *From this day on, each time you anticipate a social situation you will be happy. You'll be looking forward to an interesting experience. You'll look forward to learning something new, to meeting someone new, to having a new adventure.*

- *You will eagerly look forward to social situations. You will not be tense. You will be relaxed. You are feeling calm and comfortable, relaxed and at ease as you think about the event you'll soon be attending.*

- *Now that you know how capable you are and how competent you are you may begin to leave hypnosis for today.*

Now your hypnotist will take you out of hypnosis in his or her customary fashion.

Please use hypnosis. Hypnosis will make you a winner and you'll have a wonderful time socializing.

The Least You Need to Know

◆ Friendships are important for your health.

◆ If you were born shy, you can learn how to overcome your shyness.

◆ To succeed in a friendship it's important to focus on the other person, not on yourself.

◆ Serious shyness is called social phobia. It can be helped with hypnosis, and there is medication for it, too.

◆ Hypnosis can help you act as if you are enjoying yourself in a social situation, and soon enough you do enjoy yourself.

Chapter 16

Becoming Game at Your Game

In This Chapter

- ◆ Sports psychology
- ◆ Improving your game using hypnosis
- ◆ Hypnosis to get in the zone
- ◆ Hypnosis for quiet competition

Can a hypnotist help you win your game? The results are in and the answer is *yes!* Mental rehearsal, visualizations, and hypnotic suggestions for focus, give you the extra edge. Your mind comes along with your body. Wherever you go, your thoughts and attitudes go with you. Your body is influenced by your mind, so it's not enough to train only your body.

Whether you're a weekend tennis player wanting to improve your backhand or a professional golfer wanting to improve your swing, hypnosis can help you.

If your game is indoors and quiet—say, bridge, poker, or Scrabble—hypnosis can sharpen your mind, focus your attention, and give you a competitive advantage. Read this chapter and find out why the *Jeopardy* contestant came for hypnosis. (It's not what you think.)

Hypnosis on the Field

Iwan Thomas of Wales is about to begin the race that he will win. Before he starts running he gently touches his left ear. Did you catch that subtle movement? Those in the know were looking for it.

In previous races Mr. Thomas had been distracted by the runners on either side of him. This time he paid no attention to them. In previous races Mr. Thomas was distracted by the clamor of the crowd. This time he heard nothing. All he had to do was touch his ear and his posthypnotic suggestion kicked in. My guess is that the suggestion was *You will focus on yourself and ignore those around you.*

Focus On This

Bob Reese says that the only drawback to hypnosis is its image. "I often wish I could call it a high-powered visualization technique, and not mention the term 'hypnosis' because that scares too many people. After they experience it and benefit from it, then I'd tell them they were hypnotized."

Hypnoscript

Sports psychology is the study of the psychological and mental factors that influence performance and the application of that knowledge to real-life situations.

Bob Reese, for decades the New York Jets trainer, uses hypnosis with his clients. Some are athletes, some are other professionals who must perform under pressure—musicians, executives, and dancers.

It wasn't too long ago that *sports psychologists* were consulted by team members under cover of darkness. Admitting the need for help was considered a sign of weakness, certainly not the image an athlete wanted to project. Today sports psychologists are employed by college teams, recreational athletes, professional teams, Olympic athletes, and businesses and corporations, too.

Sports psychologists help with …

- Building team cohesiveness.
- Stress management.
- Goal setting.
- Mental rehearsals.
- Increasing concentration.

It's hard to imagine that these areas used to be managed by the overburdened coach, or not attended to at all.

Many sports psychologists use hypnosis, and many hypnotists accept athletes as clients because hypnosis …

♦ Improves performance.

♦ Helps relieve pain from injuries.

♦ Increases competitiveness while easing the pressure of competition.

Hypnotists ease the pressure of competition by encouraging their clients to focus on competing with themselves. By setting increasingly higher standards of personal performance, through visualizations, the player competes tougher, but with less pressure.

The effectiveness of hypnosis on athletic performance has been scientifically documented. One study took 24 college basketball players (12 male, 12 female), interviewed them, and gave them individual and group sessions with a hypnotist. They received suggestions for playing a better game and for visualizing themselves winning. When shooting scores were compared with the scores of a comparable group of players who were not exposed to hypnosis, the hypnosis group showed consistently higher scores.

Focus On This

The spirit, the will to win, and the will to excel are the things that endure. These qualities are so much more important than the events that occur.

—Vince Lombardi

Many of the athletes I work with are very talented; they are truly excellent. The problem is that their competitors are just as awesome, just as talented. The winner will be the one who has best access to that talent, the one who can harness it. When you get to the professional level, every team member is superior, otherwise they'd still be in the minor league or on a farm team. Psychological skills make the difference between those who are very good and those who become superstars.

If a ballplayer is in a slump and then starts to see himself as a failure, it's my job to change his image of himself to a more realistic one. Sometimes I use age regression to remind him of his previous successes.

In slumps a player loses his ability to play automatically. Something interferes with the motor skills that are already established. The player must find a way to return to his center and become internally focused. Hypnosis can do this.

Visualizations

When he worked with the New York Jets, Bob Reese was impressed with the power of hypnosis in controlling the chronic pain of his players, but he became truly hooked on hypnosis when Dennis Byrd, a defensive end for the New York Jets, was recovering from a frightening injury. Says Reese, "Dennis Byrd did it for me. After a collision on the field he was paralyzed from the neck down. The doctors said he'd be lucky to be able to feed himself breakfast in two years. But Dennis said he was going to walk out of that hospital in a few months. No one thought it could be done, except for him."

Hypnosis helps with setting your goal and with achieving your goal. Of course, it's not foolproof; this is real life, not a movie, and there's only one Dennis Byrd. Trying your best is what it's about. Bob Reese tells his athletes, "There is no guarantee that if you create a vision it will happen. There is a guarantee that if you don't have the vision it will never happen."

Scientists have proven an amazing fact: When people visualize themselves performing an activity, changes occur in the muscle groups that would have been activated if they had actually performed that activity.

This means that in your brain a neural pattern can be created either by a physical action or by a mental process. Impulses are sent by your brain to the appropriate muscle site when you visualize yourself performing an action.

CAUTION

Look into My Eyes

Be careful not to blame the victim. Sometimes recovery is not possible. There is such a thing as bad luck, and there are bad genes, so there'll always be people who will not recover. It's important for them to understand that it's not their fault that they can't overcome their body's limitations.

When you alternate periods of mental practice with active training, your results are as good as, or even better than, active training by itself for the same amount of time. Even more impressive is the news that actions learned by visualization are better retained than actions learned by actual performance.

Visualization, along with a formal hypnotic induction, produces significant improvement in performance level. Visualization, with or without a formal hypnotic induction, is now an established part of athletic training.

Hypnotic Suggestions for Your Game

The general suggestions that I find most useful to improve athletic performance are ...

♦ *You will adhere to a strict practice schedule.*

♦ *You will consistently think in a positive way.*

If I could give only two suggestions, those would be the ones, and I encourage you to use those as part of your script for enhanced performance. Players do have individual needs, problems, and situations that we talk about during their interview and address with additional hypnotic suggestions.

In the Hypnotist's Office
Milton Erickson, the renowned physician/hypnotist, believed that he could predict winners and losers when watching a sporting event by observing the unconscious behavior of players. He said that potential winners appeared to have their own inner focus and sense of direction. He could spot the potential losers because they fell into step behind the winners. Erickson said that during the preliminary warm-up exercises those players who followed others were the ones who turned out to be the losers. Erickson knew that the mind controls the body.

According to researchers at UCLA, athletes must enjoy both practicing and playing their game in order to keep up their motivation. Enjoyment comes from ...

- Mastering skills.
- Improving performance.
- Winning competitions.
- Receiving praise.
- Working with peers.
- Getting audience recognition.

Hypnosis can help the athlete achieve all of these—with a simple suggestion such as *You'll have fun with your teammates during the next practice,* or *Remembering how you feel when the audience applauds is enough to maintain motivation.*

If athletes are motivated only by winning, they're likely to drop out when their chances look grim. But if they are focused on having fun and learning new ways to play the game, they'll stick out the tough times. I sometimes give an athlete the hypnotic suggestions, *You will measure your success by your daily improvement,* or *You'll notice that you're having a good time.*

Billy is a runner who comes in for occasional hypnosis suggestions when he feels his motivation waning. We find a goal that will be easy for him to accomplish and use that as his first hypnotic suggestion. Then we begin visualizing and suggesting incremental improvements. By the end of the session Billy is seeing himself running at a faster pace and covering a longer distance. The final hypnotic suggestion I give him is *You will be proud when you have mastered the task of running to the end of the boardwalk in your best time.*

Billy regains his enthusiasm for running by focusing on daily increases in distance and then improving his speed.

Hypnotic suggestions vary according to whether the sport is one that relies upon skill or upon effort. Of course, all athletes need huge amounts of both skill and effort. But every sport does favor one over the other.

Among the sports that primarily rely upon skill are diving, gymnastics, golf, tennis, and team sports such as baseball, football, basketball, hockey, and soccer. Casey Stengel, baseball manager, once said, "I was not successful as a ballplayer, as it was a game of skill."

Among the sports that primarily rely upon effort are running, weightlifting, swimming, and biking.

If you participate in a skill sport, you know that trying harder doesn't help you. Your muscles have learned what to do and they do their tasks automatically. Practice has taught them what to do and how to do it. It is not necessary for you to pay conscious attention. In fact, paying attention can make things worse. If there's lots of competitive pressure you may find yourself attending to what you're doing and that will detract from your performance. You can use the hypnotic suggestion *Ignore the fans, ignore the competitors, act as if this is a practice.*

If you participate in an effort sport, the pressure of competition can help you. Public scrutiny makes you try harder and you will run faster or pedal harder. You can use the hypnotic suggestion *Listen to your fans as they cheer you on.*

In the Hypnotist's Office

When Rick McKinney was 24 years old, he won the world championship in archery. When he looked at this victory from a competitive viewpoint he had nothing left to strive for and became depressed. When he reframed the situation, he realized he could compete against his own record. He resumed his sport and became interested in achieving his personal best. Competition was important to McKinney, and he had to create his own challenges to motivate himself and to try harder. It worked. When he was 31, he won an Olympic silver medal.

Peak Performance

You may call it being in the zone or on a roll or going with the flow. You know what I mean. It's that fabulous feeling when everything you do is right. It's why you went out for sports in the first place. The characteristics of this state are similar to those of hypnosis.

You know you are in the zone when …

- ◆ You are alert and energetic, but calm.

- ◆ You believe in yourself and know you are a winner.

- ◆ You are totally absorbed in what you are doing, oblivious to everything else.

- ◆ Your body is on automatic and seems to know what to do by itself, with no advice from you.

- ◆ You're enjoying every minute of this activity.

Focus On This

Chief Justice Earl Warren, when asked why he liked to read the sports section of the paper, replied, "I turn to the sports pages first because they record man's accomplishments. The front page has nothing but man's failures."

Peak performance and being in a hypnotic trance, for some people, are one and the same. Practicing going in and out of trance is useful. It gets your mind familiar with the state you want to achieve when you are on the field. Hypnosis can prepare you for your athletic event by mentally rehearsing your moves.

Football

Do you remember Jim Taylor? He was the NFL's Most Valuable Player in 1962. A fullback with the Green Bay Packers from 1958 to 1966, he is one of the "greats" and is in the Pro Football Hall of Fame. Jim Taylor graciously took time away from his busy life (he plays in more celebrity golf tournaments every year than most of us ever watch) to speak to me about his use of visualization and mental rehearsal.

RT: *Were there any hypnotists around for you or the other players? Did anyone develop training scripts or visualization scripts for the team? How did you guys mentally prepare for the game?*

Jim Taylor: *Nobody ever spoke to me about hypnosis scripts. The way I prepared for Sunday's game was that on Friday night and Saturday night I would fall asleep visualizing all possibilities.*

RT: *How did you see all those possibilities?*

Jim Taylor: *By confronting pressured situations in my mind. Out on the field is not like the blackboard. At bedtime, falling asleep, I did not see the blackboard, I saw the field in my mind. I did a lot of visualizing.*

RT: *Did the bedtime visualizing help you?*

Jim Taylor: *Sure. You never know what your opponents are going to do. They're trying to confuse you. Football is a spontaneous game, you have only a few seconds to execute a new play. It helps if you already did it in your mind.*

RT: *What else helped you mentally?*

Jim Taylor: *Concentration. For the execution you need concentration. I used to love to get the ball at the time of most pressure and intensity. I thrived on the pressure. It was my way of being right up there with the toughest and the best. If I was confronted with pressure enough times, then I'd be comfortable with it. Those highly pressured situations are the ones that bring out the best in you.*

RT: *What helped you concentrate?*

Jim Taylor: *I'd go through it all in my mind—the run, the pass, the down, the distance. And then on Sunday, coming out of the huddle, when there's only a few seconds to accomplish what you need to do, I could focus on every play. It was familiar to me. All that intensity; it's all about intensity. Intensity and concentration are necessary for every game.*

Jim Taylor didn't need a sports psychologist or a hypnotist. He intuitively knew how to be a winner. The rest of us, alas, need the benefit of hypnotic suggestions.

In the Hypnotist's Office

Athletes tend to respond very well to a particular deepening suggestion. Probably because they are so accustomed to using their bodies, they go into immediate, deep trance when told to gradually tighten their arms, shoulders, and chest muscles. I count from one to five and ask them to get tighter and tighter with each number. Then I count backward from five to one, asking them to become more and more relaxed. Repeating the exercise twice, and then ending at number one or sometimes zero, produces a very deep hypnotic state. Athletes are usually pretty good at hypnosis to begin with because they have lots of experience in focusing.

Hypnoscript ⎯⎯⎯⎯

Imagery is the term for the pictures in your mind that represent specific objects or events, as well as the feelings that you associate with those pictures. When you visualize without imagery, you see the pictures but don't necessarily feel the accompanying emotions.

Skiing

Kerrin Lee Gartner, 24, won the Olympic Women's Downhill gold medal for Canada at the Winter Olympic Games in Mirabel, France, in 1992. Her mental training coach, Terry Orlick, started working with Kerrin when she was 16 years old. Her talent for *imagery* has changed over the years.

Kerrin: *It used to be pictures in your mind, very much like watching a videotape. Now, it's more of a feeling. I can feel the feelings of skiing, and the motions. My thoughts almost turn into feelings.*

Terry: *Did you do much* imagery *in preparing for this race?*

Kerrin: *I've been doing imagery of the Olympics for about four years, and have run it hundreds of times in my mind. So by the time I actually had the race day run I had done it many times before; I just hadn't won it in reality yet.*

Terry: *How else have you benefited from using imagery?*

Kerrin: *When I had injuries, even when I was on crutches and in a cast, I kept doing my imagery. After recuperation, when I put my skis on, it was like I hadn't been off them.*

Terry: *You've told me that focus makes a difference for you. What do you mean?*

Kerrin: *My very best focus is when everything happens so naturally, I don't even think about it. The focus is so clear that I shut off my thoughts. I just trust myself and believe in myself. When you've already prepared for years and years, all you do is go; it's very natural. You're very relaxed. There are many words to describe that kind of focus. There's autopilot, connection, tunnel vision, there's just being 100 percent focused. It turns from thoughts to feelings to natural motions on skis. You don't see anything. You just naturally do what you do.*

Terry Orlick had this to say about mental training:

> Like all great performers Kerrin Lee Gartner overcame many obstacles to reach the top of her field. In addition to her positive attitude, strength of character, and passion for skiing, it is her commitment to work, every day, on the mental aspects of her performance that are an inspiration to all who have visions of excelling. It's those little steps, executed with passion and persistence, that take you to your dream.

Another skier, Jean-Claude Killy, is a three-time gold medal skier. For one particular race, which turned out to be one of his best, he never practiced on that slope. He was recovering from an injury and was not well enough to ski until the actual event. However, he told a surprised audience, he prepared for the race every day by skiing it mentally!

Golf

A golfer is a hypnotist's delight because the game is dependent upon concentration. Mental rehearsal and focusing techniques are perfect golf companions. Several of my colleagues have moved from the office to the fairway because of the satisfaction they derive using hypnosis to improve a golfer's game.

Tour-level pros, including Tiger Woods, Tom Kite, and Nick Price, consult sports psychologists, and so do weekend players, too. What can hypnosis do for your game? Here are some of the benefits:

- Relaxation techniques can block out noises and any disturbing, irrelevant thoughts that might impede your game.

- Hypnosis techniques can increase your concentration. Focusing on the here and now is crucial to the game.

- Hypnotic suggestions can remind you that your brain and nervous system are capable of performing the skills they know without any interference from you. You learn to go with the flow and leave your conscious mind out of the strokes.

- Hypnosis can teach you rituals to do in the down time, to stay calm.

- Hypnosis can train you, with mental rehearsals, to swing the club in a predictable way over which you have full control.

Arthur, a weekend golfer, declared he was ready to graduate from "hypnosis school"—his term for our golf-oriented sessions. When I asked how he knew it was the right time to do it on his own, he replied, "I'm finally able to step out of my way."

Look into My Eyes

Psychologist Steve Hendlin, Ph.D., who specializes in helping golfers improve their games, says that "Golf's slow pace means there is a tremendous amount of time between shots in which to scare yourself."

A UPI report from England about the British Open Golf Tournament quotes Gary Player's victory statement: "By using self-hypnosis I put myself in a state of perfect concentration and was confident all the way." Carol Semple, noted golf champion, has said that upon winning she often says thank you to her hypnosis cassette tape.

Indoor Games

I've hypnotized a Scrabble tournament player to pay no attention to distracting noises, and a bridge player to have a sharper memory. Chess players are known to utilize hypnosis for enhanced concentration. A sixth-grade boy, Matt, once came to be hypnotized to perform his magic tricks at the school fair. He benefited from these suggestions:

- *You'll be calm.*

- *You'll remember the sequence of steps for each trick.*

- *You'll slowly and carefully concentrate on every move you make.*

- *You won't give in to the temptation to divulge your secrets.*

Matt told his parents that the hypnosis worked well for the magic tricks, so he tried hypnotizing himself with those same suggestions whenever he played Clue or Monopoly. He said it worked; his actions were more deliberate than usual and he stopped his old habit of inadvertently revealing his strategy.

Jeopardy!

It was fun hypnotizing Barbara before she left for California to appear on the game show *Jeopardy!* She had successfully used hypnosis many years ago to stop a 2½-pack-a-day cigarette habit. She entered the office saying that she felt competent, after all she had passed the qualifying test to be a contestant. "But," she said, "the pressure of playing in front of cameras in a real studio might cause me to be a scared rabbit. Can you help me reinforce my positive thoughts and personal strengths?"

We wrote a script saying:

- *Stand tall.*

- *Smile.*

- *Remember how good you felt at the tryouts.*

- *You will have easy access to all the information you know.*

- *It's going to be fun.*

- *You will have quick thumb action!* (The suggestion I thought was most important.)

Focus On This

Jeopardy! tests three things: how much information you have accumulated over your lifetime, how quickly you can recall that information, and how calm you remain while 30 million viewers watch you compete. Hypnosis can help with all three!

I am pleased to say that when the announcer called, "Now entering the studio audience, a computer consultant from New York, Barbara ..." I saw her standing tall, smiling, and looking like she was prepared for fun. Barbara played three games, was a two-time champion, and won $24,000!

The Least You Need to Know

- Hypnosis is useful for improving performance in sports and games.

- Sports psychologists and hypnotists are important members of athletic teams.

- Visualization can create a brain-to-muscle connection.

- Hypnotic suggestions can motivate you to practice your sport, and enjoy it, too.

- Peak performance is similar to the trance state.

Throw Out the Viagra

In This Chapter

- ◆ Where do your sexual attitudes come from?
- ◆ Hypnosis for a better sex life
- ◆ Use hypnosis to think big
- ◆ Too much of a good thing?

Kings have abdicated their thrones, mothers have sacrificed their children, dads have left their families, corporate officers have fled their companies, and heads of state have ruined their reputations, all for sex. Do you ask yourself, "Am I missing something?"

Sex is extremely powerful. It causes some people to suspend good judgment. Of course, if you're lucky, it causes you to feel really happy and content. If you're not that lucky, please read on, because hypnosis can help you improve your sex life.

Mixed Messages

Cultural context makes a difference. Your religion will give you some messages about sex, and so will your friends. Your social circles may be of the "let's have fun in our California hot tub" variety, or of the "no sex and proud of it" style. Some people are socially, emotionally, and psychologically ready for a serious sexual relationship when they're very young; others don't reach that maturity until they're ready to retire.

The clients who come to me for hypnosis for sexual issues all have different agendas. They each have information that they're certain is accurate, and they wonder why their sex lives aren't perfect. Here's a sampling of some of the "facts" they tell me:

- Sex is good for you; if you don't do it, you can become very ill.

- Sex is bad for you; if you do it, you can get a fatal disease.

- Don't do it before you marry.

- Don't marry the only one you ever did it with.

- You should enjoy it.

- You should pretend to enjoy it.

- You should pretend you don't care about it.

- It's not normal to have a sex life after age 65.

- It's not normal to have no one to have sex with; I'm only 72.

Look into My Eyes

Times change, and the definition of acceptable sexual conduct changes, too. Today you can get arrested for behavior that just a few years ago brought you compliments. Fear of sexual abuse allegations forbids a teacher or camp counselor from putting a comforting arm around a crying child. Increased sensitivity to sexual harassment forbids a male worker to call a female worker an endearing term in the workplace.

We all have the same human body but receive different sexual instructions. Our information may come from our families or from the experts. In America we have no lack of sexual authorities. Sigmund Freud was sure he knew the answers; then came Alfred Kinsey and the Kinsey Report with its own brand of expertise; and then came Masters and Johnson with their unique research.

Ladies brought up in Victorian times were told to be dutiful wives and mothers and ignore whatever sexual desire they might feel. My client, Wendy, has the same body and sexual equipment as did those Victorian ladies. But, Wendy was brought up in America in the 1960s, burned her bra, chanted to government officials that they should make love not war, and watched porno movies as part of her undergraduate film studies program.

Wendy wanted hypnosis to help her adjust to a lowered sex drive. She was judging herself harshly for no longer being interested in long nights of passion. Nowadays she prefers to soak her feet, put on a flannel nightgown, and conk out before the nighttime news. She got the same hypnosis suggestion that I gave to one of my other clients, Joanne.

Joanne wanted hypnosis to help her accept her husband's ideas of lovemaking. They have a good relationship and Joanne says she enjoys sex, but afterward when she thinks about what she's done it bothers her. She referred to her husband most lovingly, and then added, "he's into some weird stuff." Because I've been in practice for decades, I know that one person's idea of weird stuff is another person's idea of heaven, and yet another person's definition of boring. So the questions I ask are ...

Focus On This

Most people do not believe their parents have a sex life. Yet, Masters and Johnson proved that if you're in reasonably good health there is no physiological reason for stopping sexual activity with advancing age. Contrary to popular belief, the joys of youth persist into old age.

1. *Does it hurt you?*

2. *Does it hurt him?*

3. *Does it hurt anyone else?*

4. *Does it frighten you?*

5. *Does it disgust you?*

6. *If you knew other people did it, would you enjoy it?*

Joanne answered "no" to questions 1 through 5, and "yes" to question 6. Then I knew, without having a clue about the act she was referring to, that she'd be well served from the hypnotic suggestion that Wendy benefited from. They each were hypnotized and told the following:

◆ *Please accept yourself and your sex life.*

◆ *The way you are feeling about sex now is the right way, for you, at this time.*

◆ *Enjoy yourself, enjoy your feelings.*

Even though we're in the twenty-first century and think we're sexually sophisticated, people still need reassurance that they can listen to their hearts.

Improving Your Sex Life

Wherever you go, there you are. When you're in bed, your personality goes with you. Marty's feelings of sexual inadequacy were similar to his thoughts when he picked up the telephone—"maybe they'll hang up on me"—and when he walked onto the basketball court—"maybe I'll embarrass myself." If you're self-conscious out of bed, you'll probably be self-conscious in bed. There's a simple hypnotic suggestion that will help you to feel comfortable in bed. It is this:

- *Think about pleasing your partner.*

- *Do not think about yourself. Don't ask yourself how you're doing. Think only about pleasing your partner.*

These few sentences always help both men and women who feel concerned about their body or their lovemaking skills.

Years ago, a man might walk into my office to complain that his wife had too many headaches, and was simply uninterested in making love. Today, it is the wives who are complaining about their husbands' lack of interest in sex. Hypnosis can remedy that. It usually requires that both partners reorganize their schedules.

How can you possibly expect your mate to be ready, willing, and able when the window of opportunity is only on Thursdays from 9 to 9:45 P.M.? I encourage couples to make appointments with each other for a sexual encounter. Although some couples object to that because they think sex should be spontaneous, statistics show that busy couples who wait for spontaneity are rarely awake and in bed at the same time. After we talk I give both husband and wife the suggestion that …

- *You will sit down with your date book and schedule a few hours to be with each other.*

- *You will honor that time commitment.*

In the Hypnotist's Office

Many couples are so busy working that they don't do anything as a couple. They have no time for sex, for friendships, for going out with other couples, for entertaining, or for visiting with the extended family. Those couples, if they want to stay married, must set aside time to do something—anything—as a couple. Sometimes I prescribe going to a movie, taking a bike ride, or even going to the supermarket. It's important, too, for couples to socialize with other couples. Every activity done as a couple reinforces a marriage.

These planned hours are often cherished as the only stress-free times in the week. Some couples begin with a glass of wine, and then add some music, in an effort to minimize the prearranged aspect of their rendezvous.

For some couples the bed becomes a battleground. Their sex life is a microcosm of their relationship, and the relationship is not all that good. Marriage counselors insist the relationship must first be worked on and then comes the sex part. But I've had some success with married couples who began by improving their sex lives, and the rest of the relationship soon followed. For such couples I use the following suggestions:

- *Concentrate on pleasing your partner.*

- *Try to figure out what your partner really wants and give it to him or her.*

- *After you please your partner, you will feel happy.*

- *When your partner pleases you, you will show your appreciation in a very special way.*

- *After sex, you will notice strong feelings of emotional intimacy.*

Couples who get these suggestions and actually put them to use find that their anger dissipates, and they are ready to let go of some past resentments. Pleasing your spouse in bed usually leads to pleasing your spouse out of bed.

Connie, a widow who recently remarried, came for hypnosis after realizing that her second husband had the same complaint as her first husband. They both said, "You're a great gal. I love you. Why can't you enjoy yourself sexually? You are very uptight." Our conversation went like this:

Connie: *I grew up thinking only sluts had a good time in bed.*

RT: *Do you still think so?*

Connie: *No, my mind knows better. It's my body that hasn't received the message.*

RT: *Would you like to learn how to use your mind to control your body?*

Connie: *If it's possible, yes, I would.*

RT: *Hypnosis can make it possible. I'll explain it to you, and if you agree, we can take care of your problem today.*

Connie: *You won't make me bark like a dog, will you?*

RT: *Misconceptions never go away. Of course, you won't bark and I won't make you do anything. Hypnosis is a mutual, cooperative endeavor. If you'll lean back in your chair and focus your eyes on that drawer handle while I speak to you, we'll soon have your problem resolved.*

Connie: (Leans, stares, listens to me.)

RT: *While you stare, please listen to my words as I tell you that hypnosis is an interesting experience. You'll become aware of the gentle rhythms of your breathing as I speak, and you'll find yourself becoming more and more relaxed and rested. Throughout this experience you will be safe and secure …. You will be calm and comfortable. You will have no thoughts on your mind. Instead, your mind will be delightfully light … and carefree. Please give yourself permission to feel your body relaxing …. Feel your body slowing down …. Your mind is slowing down, too …. Your muscles are slowed, your thoughts are slowed …. You are calm and quiet. Quietly you are entering a deep state of relaxation. Your body is feeling heavy … so heavy … heavier and heavier. Your eyes are heavy, too … your eyelids will close now.*

(Now I do an eye-roll exercise for Connie to become even more involved in hypnosis.)

Remember the eye-roll susceptibility test from Chapter 1? Rolling your eyes back into your head is a way to determine your hypnotizability. Eye-roll exercises also can be used as an induction, to help you become hypnotized, and as a deepening technique to further your depth of hypnosis.

RT: *Please visualize the number one …. Good … now, keeping your eyelids shut, please visualize the number two … very good. Please visualize the number three and roll up your eyes as far as they'll go—way back … good; then please visualize the number four and roll down your eyes … excellent.*

Throughout this experience you will be able to speak, to hear, to move. You can awaken anytime you wish simply by opening your eyes. For now, though, we'll use our time to help you overcome your problem.

You don't even have to listen to me; your mind can do that all by itself. You just need to concentrate in your mind on something very pretty. [Connie appears to be deeply hypnotized.]

Please visualize a beautiful piece of fabric. It's soft and delicate and pretty. It's large. Look carefully at it and you'll notice it is a bed sheet. Please pay attention as you watch yourself place it on your bed and tuck in the sides … and place some pillows on the bed, too …. Good. Now please keep looking at that beautiful sheet and your beautiful bed while I tell you a story.

This story is about a girl who is on her first journey without her parents. She is on a plane, traveling to her grandparents' home in Florida. She's a bit nervous. She looks out the window and wishes the pilot would straighten out the plane. It looks tilted to one side. Then the captain makes his introductory announcement. The girl doesn't like that, at all. He should be paying attention to his job, not chatting. She wishes she could tell him to stop talking. Soon the flight attendant comes by to offer a snack. The girl is too nervous to eat and too nervous to say "no, thank you," so she accepts the tray.

She looks around and wonders how everyone else manages to stay calm. She thinks and thinks and finally decides that (at this time, I change my voice tone and my speaking rhythm) *sometimes you have to trust that things will go smoothly … things will go your way and be right for you …. And sometimes if you allow someone to follow their own method, their own rhythm, their own ways, you will soon be following your rhythm, doing what you need to do. It seems scary at first to let go and relax … but worrying doesn't help …. After a while you can relax and let things happen automatically, and you don't have to try hard … you can just enjoy each moment. It's reassuring to know how safe you are … so safe that you can let your mind drift away, and feel all the pleasant feelings in your body …. So relaxing … so pleasant … allowing your unconscious mind to experience everything it needs to experience … allowing your unconscious mind to direct your body to safety and to happiness. Sometimes your body knows what it's feeling before your mind can figure it out. Sometimes your body knows that feeling calm and safe and happy and relaxed is a gift … and you deserve a gift. You can forget to remember to be nervous …. You can remember to forget to be nervous.*

And now, the girl has successfully arrived at her destination. And now it is your turn to arrive at your destination. You are already in the bedroom, so just place yourself on the bed, in your mind's eye. You can be sitting up and fully clothed, that's just fine. Please nod your head when you see yourself sitting on the bed.

Connie: (Nods, still deeply in trance.)

RT: *And now my words will tell you that you are supposed to let go and have a good time in your bed. You are entitled to fun in bed. You have the ability to have fun in bed. You no longer have a need to be vigilant. You can relax and let go. You are supposed to relax and let go. You will want to relax and let go whenever you and your husband are making love.*

And now please see yourself in your bed, in the morning, waking up next to your husband …. Please feel the love in your heart. (Connie smiles.) *Good, now watch yourself as you reluctantly get out of bed; you wish you could stay, but it's time for work.*

And now in your mind's eye please visualize that piece of fabric, the bed sheet, and listen to my words as I explain that you know that you are supposed to have fun in bed. And every time you see a lovely sheet on your bed you will be reminded of just how enjoyable making love can be.

Look into My Eyes

Remember that unless your sexual partner is your lifelong lover, you must practice safe sex. Safe sex means there is no exchange of body fluids. Going to bed with one person whose sexual history you do not know is equivalent to going to bed with every one of his or her sex partners. Watch out!

I begin reawakening and reorienting Connie. She takes a while to open her eyes and get going. She schedules another appointment for two weeks later. But Connie does not keep her next appointment. She calls to proudly announce that she does not need any more help!

Expanding Your Options

Hypnosis can help you do more with less. As you already know, hypnosis is capable of getting your mind to control your body. During surgery, blood flow can be directed away from the surgical site if the patient has been given such a suggestion while hypnotized. (See Chapter 22 for more about hypnosis and surgery.)

In your regular, unhypnotized state you can become sexually aroused when you think about a particular person or a particular erotic situation. Among the things that happen to you during arousal is that blood flow is directed toward your sexual organs. You can control this blood flow by your thoughts.

Focus On This _____

The last time I tried to make love to my wife, nothing was happening. So, I said to her, "What's the matter? You can't think of anybody, either?"

—Rodney Dangerfield, comedian

You do not become sexually aroused by someone who does not appeal to you. It's only when that person has some attraction for you that your mind tells your body what to do.

It's your thoughts, words, feelings, and mental images that produce the changes in your body. If you're easily able to conjure up sexual fantasies, you can easily put yourself into a state of sexual readiness. It's your deliberate focus on certain thoughts and images that does it for you.

What if you want to have sex but you're not sufficiently aroused? You can use hypnosis …

- To plant the appropriate images in your mind.
- To do an age regression to a time when you had the feelings you want to recapture.
- To give you suggestions about being open to pleasure.
- To relax, if tension is stopping you from enjoying yourself.
- To visualize yourself responding the way you want to.

Choose your hypnotic method from the options above and you'll solve your problem.

Luke arrived at my office upset and anxious. He was newly married and had not yet consummated the marriage. Luke was pleased that his wife was a virgin, but he was annoyed at himself for his inexperience. Usually couples need a little experimenting time to get it right, but Luke seemed extremely nervous. I suspected there might be more to this, so I asked some questions:

RT: *Are you comforted when you realize that everybody is unsure the first time they do anything? No one can do anything well until they've done it a few times. Practice will make perfect. When you get started there'll be no stopping you. Why do you doubt this?*

Luke: *Because I'm probably different than most other guys.*

RT: *How so?*

Luke: *I'm not the right size.*

RT: *You mean you? Or your penis?*

Luke: (Looking down and mumbling.) *Penis.*

RT: *What makes you think so?*

Luke: *In high school, the only time anybody ever saw me undressed, the guys in my locker room pointed at me and said horrible things.* (Pause) *That was the worst day of my life. It amazes me that Anna loves me and agreed to marry me. I think it's because she doesn't know how I'm really supposed to be.*

RT: *Have you ever been to a doctor?*

Luke: *Yes.*

RT: *Did the doctor see you naked?*

Luke: *Yes.*

RT: *And did that doctor gasp in horror and recommend immediate treatment?*

Luke: *No.*

RT: *How come, if it's so apparent?*

Luke: (Shrugs.)

RT: *Do you think there's a possibility that the guys in the locker room were simply being sadistic?*

Luke: (Shrugs.) *I dunno.*

RT: *Is there a possibility that if that incident didn't occur you might be home now, with your bride, in bed?*

Luke: (Thinks a minute or two.) *Maybe.*

RT: *Would you be interested in erasing that scene from your mind, and, even better, replacing it with a positive scene?*

Luke: *How?*

RT: *Watch me. First I'd like you to tell me about that locker room scene. I'd like to know everything—who was there, what each of them said, where you were and where they were, what the room looked like, what time of year it was, what you were doing right before you walked into the locker room, everything.*

Luke: (He describes the scene fully and then agrees to be hypnotized. In trance he went back to the morning of the incident and slowly we worked up to his entering the locker room.) *I'm walking in now.*

RT: *This time, you are standing tall and feeling pretty terrific about yourself. Nod your head when you see yourself like that.*

Luke: (Nods.)

> **Look into My Eyes**
>
> Sex is supposed to be pleasurable. It's not a task or a chore. It's not a competitive activity, and it's not a performance. Sexual activity is a mutually enjoyable act of sharing. Don't look to experts or, worse, to nonexperts to judge how you are doing. There is no judgment necessary. Pleasure your partner and express emotional closeness to experience good sex.

RT: *Some of the guys are starting to talk to you. Watch yourself as you immediately take charge of the conversation. Now you are changing into your gym clothes. While they are watching, you look at their faces. They are in awe. You continue to stand tall and proud. The guys are all, every one of them, impressed with your body, with your physique, with you. Listen to them talk …. Now, feel the feelings you have …. This is your new reality. This is who you really are …. Anytime you think about your body and your penis, in particular, you will remember how impressed the other guys were. But, you won't spend much time thinking along those lines. You have more important things to think about. You have a loving bride waiting for your attention. You'll be thinking about her.*

Luke comes out of trance, our session soon ends, and about one month later he calls to make another appointment. He tells Jeanne, my secretary, "Now that I know hypnosis is not a scam, and it really works, I want to come in to talk about some other stuff."

Too Much of a Good Thing

The National Council on Sexual Addiction and Compulsivity says it gets about 50 e-mails and 40 phone calls every week from people seeking help. Some psychologists think that sexual addiction does not really exist. They claim that what looks like sex addiction is actually an emotional disturbance, such as an anxiety disorder or a mental condition such as bipolar disorder. Nevertheless, there are people who feel out of control sexually, and their behavior lands them in trouble.

Certain environments—Wall Street, Hollywood, the music industry—tend to attract employees who are risk-takers. Risk-takers at work are more likely to take sexual risks, too. Different companies have different standards of behavior. When one company president propositioned many female employees, he was quickly dismissed, whereas

at another firm people laughed at their CEO who behaved the same way. Nowadays, though, everyone is afraid of a lawsuit, so sexual-addiction treatment centers are being established. The Meadows, an inpatient program in Arizona, says that among its residents last year were four Fortune 500 chief executives!

Focus On This _____

To find a sex therapist or marriage counselor, contact the American Association for Marriage and Family Therapy (AAMFT) at 202-452-0109, or the American Association of Sex Educators, Counselors, and Therapists (AASECT) at www. aasect.org.

Hypnosis is useful for self-control, and can be used to treat sex addiction just as it is used for other addictions. (See Chapter 11 for more about hypnosis and addictions.)

Dr. Whipple Speaks

Professor Beverly Whipple is known around the world for her scholarly research on human sexuality. She agreed to chat with me about using hypnosis to have a better sex life.

RT: *What does your research reveal? How can we all have more fun in bed?*

Dr. Whipple: *By focusing on a four-letter word that means intercourse. The word ends with the letter K.*

RT: *Oh, oh, this interview is going to be published in a book. Are you sure you're the great Dr. Whipple?*

Dr. Whipple: *Relax. The word is* talk. *I believe that good sex concerns far more than your genitals. It concerns communication that is dynamic and honest.*

RT: *The hypnotic suggestion for that one can be, "Talk to your partner. Communicate what you like and what you don't like. You will feel at ease talking about sex."*

Dr. Whipple: *Sexuality is about all aspects of you—your spiritual life, your emotional life, as well as your physical life. You know yourself better than anyone else knows you.*

RT: *So the next suggestion can be, "You are the expert on yourself."*

Dr. Whipple: *Yes. And you must take your time, and arouse yourself and your partner by using all your senses—focus on smells and sounds. Use music or talk, flowers or perfume, silk or satin—you get the idea.*

RT: *And that suggestion could be "Engage your five senses, and don't rush."*

Dr. Whipple: *If your attitude about your body leaves something to be desired, work on changing your attitude.*

RT: *That's easy with hypnosis. Next suggestion could be, "Your body is fine just the way it is."*

Dr. Whipple: *If a man reaches orgasm too quickly and wants to slow down he'll make matters worse if he concentrates on slowing down. Instead, he should distract himself by concentrating on his partner's eyes or shoulders.*

RT: *So the next hypnotic suggestion could be, "Slow yourself down, concentrate on your partner, not on yourself."*

Dr. Whipple: *I think hypnosis is a good idea for enhancing sexual pleasure because it can help partners to be open to new experiences, to accept their body, and to focus on giving pleasure.*

RT: *I know one of the things you're famous for is discovering a part of the female anatomy that's particularly sensitive to stimulation. Can you talk about that?*

Dr. Whipple: *It's the G spot, named after Dr. Ernst Grafenberg who first described it. It's a spot felt through the front wall of the vagina that is extremely sensitive to deep pressure. My colleague, John D. Perry, and I wrote a book aptly called* The G Spot, *which tells about our research and how you can use it to enhance your sex life.*

RT: *Thank you, Dr. Whipple.*

In the Hypnotist's Office

Kathy wanted help with her sex life. She liked her boyfriend but didn't like the way he made love to her. When I asked what she told him, in her attempt to change the situation, she said, "Oh, I'm not comfortable talking to him about sex. I don't know him that well." I told Kathy she was not a candidate for hypnosis, but perhaps some counseling was in order. If you don't know your partner well enough to discuss intimacies with him, to talk explicitly about sex, you surely don't know him well enough to be in bed with him!

Suggestions for a Better Sex Life

Adding the suggestions derived from Dr. Whipple to those I've amassed from years of working with clients, I've compiled a list of the hypnotic suggestions I think are most useful for improving your sex life. Take this list to a hypnotist, or use it with self-hypnosis:

- *Your body is fine just the way it is.*

- *Concentrate on pleasing your partner.*

- *Enjoy yourself, enjoy your feelings.*

- *Do not think about yourself. Don't ask yourself how you're doing.*

- *Try to figure out what your partner really wants and give it to him or her.*

- *Talk with your partner. Communicate what you like and what you don't like. You will feel at ease talking about sex.*

- *Engage your five senses, and don't rush.*

- *You are the expert on yourself.*

- *To slow yourself down, concentrate on your partner, not on yourself.*

- *You are open to pleasure. You are relaxed.*

- *In your mind's eye you can see yourself responding just the way you want to.*

Good luck!

The Least You Need to Know

- Every generation invents new sexual ethics. Today's standards say you are supposed to enjoy sex.

- If you're self-conscious out of bed, you'll probably be self-conscious in bed.

- Busy couples need to set aside time for their sex lives.

- Hypnosis can help with many sexual issues, including problems of arousal and undoing a past sexual trauma.

- Dr. Whipple, a leading sex researcher, insists that the most important thing you can do is concentrate on pleasuring your partner.

Chapter 18

Be a Better Parent

In This Chapter

- Hypnotize your child with superheroes and fairy tales
- Parents count, too, in a child's hypnotherapy
- Inducing hypnosis in children
- How to make children feel safe and secure during hypnosis
- Self-healing for kids

Children are naturals when it comes to imagining things. They're accustomed to watching TV cartoons where animals speak, and they believe in Santa Claus and the Tooth Fairy. It's easy for kids to be hypnotized because they're accustomed to going back and forth between reality and fantasy.

Hypnosis can help children write better, play soccer better, and cooperate in the pediatrician's office.

Imagination

Children are much more hypnotizable than are adults. When I work with some kids I don't even need to do a formal induction. I just talk to them about TV characters and before long they're in a deep trance. Of course, it doesn't look like a trance as you know it. Kids tend to wiggle around and usually they keep their eyes open.

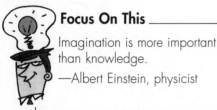

Children who do best with hypnosis are ages 8 through 13. In that age range they have fun with hallucinations during their sessions. They visualize animals that talk and superheroes who fly. Interestingly, children respond very well to the suggestions that are given, yet afterward, when I ask them a question about their experiences in hypnosis they have *amnesia* for the sessions. Unlike adults, who usually remember everything that is said to them, children remember little or nothing.

Children are comfortable with fairy tales and with superheroes, so the imagination of hypnosis is not strange to them. Children's affinity for hypnosis makes hypnotherapy a powerful tool for tackling childhood problems ranging from bed-wetting, to test anxiety, to performance on the soccer field.

Saying No to "Yes, Master"

Some children approach hypnosis with misinformation. Typically, they believe that they will be put to sleep and be under the absolute control of an evil hypnotist. This misinformation usually comes from television. There's a children's program that portrays a mad scientist who uses a shiny ring to bring people under his spell. When his victims wear the ring they walk around in an obvious trance state, follow his instructions for embarrassing and antisocial behavior, and mutter, "Yes, Master."

Fortunately and ironically, the effect of such misinformation is usually more positive than negative because it arouses children's curiosity. They're intrigued by the magic of it. It's important that I inform the child that on television the power of the hypnotist is supreme, but in my office the child holds the power. I am the guide, coaching the child to use his or her mind's power to control his or her body.

Parents and Hypnosis

You are an integral part of your child's treatment. Just as you would accompany your child to the pediatrician, so you should go to the hypnotist's office, too. As you learn about children and hypnosis you may decide to make some changes in your daily communication patterns with your children.

Hypnotic Communications

Children regularly use imagination and fantasy. They seem to be in a ready state of susceptibility, and their minds are eager to absorb suggestions. Because children easily absorb what you say, you need to watch what you say to them. It's as if your words can program your children without them being hypnotized. The very essence of being a child is being impressionable.

You can unknowingly hypnotize your child into believing the world is a bad place, dangers are everywhere, and failure is inevitable. Or you can produce optimistic children who look at life as an adventure.

When you speak to your children you have the choice of saying something that threatens impending doom, or something that conveys your confidence in your children and the world around them. For instance, you can say something scary like, "Be careful, don't run, you'll fall," or you can be reassuring and say, "Have fun, I know you'll watch where you're going." You can tell your child, "I wonder how brave you can be today. Let's think of all the happy things you'll think of while you're in the dentist's chair," or you can say, "Let's go to the dentist now. Don't cry when he hurts you, you're a big girl."

Your words determine how your child will face new experiences. Your choice of words determines whether your child will look at the future with enthusiasm or with dread. You have so much authority as a parent that you don't necessarily have to formally hypnotize your child to achieve tremendous impact and influence.

> **Focus On This**
>
> A torn jacket is soon mended; but hard words bruise the heart of a child.
>
> —Henry Wadsworth Longfellow, poet

> **Look into My Eyes**
>
> Words are powerful, particularly when they come from an authority figure. Teachers can imprint a lifelong viewpoint on their students' minds. When a teacher refers to a child as bright, that child incorporates brightness into his or her self-image and begins to act like that ideal. Unfortunately, a teacher can just as easily instill feelings of stupidity in a child.

Parents in the Hypnotist's Office

I invite the parents to stay in the room with their child while I do the hypnosis. Younger children are encouraged to sit on Mom's lap for the entire session. The advantages of parents being in the room are the following.

- The child feels more secure.

- Hypnosis is demystified for the parents, and they don't worry that their child is being traumatized.

- The parent develops a positive attitude toward hypnosis, which is easily transmitted to the child.

Your hypnotist should encourage your involvement with your child's hypnosis. If you are forbidden to be present you are entitled to a good explanation. Parents can learn some simple hypnotic techniques by watching the hypnotist, your hypnotist should be willing to talk to you about when and how to use those techniques with your child.

I don't ask parents to come into the treatment room when I think the issues bothering the child might have something to do with the child's relationship with the parents, when the parents seem intrusive or highly agitated, or when the child is a teenager wanting to be independent.

I like to include the parents when I teach children how to do self-hypnosis. They need to practice often, and it's a good idea for parents to know what their kids are doing. I don't want the parents to think their child is holed up in his room putting spells on people, practicing a cultlike chant, or playing around with voodoo.

Matthew learned how to put himself into trance when he came for help before a citywide eighth-grade math test. His dad sat with us and observed what I did. Afterward Matthew did well on his test and on subsequent tests, so he knew hypnosis could work for him. His dad helped Matthew hypnotize himself before a big soccer game. It worked, too!

> ### In the Hypnotist's Office
>
> Parents are usually wary of hypnosis at first. They almost challenge me to try to help their child, implying that the cure will never be found in hypnosis. Yet, when I work with a child whose parents are in the room with us, those very parents, who may have at first been skeptical, often ask, "Say, Doc, excuse me, but do you think while you're at it you can direct a suggestion to me? I'm having some trouble sleeping at night."

Kids in the Hypnotist's Office

Children can be treated individually or in a group—same as adults. The advantage of individual treatment is that the script can be tailored to precisely fit the child. However, to save time and money, sometimes a group is the method of choice.

Groups of Kids

Last summer a day-camp director brought a group of campers to my office. They all had poison ivy and were scratching fiercely. They responded well in a group hypnosis session when I gave them the suggestions that …

- *Your skin no longer feels itchy.*

- *Every few minutes you'll feel as if cool water is being poured over all your rash spots.*

- *The cool water is very soothing.*

Scientific studies have been conducted to test the validity of hypnosis on kids. One study took place in the New York City school system. Forty-eight elementary school children who were having trouble in school because of short attention spans and poor tolerance for frustration were part of an experiment. Every morning their teacher played a 15-minute audiotape that hypnotized them and gave them the following suggestions:

Focus On This _____

Children must find a way to learn in school, even if they have problems that prevent them from sitting still or concentrating. Hypnosis can be a child's ally. To quote civil-rights activist Malcolm X, "Without education you are not going anywhere in this world."

- *You will feel relaxed, not nervousness, today.*

- *You can learn as well as everyone else.*

- *When you put your mind to it, you can cope with school.*

- *When you write, you won't reverse your letters.*

- *You're as good and as smart as the other children.*

- *As soon as you start to learn something, you'll feel so good you'll want to learn more.*

- *When you're learning, you'll think only about the words and letters right in front of you.*

At the end of the school year, 45 out of the 48 kids improved in school, concentrated better, and were less hyperactive. A similar group of students who were not exposed to the hypnosis tape showed no change in their schoolwork or their behavior.

Children One at a Time

It is very satisfying to hypnotize children because they readily respond to suggestions and are so proud of themselves when they achieve their goals. And they almost always achieve their goals. Parents who've learned hypnosis skills can hypnotize their children when necessary. Until such skills are taught as part of parenting education programs, parents will continue to send their children to hypnotists and hypnotherapists. Now read about the three children I recently saw in my office.

Stacey

You already know that visualization reinforces the hypnotic suggestions. Stacey is proof. She's a high school student who stuttered whenever she felt nervous. She devoted her entire session with me to visualizing herself in various situations where she didn't stutter. She saw herself volunteering answers in her English, French, and history classrooms, chatting in the lunchroom, and talking with friends on the school bus. She watched and heard herself speaking fluently, no hesitations, no stuttering. Months later she returned for additional hypnosis. She wanted to visualize herself flirting!

Stan

Fifth-grader Stan has trouble concentrating on his homework. When he sits down to do his work at the dining room table after dinner, his eyes wander, his thoughts wander, and he hopes hypnosis will help him focus. Stan is a good ball player so his induction and suggestions were all about ballgames. For the induction I asked him to visualize his best game ever. I encouraged him, with his eyes closed, to see the field, all the players on both teams, the bleachers, the sky, the refreshment stand, and the parking lot in the distance. Then we engaged other senses. He felt the breeze on his arms, he smelled the fresh air, and he heard the cheers from the stands. I suggested he spend a few minutes watching himself and his teammates at their best. Then I said …

- *Watch how you're playing. You're doing a great job. Watch as you do each action at the right time.*

- *When you are at the dining room table doing homework you will have the same competence as you do on the ball field. You will be alert and pay attention and focus on one thing at a time.*

- *Watch yourself doing your homework without popping up, without your thoughts wandering. Good job!*

Rachel

When Rachel and her mom walked into my office they both looked scared. Rachel was afraid of doctors, particularly when she thought she might need an injection. Mom was nervous, anticipating Rachel's tears and tantrums.

I instructed Rachel's mom as follows:

When Rachel is on the examining table waiting for the doctor to come in, please have her look up at the ceiling. There are some cracks in the ceiling that look like funny, squiggly lines. Carefully watch those lines. Pay no attention to the doctor when he comes in to give Rachel the injection. Instead, follow those lines and see what interesting designs they make. Look for animal shapes, geometric shapes; maybe you'll find a ball or an ice-cream cone up there.

I was actually teaching Rachel and her mom to engage in a form of hypnosis. As you know, hypnosis is a state of deep concentration where you are so focused on your task that you cannot pay attention to anything else around you. If her mom keeps Rachel very busy locating shapes, the doctor can come and go and Rachel won't pay attention to him; she'll be too busy searching for shapes. Mom, too, will be distracted and her own nervousness will be diffused.

I recommended to Rachel's mom that she ask her daughter some nonsense questions, too. This is a technique advocated by Dr. Milton Erickson, the physician/hypnotist responsible for championing hypnosis during the twentieth century in America. It's a confusion technique that gets the brain to try so hard to figure out an answer that the child becomes oblivious to everything else going on around her. Among the questions Dr. Erickson liked to pose are …

- ◆ *Is your thumb telling you something?*
- ◆ *What color is the weather today?*
- ◆ *Are you married?*
- ◆ *How high can an elephant jump?*

The process of shifting Rachel's attention from the anticipated pain to a fantasy world that absorbs her attention is hypnosis.

> **CAUTION**
>
> **Look into My Eyes**
>
> Your hypnotist should interview your child to know which sports, school subjects, and interests are appealing and which ones to stay away from. A child who struggles at softball should be far away from the ball field during hypnosis.

Confusion and Distraction

Confusion and distraction techniques are recommended for children who are in pain or who are frightened. Dr. Milton Erickson told the story of one of his own children falling and bleeding. To distract the child Mrs. Erickson asked, "Let's see how red your blood is. Oh, look, it's a good bright red. You're a healthy boy." The distraction also gave the embedded suggestion that he was healthy and nothing was wrong because of the fall.

Focus On This _____

Some pediatricians have learned magic tricks and perform them for their patients. This is a form of hypnosis—a distraction to occupy the child's mind and prevent the child from focusing on the upcoming treatment.

Dr. Erickson recommended similar confusion/distractions for a child who got hurt. He liked the idea of asking these silly questions:

- *I wonder whether the pain will stop in 40 seconds or in a minute and a half or maybe right now. Let's see.*

- *Which eye will cry more tears?*

The first suggestion implies that the pain will soon stop. The second suggestion evokes curiosity and incredulity.

Distraction/confusion suggestions are recommended for children who are frightened and for children in pain. The child becomes curious and concentrates on stopping the pain, rather than feeling more pain.

Dr. Steve Bierman is an emergency room doctor who presents two possible scenarios when a child comes in and needs an injection.

- The doctor, in an effort to tell the truth and get the child's trust, says, "I'm going to give you a shot, and you'll feel a little pin prick. And then it will be all over." The doctor feels virtuous because he remembers his doctor from his childhood, who lied and said, "This won't hurt a bit."

  But, even though these are good intentions, saying this is not in the child's best interest. The use of the word "shot" triggers past painful memories. The child tenses in expectation, and can think of nothing but the impending pain. When the shot is delivered, the pain is sharply felt because the body is tensed.

- The doctor says, "I would like you to please look at that orange circle-square over there and tell me if it's getting bigger or smaller. Just look there and tell me, please." While the child is searching, the injection has been given. The child is still focused on finding the circle-square and is amazed when informed that it's time to leave.

  In this scenario the child is confused by the term circle-square and is paying attention only to figuring out what that means. Also, when the doctor says "just look," the child's unconscious hears that as a suggestion to look and not use any other senses—therefore no feeling.

Children really want to cooperate and therefore appreciate being distracted. It helps them act the way they want to and not behave fearfully.

Confusion and distraction will serve you well when your child has a temper tantrum. Think of the interesting comments you can make. Instead of addressing your child's behavior you can ask:

◆ *Did you hear that bell ringing?*

◆ *Can you cry in a different voice? Can you sound like a baby? Like a grownup?*

You get the idea. Now you and your children can drive each other to distraction.

Inductions for Children

Confusion and distraction techniques work as inductions and sometimes as hypnotic suggestions, too. If a formal induction is necessary I ask the children about their favorite TV show and then wonder aloud if they're smart enough to recount an episode to me. When they begin describing a scene I mention that they'll see the screen in their mind more clearly if they close their eyes. From there the session is easy. Girls usually choose sitcoms, boys go for superheroes, and I need to brush up on my Saturday morning television to prepare for the week's clients.

When Laurie was hypnotized, she was watching the television screen in her mind. I spoke to her as follows:

◆ *See yourself watching TV and not biting your nails.*

◆ *Notice that you have no interest in nail-biting.*

◆ *Watch yourself as you begin to put your fingers toward your mouth and then immediately lower your hand.*

◆ *You are repulsed by the idea of biting your nails.*

 **Focus On This** _____

Many children and adolescents enjoy having a relationship with a hypnotist; they consider it a form of security. If things go wrong they can call. Some kids have told me that knowing I'm there, without even speaking to me, is enough to help them solve their own problems. When in the office, they learned techniques for self-mastery that can transfer to any situation.

Watching herself try out a new behavior—not biting her nails—helped Laurie eradicate her old habit—biting her nails. These suggestions aim at more than changing a behavior. They also say to the child that …

◆ *Feelings can respond to changes in thinking.*

◆ *You are capable of mastering your thoughts.*

◆ *You can become your own medicine!*

Sometimes children (and if the kids are very young, their parents, too) sit on my "magic carpet." The rug on my office floor will travel to any destination the children want. After we play a game or do a puzzle, and they're feeling comfortable with me, I suggest a trip. It may be to the land of a favorite video or movie, to Grandpa's house, or to outer space. While on the magic carpet, the children close their eyes and see themselves being transported to that special place. When they arrive, I deepen their hypnotic state by saying ...

- ◆ *It's so clear; it's just like being there.*

- ◆ *You can hear interesting sounds and smell interesting smells.*

- ◆ *Look around and you'll see something very special.*

Look into My Eyes

Not everyone, child or adult, responds to visual suggestions. Some people get hypnotized by listening to sounds that they create in their minds—the sound of ocean waves rolling in and out, or the sound of a tennis ball being hit back and forth, for example. Others go under while petting their dog's fur or stroking a silk fabric—in their minds, of course.

After the deepening I offer the hypnotic suggestions and ask the children to visualize them. Traveling back on the magic carpet the children are instructed to visualize themselves in new ways, with the suggestions already making a noticeable change.

When very young children need hypnosis I prefer to instruct the parents on how to get their children into trance. Mothers do so every day by stroking or rocking their babies. A preschooler can become hypnotized by rubbing his or her hand back and forth on a Beanie Baby, or by performing any other repetitive action. Repetitive motions facilitate hypnosis. Ask your child to picture him- or herself on a swing, going back and forth, back and forth. Soon your child will be in trance.

Young children don't respond to suggestions to relax or close their eyes. You know kids—they'd rather fall asleep standing up than admit to a grownup that they're tired, so encouraging children to feel drowsy will never work as an induction. But trance can be created in a few seconds by focusing a child's attention on something playful, unusual, and interesting.

New York City hypnotherapist Naomi Sarna tells of an active little girl who jumped around and twirled around the office while Sarna tried to hypnotize her to help her with her insomnia. Finally, Sarna engaged the child by asking, "How many jumping jacks can you do at one time?" While the child was jumping toward 100, Sarna was praising her activity and at the same time interspersing induction phrases, such as, "When you finally stop, your breathing will slow down," and "When you stop your muscles will be relaxed," and "Soon you'll be ready to learn tricks about how to fall asleep."

After reaching 100 the child curled up on the floor, closed her eyes, and was in trance.

The foolproof induction for teenagers is driving a car. I tell them to get behind the wheel in their minds and go. I suggest that they are in control and can go exactly where they want. The car then takes them on a monotonous freeway ride where they easily enter trance. If I need to deepen the trance, I give the suggestion that everything they see on the side of the road is a signal that they are more and more hypnotized. If further deepening using a different sense is necessary, I've learned that teens can smell pizza at the slightest suggestion.

Hypnotizing a child consists of …

- ♦ Establishing rapport.
- ♦ Capturing the child's interest.
- ♦ Developing the trance state.
- ♦ Giving suggestions.

Games, stories, and magic tricks are excellent ways to capture a child's interest. A formal induction is not always necessary. After the hypnotist has the child's attention, the trance may occur spontaneously.

Child, Heal Yourself

Should you teach your child self-hypnosis?

Yes, says Dr. Karen Olness, professor, pediatrician, and world-renowned hypnosis researcher. Dr. Olness believes that parents have a responsibility to teach their children self-regulation techniques. Just as you teach little Joey not to crawl toward the hot stove when he's one year old, so you should be teaching him at five years old that when he gets a blood test he can control how his body responds. He can teach himself to feel no pain. When Dr. Olness instructs a child, she does so in a fun way: "Would you like to learn a trick so that injections won't hurt you?"

 Focus On This

Pablo Casals, the great cellist, conductor, and composer, suffered from nervousness at his Viennese debut. When he picked up his bow to play, it flew from his trembling fingers into the orchestra. He regained his composure by remembering his mother telling him when he was a boy to calm himself by concentrating on his goal and purpose. He played one of his greatest concerts ever.

Dr. Olness recommends teaching kids hypnotic techniques to help with headaches, nail-biting, fear of pubic speaking, and other frightening situations. She also advocates teaching children relaxation techniques by age five or six. That way children will always have the skills of calming themselves in emergency situations. Don't you wish someone taught you that lifelong skill when you were a small child?

Hypnotherapist Naomi Sarna teaches her hypnotherapy patients to knit! Says Sarna, "Knitting is a repetitive, rhythmic process that creates a calm, trancelike state." Sarna teaches knitting to the children in her hypnosis practice as a way of teaching them to calm themselves.

Repetitive hand motions are important stress reducers—they soothe. That's part of the appeal of cooking and baking, and of clicking the mouse, too. And, at the end of a session with Sarna, the kids who knit have something to show for their efforts.

You can learn the following self-regulation methods and work with your child, or you can go with your child to a hypnotherapist to learn these techniques. Before you begin, however, refresh your memory about dissociation.

Remember dissociation from Chapter 4? It's that feeling of having two simultaneous experiences, but being aware of only one. You were dissociated that time that you arrived at your destination but couldn't remember driving down the freeway. Dissociation is a way of being "here" and "there" at the same time. It's being aware of only one part of what you are experiencing and ignoring the other parts.

Dissociation during hypnosis helps your child reach his or her goal. One way to encourage dissociation while giving suggestions is to refer to parts of your child's body as if those body parts were separate from the rest. I suggest you say, "the" leg rather than "your" leg, "that" arm rather than "your" arm.

Here are some useful techniques you can use if your child is in pain. Each exercise is suitable for a different situation and a different child. You know your child best—use your best judgment:

- Ask your child to picture a woodpecker. Describe the woodpecker as a nasty bird that wants to peck and peck, and is the cause of the pain in whichever body part is ailing. After full pictures are formed in your child's mind, tell your child to firmly shoo away that woodpecker. In your child's mind, he or she is to see the woodpecker fly away and then watch the pain fly after it.

- Help your child create an image of a bucket of paint and a paint brush. Allow your child to choose the color. Place magic medicine in that bucket and ask your child to mix it well. Then add some numbing medicine. Mix it again. Instruct your child, while in hypnosis, to paint the magic paint over all body parts that hurt.

◆ Tell your child to visualize a light switch. It has three buttons on it: on, off, and dim. It is actually a pain switch. Your child can control the pain and take it from "on," to "dim," to "off." Sometimes it may get stuck on dim and your child will need to do extra work to get to "off," but he or she can do it.

◆ Suggest the following to your child: In your mind see your body with that painful foot. Watch as that foot begins to detach itself. Watch that foot as it floats away into outer space. You are fine without it. The pain is in outer space, not in your body.

◆ Teach your child to tense and then relax muscles. Go through the body, from one end to the other, mentioning all muscle groups, and give your child the opportunity to become proficient at relaxing.

◆ Instruct your child to rub a pebble, to knit, or to keep lucky pennies in his or her pocket. Tell your child that the activities and the lucky coins can create a magic relaxation effect.

All of these techniques (and some more that you'll think of), when practiced several times each day, eventually become easy and successful. Soon your child is relaxed, unafraid, and pain-free in less than one minute by knowing how to quickly visualize a scene of safety and comfort.

Children who are taught self-hypnosis and stress-reduction techniques have fewer colds, fewer flu symptoms, and fewer upper-respiratory infections. These techniques make a measurable physiological change. They boost the level of one of the immune system's disease-fighting components called IgA. The children do this to themselves, by themselves. Hypnotic technique makes them less vulnerable to disease. It is clear that children can be taught to influence the complex interaction of mind and body.

The hypnotist uses words, the children use imagination, and the results are very impressive. Children can enhance their own healing, and you can, too.

 Focus On This

Hypnotists who work with kids all agree about one thing. Kids must practice self-hypnosis at home several times a day.

Dr. Howard Hall says it best: "Hypnosis is a skill, not a pill. It takes practice."

The Least You Need to Know

- Kids are easy to hypnotize. Often they go into a fantasy world without a formal hypnotic induction.

- You should be involved in your young child's hypnosis experience. Choose a hypnotist who encourages your participation in the process.

- Some of the methods used to hypnotize children are interesting, amusing techniques that you can learn to use, too.

- It's important for children (and adults, too) to know how to induce calmness during stressful situations. Hypnosis can teach these skills.

Part 5

Get Well Soon—and Stay That Way

Please, please read Part 5 before you go into the hospital. Hypnosis makes a difference in healing and in recovery, and there's scientific evidence to prove it.

You'll be amazed at what your mind can do for your body. You can help yourself breeze through surgery, breeze through childbirth, eliminate pain, and get through medical procedures with ease. Learn about clinical trials and hypnosis in medical research, too.

Read the chapter on dentistry and you'll never again fear a root canal. You'll know exactly how to prepare yourself for your next dentist appointment.

Chapter 19

Hypnosis and Medical Research

In This Chapter

- Research for your good health
- Heal broken bones
- Calm a nervous stomach
- Smooth your skin
- Visit the sick

While you are reading this, doctors, nurses, and scientists are discovering more and more about hypnosis. They are studying groups of patients and trying to figure out how hypnosis can be used in medical treatments.

We know that one hypnotist can help one patient by offering a couple of suggestions. Imagine the benefit when hundreds of patients are studied in formalized medical test situations in hospitals and in doctors' offices and clinics.

Clinical Trials

When expert health professionals try to find answers to specific medical questions they set up a study called a *clinical trial*. The word *clinical*, when used in medical situations, means having to do with patients. The *clinical trial* is a research project that tests a particular theory. Volunteer patients who all have a specific condition are recruited to help the medical folks determine what works and what doesn't work. Eventually the theory is either proved or disproved.

Hypnoscript

Clinical pertains to the direct observation and treatment of patients. When patients with a specific disease volunteer for a research study designed to evaluate a new treatment, answer scientific questions, and find better ways to handle that disease, the investigation is called a **clinical trial**.

Question: How is the best treatment for a particular disease determined?

Answer: Research, research, research.

You've probably heard of drug companies conducting clinical trials to test the power of a drug. Alas, when it comes to testing the power of hypnosis there is no interested drug company.

Why would a pharmaceutical corporation be willing to come forward and pay for an investigation of hypnosis? After all, if they are testing a drug and it proves to be effective, they will earn a tidy sum. But, if hypnosis proves to be effective that same drug company gets no benefit, no profit.

Treatment Plans

Ideas for hypnosis clinical trials sometimes come from patients themselves. After *Good Housekeeping* magazine ran an article about medical uses of hypnosis, in March 2003, many readers requested that their doctor add hypnosis to their treatment plan.

What do you think? Should doctors change their medical treatment plans on the basis of one patient or one magazine article?

Finding Answers

Most physicians would feel more confident recommending hypnosis if there were proof that a significant number of patients benefited by having it added to their protocol. It would be encouraging if there were proof, too, that the patients who did not receive hypnosis didn't fare as well.

It's a clinical trial that provides such information to doctors around the world. During a trial, a massive amount of data is collected about the usefulness of the procedure being investigated. These days more and more patients are asking about hypnosis, so there are more and more clinical trials being established that explore the value of hypnosis.

> **CAUTION** **Look into My Eyes** _____
>
> The American Medical Association (AMA) has accepted hypnosis as an adjunct to standard medical care since 1958 and recommends that it be taught in medical schools. Yet, most practicing physicians know little about it and haven't used it since they learned it in medical school—if they learned it at all. It's possible that your doctor is not recommending hypnosis because he or she doesn't know how to do it and doesn't know a good hypnotist to recommend.

Current Research

Right now, on the very day I am writing this page, our government is in the midst of conducting several tests involving hypnosis. Two of those tests are discussed here.

Hypnosis Instead of Anesthesia?

Clinical Trial 1:

Is hypnosis useful in reducing the distress of patients during a surgical intervention to stop the flow of blood to a tumor? Can hypnosis be used instead of anesthesia? Can hypnosis reduce pain after the surgery? Can hypnosis take away worrisome thoughts before, during, and after the procedure?

No More Muscle Tension?

Clinical Trial 2:

Can hypnosis help a patient who has cerebral palsy relax, and thus decrease tension in his or her muscles? Can hypnosis do a better job than acupuncture? Would self-hypnosis work with these patients?

In a few years the results will be in and we will all know the answers to the preceding questions. Increased consumer demand—that means you, the patient, asking for more alternative medicine treatments—will encourage more and more research about hypnosis. Talk to your doctor.

In the Hypnotist's Office

Just one generation ago a patient would never have thought of demanding anything of his or her doctor. Doctors were to be idolized and obeyed. That's all changed. Today's patient is an informed consumer and often demands that the doctor look into a certain treatment or medication. Patients are consulting the Internet, as well as reading, and finding out about new medical techniques at exactly the same time that the doctor is learning that same information.

Focus On This

The two most famous medical journals are *JAMA* and *The Lancet.* They both publish scholarly research papers of the highest scientific merit. *JAMA* is published by the American Medi-cal Association, and *The Lancet* is published in London,

Research Results

When major medical journals publish results of a clinical trial, everyone listens. You listen, your doctor listens, and hospital directors listen, too. Changes in procedures are implemented to reflect the new knowledge. Below are the very latest findings of several studies. Pay attention to medical care in your city and notice if medical professionals are starting to change their ways because of this new research.

Your Bones

Can hypnosis help a broken bone mend? Sounds impossible, right?

Researcher Carol Ginandes, Ph.D., from Harvard Medical School, has reason to believe that hypnosis may accelerate bone healing. She conducted a clinical trial with patients who came to the orthopedic emergency room at her hospital. All of her patients had broken bones in their foot, but were otherwise healthy.

The Experiment

Dr. Ginandes divided the patients into two groups:

Group A received standard orthopedic care, including weekly examinations and x-rays for 12 weeks.

Group B received standard orthopedic care, including weekly examinations and x-rays for 12 weeks, and also received hypnosis. They received individual hypnosis sessions and then hypnosis audiotapes to take home and play daily.

The Procedure

At every visit back to the hospital each patient …

- Had his or her foot examined by a nurse.

- Had x-rays taken and scrutinized by a radiologist.

- Filled out a questionnaire that asked questions about how they were progressing.

(Neither the nurse nor the radiologist knew which patients had been hypnotized.)

In the Hypnotist's Office

Kevin came to my office asking for hypnosis to get rid of the pain in his arm. He had fallen while skateboarding. I refused. He had not had x-rays. Although he said he had similar pain before and it was a bruise that simply required time to heal, I could not take a chance. What if he had a broken bone this time? The hypnosis might take away the pain but then his arm would never be properly set.

The Results

The doctor and nurse noticed that certain patients had faster healing than other patients. In fact, at six weeks some foot x-rays looked exactly like the usual healing level of eight and a half weeks.

Certain patients had improved ankle mobility, had an easier time walking down stairs, and had a decreased need for painkillers.

When the patients' identities were revealed, it turned out that the fast healers were all members of the hypnotized group.

Your Stomach

Irritable bowel syndrome (IBS) affects so many people that gastroenterologists around the world say that half their patients come in with IBS symptoms. (You may know IBS as stomach trouble, or spastic colon, or colitis, or nervous stomach.) And, many, many of those patients do not respond to typical treatments. Gastroenterologists who use hypnosis say that patients with IBS are helped when receiving suggestions for slowing down digestion.

Health researchers in England have been studying IBS and hypnosis for quite some time, and now their colleagues in the United States are doing the same. The results are so astonishing that Adriane Fugh-Berman, M.D. of Washington, D.C., has said, "All severe cases of IBS should be treated with hypnosis."

Not only does hypnosis provide quick relief from symptoms, but in one clinical trial the doctors checked on patients 6 years after their hypnosis and found that 75 percent of the patients were still feeling fine.

The clinical trials have given us proof that hypnosis works for IBS, but we still don't understand what's going on scientifically. So some doctors are not yet recommending hypnosis for their IBS patients. They're waiting until they know how the improvement occurs. What do you think? If you were the patient would you wait or would you find a different doctor? Or might you just find your own hypnotist to go to?

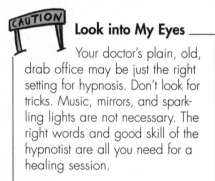

Look into My Eyes

Your doctor's plain, old, drab office may be just the right setting for hypnosis. Don't look for tricks. Music, mirrors, and sparkling lights are not necessary. The right words and good skill of the hypnotist are all you need for a healing session.

Birmingham, Alabama, hypnotist Melissa J Roth specializes in treating IBS. Jackie is one of her typical patients in that she did not think hypnosis would alleviate her symptoms, but she tried because she was desperate. After two sessions Jackie reported, "I actually got out with my family and went a few places for the first time in four years." After a few more sessions she was able to stop her medications, and she now is symptom-free.

Your Skin

Clinical trials have established the usefulness of hypnosis in treating a number of skin problems, including psoriasis, warts, dermatitis, hives, acne, and skin itching.

Focus On This

Hippocrates (460–377 B.C.E.) was the Greek physician considered the "Father of Medicine." He must have been a believer in hypnosis because he said, "The affliction suffered by the body, the soul sees quite well with the eyes shut."

How can hypnosis affect acne? Listen to Dr. Philip Shenefelt explain:

People who have acne lesions on their face often pick at their skin, making their condition worse. I had a patient who had been picking at her face for 15 years when I hypnotized her to stop that behavior. When she stopped picking, her appearance improved dramatically because the picked open acne areas are much more noticeable than the acne itself.

According to Dr. Shenefelt, the skin is a mirror of emotion, and many diseases of the skin get worse when the patient is stressed. Using hypnosis to reduce stress thus reduces the skin flare-ups.

Warts

Did you ever have warts? Did anyone give you advice on how to get rid of them? Through the ages wart sufferers have been told to bury a steak in the backyard, under a full moon; tape lemon rind to each wart; or imagine each wart disappearing.

Guess what? There's evidence that all these methods work, to some extent or another. There is particular evidence, substantiated by scientific studies and clinical trials, that a formal hypnotic induction followed by a specific suggestion will eliminate warts.

The specific suggestions to get rid of warts are …

- *Your body will cut off the blood supply to the wart.*

- *Now you will focus on the next wart, and your body will cut off the blood supply to that wart.*

You simply focus on each wart, one at a time, and instruct your blood to stay away from that site. This works!

Getting Your Doc Up-To-Date

How come you've been to the *dermatologist* and never been hypnotized? It could be for any one of the following reasons:

- Hypnosis takes too much time.

- The doctor doesn't know about the benefits of hypnosis to your skin.

- The doctor does not know how to do hypnosis.

- You've never asked about the usefulness of hypnosis for your skin condition.

I advise you to talk to your doctor about hypnosis. Educate your doctor about hypnosis. Mention that there are clinical trials that have proved the effectiveness of hypnosis for particular conditions. Ask for a referral to a hypnotist if your doctor does not know how to use hypnosis.

Hypnoscript

A medical doctor who specializes in treating disorders of the skin is called a **dermatologist**.

House Call

Doctors are not the only ones who can use hypnosis research to make a difference in a patient's life. You can, too.

If someone you love—or even just like—is ill and you go to visit him or her, either at home or in the hospital, there are some hypnotic interventions that you can do that research has shown will help.

No, you won't be putting them into a deep hypnotic trance and miraculously eradicating their fever, their illness, and all their symptoms. No, they won't jump out of bed and dance with you after a few moments of your expert care. But you can make a difference.

Let's say you are visiting Mike who just came home from the hospital after surgery. You know from your understanding of hypnosis that when people are concentrating on something they often are oblivious to everything else around them. Maybe Mike would like to forget about his situation for awhile. Perhaps you can give Mike something to concentrate on that will distract him.

Words That Heal

Consider talking about a movie you just saw or a TV show. Don't just chat about it but actually take Mike there—in his mind, of course. That means you must describe it in detail. Talk about the plot from beginning to end. Talk about the main characters. Depict them so clearly that Mike could recognize them in a minute. Make sure he knows what they wore, what they said, what dilemmas they face and more. You are helping Mike by giving him an opportunity to escape from reality. The more vividly you speak, the more clearly he sees the scene and creates a safe place to go to in his mind.

Images That Heal

Ask Mike to share some memories with you. Ask about vacations or any outdoor activities he has enjoyed. Listen to him reminisce about hunting, swimming, or canoeing. Ask if he has a favorite place. Then, together, you can create a replica of one scene of nature—again, this is in his mind.

When he specifies a scene help him add to it by engaging all his senses. It's okay for you to take notes. That way you won't leave out anything when you describe the scene to him later on. Ask Mike to think of that scene and then ask him …

- What do you hear? Sounds of nature? Cars? Music?

- What do you see? The sky? Water? People?

- What do you feel? The wind? The sun? A chill?

- What do you smell? Fresh air? Skunk? Chlorine?

Now be a good friend and take your notes and in a soothing voice read them back to him. Instruct him to close his eyes and imagine he is back in that special place. You can take him there, in his imagination, by mentioning all the facts about that place. When he is really seeing it, he will be calm and content.

Name Game

Tell him that anytime he wants he can bring himself back there, even during a medical procedure. All he needs to do is say your name and immediately he'll be transported to this place of peace!

Practice with Mike. Tell him to lean back, close his eyes, and say your name. Tell him that after a couple of minutes he will open his eyes. During those two minutes he'll be experiencing relief from whatever ails him.

You did a good job for your friend. And from now on he will associate you, or at least your name, with all things good.

> **CAUTION**
>
> **Look into My Eyes**
>
> It is important to treat ill people with respect. Losing good health does not necessarily mean also losing your mind. Don't assume that a sick person is not capable of understanding what's going on or of making sound decisions.

Touch the Towel

Here's another way to help your sick friend. Remind Mike that when he was a baby, like most other babies, he probably cried for Mommy when she wasn't around. And like most babies he was probably soothed when he held on to something of comfort, usually a special blanket. When he touched that blanket he was reminded that Mommy would return and once again all would be well in the world.

You can help Mike recapture the faith he had in childhood—the feeling that everything will soon be fine and he will soon be feeling comfortable. This time his treasured object will be a towel, not a blanket, because there are many, many towels in hospitals and in sick rooms.

In the Hypnotist's Office

When people suffering from chronic illnesses come to my office for hypnosis, they usually are looking for a suggestion that will help them stay in good control of their disease. And they regret that they didn't discover hypnosis earlier. More than one client has repeated the popular saying, "If I'd known I was going to live this long, I would have taken better care of myself."

Place a towel in Mike's hands and tell him to close his eyes and imagine he is a little boy sitting with his mom or dad. Then suggest that he visualize that picture with more detail in it, and simultaneously be aware of the towel.

Focus On This _____

Comedian Jackie Mason, lamenting about getting older, said, "It's no longer a question of staying healthy. It's a question of finding a sickness you like."

Now all you need to do is tell him that touching the towel gives him comfort and courage. Suggest that whenever he's ready he can open his eyes. When he is back from his reverie explain that from now on whenever he needs comfort or courage he can pick up any towel and he will feel better.

You've been a helpful friendly visitor. Your knowledge of hypnosis comes in handy.

The Least You Need to Know

- There are ongoing investigations about the usefulness of hypnosis in medicine.

- Hypnosis may accelerate bone healing and skin healing.

- Hypnosis has a part to play in treating digestive disorders.

- Your doctor may need information about hypnosis.

- You can use hypnosis techniques to help sick friends.

Chapter 20

Hypnosis and Patient Care

In This Chapter

- Hypnosis to prepare you for MRIs and other exams
- Hypnosis in an emergency
- When nurses know how to hypnotize
- Hypnosis in the burn unit
- Healing with hypnosis

At UCLA's pediatric emergency room, a patient is being wheeled in. Racing to keep up with the stretcher are a nurse, a doctor, a paramedic, and … a hypnotist!

Progressive hospitals throughout the country are using hypnotists to reduce pain, eliminate fear, facilitate cooperation, and more.

Procedures and Programs

Do you faint at the sight of blood? Are you dreading an MRI? Does your upcoming GI test have you in a panic? Plenty of people ignore symptoms and skip life-saving diagnostic tests, because they're scared. If you're one of these people, read on. Hypnosis can help you whistle on your way to the lab, and skip into the surgical suite.

Trouble with Your Lungs?

A 52-year-old woman who had never before been hospitalized was admitted because she needed a bronchoscopic lung exam. She was agitated and as frightened as could be. The surgeon thought she was too anxious and called the psychiatry department to send someone down for a consultation with her. Luckily, the psychiatrist on call was Dr. Gerard Sunnen, not only a compassionate man and fine psychiatrist, but an excellent hypnotist as well.

Patient: *I'm scared of the thought of a large, cold, straight metallic tube being pushed down my throat. I'll probably choke.*

Dr. Sunnen: *I'd be scared, too, but that's not what the procedure is at all. I'll draw a picture for you. It's a flexible tube and has plenty of space for air to pass. And, the more relaxed you are, the easier the air will flow. If you'll agree, let's try a hypnotic experience to help you during the procedure.* (Patient agrees.) *May I touch your wrist to begin?* (Patient agrees.)

Dr. Sunnen explains: "Gently and slowly, while holding her wrist, I bring her arm straight out in front of her. I give her images of heaviness and relaxation, and her arm slowly goes downward, her hand coming to rest on the bed. Her eyes close, all muscle tightness disappears, her respiration adopts a slow rhythm, and her face appears serene. Induction is complete."

Dr. Sunnen begins the hypnotic suggestions:

- *You will feel the tube and it will not bother you.*

- *Your throat and all your air passages can be relaxed.*

- *You will have plenty of air.*

- *With each breath you take you'll feel more and more relaxation sweeping through you.*

- *You'll be so relaxed that the whole experience will seem to be occurring some distance from you, far away.*

- *Until the time of the procedure you won't bother thinking about it.*

The patient had the bronchoscopy the next day and was remarkably calm throughout. The surgeon commented that the tube met very little resistance—an unusual occurrence.

Getting Through Procedures

Doctors use hypnosis to facilitate medical procedures. A hypnotized patient is a cooperative patient. One gastro doc who uses hypnosis during upper-GI endoscopies hypnotizes his patients and then proceeds as follows:

Doctor: (The patient is lying on his side.) *Okay, now we are going to start, and I suggest that you close your eyes and relax. Now I'm inserting the instrument into your mouth, you can relax your tongue and allow the instrument to glide down your throat like a piece of macaroni. You'll be able to swallow it—please do. That's good. You may feel some inconvenience in your throat, however your right elbow is extremely relaxed. Please focus on your right elbow and imagine that your right elbow is going to the beach on a relaxing vacation. See the beach and relax more deeply. Excellent, the exam will be over in a moment. You accomplished so much. Thank you for your cooperation.*

When the doctor talks about the right elbow going to the beach he's encouraging the patient to dissociate, which helps take the focus off the procedure. Remember dissociation? It's the ability to turn off part of what you're experiencing and attend to a different aspect of what is going on.

When the doctor talks about the beach he encourages imagery that deepens the hypnotic trance. The time required for this procedure using hypnosis is less than it would be if using chemical anesthesia because there's no need to insert an intravenous line. The other advantages are that there's no risk of drug complications or side effects, and the patient can get up off the table and go right back to work. No after effect of anesthesia, no grogginess.

Need an MRI?

An MRI (magnetic resonance imaging) is a medical procedure you may need to undergo if your doctor wants to see inside your body to detect disease. It's a painless procedure—unless, of course, you happen to have a fear of being closed in.

The MRI machine is a huge magnet and you are placed on a sliding cot and wheeled inside a narrow opening. Some people just shut their eyes and drift off to sleep during the hour or so that the procedure takes. Others cannot tolerate the confinement. Still others have trouble with the loud banging, clanging sounds that accompany the procedure.

If you live in Pittsburgh, Iowa City, or certain other cities, you have no need to worry. Progressive hospitals in these cities employ hypnotists to stand by to help MRI patients. Everyone benefits—the patient who does not experience fear and does not have to undergo a more invasive procedure, doctors who get a better look at the problem, and

Focus On This

The time slots allocated for MRIs, as well as other types of scans, are tightly booked and expensive. When a patient panics and the exam is not completed, the department can lose up to $3,000 in charges. This is a great incentive for radiology departments to bring in hypnotists.

hospitals who don't suffer financial loss. (Insurance companies don't reimburse for procedures that are not completed.)

You can go to a hypnotist before your scheduled MRI if you suspect you'll be claustrophobic. Here's the script I use:

◆ *With each loud noise you hear you'll become more and more reassured that you will get the most accurate diagnosis.*

◆ *You'll enjoy the snug feeling of security inside the machine. It's as if you're back in the safety of your mother's womb.*

◆ *Your mind will take you on a trip to a pleasant place … a place you remember … a place of beauty and comfort.*

◆ *You will enjoy your trip to the comfortable place and you'll stay there and experience everything there is to experience.*

◆ *You'll enjoy the weather, the smells, and the sounds.*

◆ *Your place of comfort will make you so relaxed that it's possible you'll be drifting in and out of sleep.*

◆ *Time will pass very quickly. You'll think the procedure is just beginning when it's already finished.*

◆ *When the MRI is over and you are wheeled out, you'll be particularly rested and content.*

Take the preceding script with you to a hypnotist or use it on yourself, following the self-hypnosis instructions in Chapters 6 and 7.

Hypnoscript

The naturalistic, **utilization** approach uses the client's personality characteristics and whatever is going on in the environment, and casually incorporates these dimensions into the hypnotic induction and script.

Why do I bother to mention the noise, in the first suggestion? I do so because it does exist; it's a noisy procedure, so I can use it to deepen the trance. I am reframing it. It is now not a distraction, but something useful. I can attach it (the noise) to something positive (an accurate diagnosis).

Dr. Milton Erickson believed in using whatever information the client revealed about him- or herself, as well as whatever the environment offered, to create a richer hypnotic experience. He called this the *utilization* technique.

Emergency Medicine

Have you ever been in an accident? Have you ever felt scared to death? Emergency situations can do that to you. That's the bad news. The good news is that when you're in that terrified state you're in a trance! Yes, you are so scared that you pay attention to nothing around you, and focus only on your urgent situation. Remember, hypnosis is a state of focused attention and concentration on only one thing, while ignoring everything else.

The good news about being in a trance is that you can easily be hypnotized. The bad news about being in a trance is that you can easily be hypnotized. The truth about being in a trancelike state is that you are extremely vulnerable and impressionable. If the people you encounter understand this and speak carefully, you'll be helped. If not, well, here's what happened to Sam: "The paramedics picked me up from the sidewalk where I collapsed after that stabbing pain in my belly. They put me on a gurney and into the ambulance. I overheard their conversation."

Driver: *He's not gonna make it.*

Assistant: *I don't think so, either.*

Driver: *Too bad. But, what can ya do?*

Assistant: *Nothing. There's no hope.*

> **CAUTION**
>
> ### Look into My Eyes
>
> There is such a thing as being scared to death. During the Northridge, California, earthquake of 1993, 15 people who were not injured died of fright. Self-calming might have helped.

By the time Sam was wheeled into the emergency room, he was dejected, hopeless, and wondering if his wife knew where the will was. The next morning, Sam was stunned when the doctors discharged him. He fearfully asked, "You mean there's really no hope for me? Nothing you can do? I just go home to die?"

Now it was the doctors' turn to be stunned. So Sam told them what he'd overheard. They tracked down the two paramedics who innocently explained, "We were talking about our buddy, Joe. He got called to an emergency just before he was supposed to leave, and there was no hope that he'd catch his plane."

Sam was reassured that all test results were in. He was declared healthy and recovering well from the bad case of food poisoning that caused him to pass out.

This never would have happened in Lawrence, Kansas. Emergency technicians there have been trained in how to speak to each other in the presence of a patient, and of course they've been trained in how to speak to the patient, too. They are aware of how susceptible an accident victim is to any suggestion of things going wrong or going right. After six months, a study determined that patients brought to the emergency room by the crew who knew about hypnotic suggestibility did better than other patients brought in by the untrained technicians. Patients brought in by the first group were less likely to need hospital admission, and if they were admitted, they were more likely to be discharged quicker.

Patients in the hospital should be protected from ambiguous comments made by hospital personnel. If you're suggestible, frightened, and traumatized and you hear the professionals around you saying "soon it'll be all over," how are you to know they're referring to the paint job in the lounge? If a patient is alarmed about his excessive bleeding, the wise ER professional can say, "You'll be healing very well because the blood does a good job of cleaning out your wound."

In the Hypnotist's Office

Patients are always extremely upset when they arrive at the emergency room. They have a serious physical problem and they have the accompanying psychological fright. The noise, bright lights, and unfamiliar faces are enough to scare most people. Dr. Dabney Ewin, professor of surgery and psychiatry, says that if patients are not traumatized when they arrive at the ER, they soon will be if they need surgery. Dr. Ewin reports, "In my hospital if a patient needs surgery, the release he or she must sign says, 'I understand that I may die, be paralyzed, lose use of a limb, or be permanently scarred.'"

Would you prefer to be told "Sorry, this is going to sting. Get ready" or "This stings for a moment before the healing begins." Would you rather hear "This will burn a little. Hold still" or "Some patients tell me this burns for 10 seconds or maybe 20 seconds before it stops. I wonder how soon yours will stop." Which would you rather be told "Your pressure is still sky high even though I gave you IV medication" or "It will be interesting to notice when your blood pressure will lower."

The good news is that a sensitive nurse or doctor can tell you to "feel no pain" or "concentrate on a relaxing scene," and you'll probably obey immediately. Use your knowledge of hypnosis to be useful to someone when they're in an emergency situation. Include positive outcomes in your statements.

Nurses

Lucky you if your nurse knows something about hypnotic suggestions. Nurse Dorothy Larkin is one such nurse. She's aware of the hypnotic technique of reframing. You remember that—it's a way to see a situation in a new and more favorable light. Nurse Larkin says that when burn patients complain about itching she congratulates them, telling them that the itching means their skin is healing. This new frame of reference permits the patients to associate future itching with healing, instead of with extreme discomfort.

Similarly, one day Larkin heard a physical therapy patient screaming in pain and yelling frightfully, "It's pulsing. I can feel it pulsing." Larkin utilized that patient's perception to distract her by reframing the fear of unfamiliar, painful feelings into a feeling of hopeful possibility. Larkin said, "Yes. I'll take your pulse now, and we'll see if your count of those beats will be the same as mine."

In the following example, Larkin sees a young patient fighting with nurses as they attempt to change the dressing over her wound. Larkin talks to the patient using a confusion/distraction technique that works.

Larkin: (Gazing into the girl's eyes) *Hi, may I call you Fred?*

Patient: *No!*

Larkin: *Oh, well, how about George?*

Patient: *I'm a girl.*

The nurses were able to accomplish their job while the girl was busy trying to figure out what was going on with the nurse who wanted to call her by a boy's name.

A nurse doing a painful treatment to a man's shoulder wisely referred to it as "the" shoulder in an effort to help the patient dissociate and feel less pain.

Nurses who understand hypnosis add healing to everything they do and often use their talents and wisdom to undo a negative statement made by an authority figure. When the patient is vulnerable, negative statements seriously impede recovery.

Every one of the nurses and physicians I interviewed for this book told me that part of their job, as knowledgeable hypnotists, is to teach patients to block the effect of statements made by unthinking persons. Dr. Alexander Levitan calls it "reversing the negative," and teaches his oncology patients how to do it.

Think of things you may have said, unwittingly, and with good intentions, to a sick friend or family member. Did you ever say, "Are you still in pain?" Dr. Levitan prefers, "How comfortable are you today?"

Focus is on the positive, not the negative. Did you ever say, "Please try to get out of bed today"? Dr. Levitan prefers, "Please get out of bed today." ("Trying" assumes the possibility of failure.)

Words are extremely powerful. Please choose yours carefully.

Nurses are often the only professionals who know what's going on within the patient's family. A nurse referred Mrs. R. to me after observing her interact with her terminally ill, hospitalized mother. Mrs. R. never got along with her mother who is now dying of stomach cancer. Mrs. R. is the only surviving relative and wants to be there so her mother doesn't spend her last days alone. But, she has to force herself to get to the hospital, force herself to touch her mother's frail, disfigured body, and force herself to be patient and kind. At the end of each day Mrs. R. is emotionally exhausted and wishing her mother would soon die, then hating herself for that wish.

Mrs. R. was not interested in hypnotherapy or psychotherapy. She had no desire to explore her relationship with her mother. She simply wanted a way to get through the next week or so. She responded very well to the following suggestions:

> **In the Hypnotist's Office**
>
> Oncologist Dr. Alexander Levitan believes so strongly in the power of words that he gives his patients the following hypnotic suggestion: "Should anyone say anything to you that is negative or less than helpful, it will have no effect. It will be as if those comments were expressed in a language that is foreign to you. You will not understand those comments."

- *You'll be interested in noticing how tolerant you can be. Things that usually annoy you will not bother you once you enter room 206.*

- *You'll surprise yourself with your gentle touch. Stroking your mother will be an exercise in compassion for you. Each day your place of compassion will grow and grow.*

- *You will relate to your mother as if she is someone who makes you feel happy about who you are.*

- *You will relate to your mother as if she is someone who brings out your sympathy.*

- *You know you are a good-hearted person. This is your last opportunity to let your mother know that side of you. It's important for her to know that you are good-hearted. You will act in a good-hearted manner when you are visiting her.*

- *You'll be so proud of yourself every day. Visualize yourself leaving the hospital knowing that you were tolerant, knowing that you were gentle, knowing that you were compassionate, knowing that you were sympathetic. Notice that you are feeling proud of yourself.*

- *Each day, when you come home, you'll know that you did everything right for your mother. You'll know you've been the best possible daughter. You'll be at peace with yourself.*

Nurses who know hypnotic techniques, and have the time and space, could accomplish what I did in my office right there in the hospital room. It's hard to hypnotize a patient when others—visitors and roommates—are looking on because the patient's privacy is compromised and the distractions are plentiful.

Burns

Have you ever stayed out in the sun much too long? You pay a price for too much sunbathing. Hours after you get home your suffering begins. You might have some fever and then the blisters start forming. This is the natural progression of a burn. You have a window of a few hours before the suffering begins to use hypnotic suggestions to head off a serious problem. Try it; it will work.

In the first two hours after a serious burn, the suggestion that the skin is cool and calmed may prevent the burn from progressing from first degree to second degree or more.

When Dr. Dabney Ewin meets a burn patient for first time he introduces himself and then asks, "Do you know how to treat this kind of burn?"

Patient: *No.*

Dr. Ewin: *That's all right because you've already done the most important thing, which is to get here to the hospital as fast as possible. You're safe now and if you'll do what I say you can have a comfortable rest in the hospital while your body is healing. Will you do as I say?*

Patient: *Yes.*

Dr. Ewin: *Good. The first thing I want you to do is turn the care of this burn over to me. The second thing is to realize that your own thoughts will make a great difference in your recovery. Your thoughts can affect your blood supply to your skin. You'll need to have happy thoughts to free up your healing energy. I'd like you to imagine that you're in a safe, peaceful place. A place where you can relax and enjoy yourself. A place where you can goof off and have no responsibility. Let's call this your laughing place and when I ask you to go there you'll imagine that place in your mind.*

Look into My Eyes

With a person who is extremely susceptible to hypnosis I find it easy to create skin responses. "Hot" suggestions can produce red marks and even blisters (!). "Cold" suggestions produce goose flesh with arm hairs standing up. You know that your mind can control your skin responses—do you blush? Or from your experiences with fright—do you turn ashen? Skin is very responsive.

Focus On This

Experiments have proved that hypnotizing clients by having them stare at a swinging pendulum or listen to the droning sound of a metronome is not as effective as having them focus on images that they conjure up, by themselves, in their minds.

From this point on Dr. Ewin cares for the patient while the patient is busy in his laughing place.

Dr. Ewin does not specify the exact areas of the burn when speaking to the hypnotized patient. According to Dr. Ewin, "I had one case where I specified the hand and forearm that I knew went into boiling oil, and neglected some oil that had splattered onto the shoulder. The hand and forearm stayed second degree and healed in two weeks. The shoulder area that I had considered inconsequential went on to third degree and required a skin graft."

Burn patients treated by Dr. Ewin and other excellent physician/hypnotists enjoy their laughing place, occasionally even dropping off to sleep, while usually painful procedures are being carried out.

Rehabilitation

How can a patient in a physical rehabilitation facility use hypnosis? Let's count the ways:

1. To master skills

2. To feel at ease in the rehab environment

3. To increase self-confidence

4. To become proficient at mental rehearsal

The more help rehabilitation patients get—both emotionally and physically—the quicker they respond to physical therapy and occupational therapy. As you'll see in the two stories following, hypnosis helps with attitude and enhances compliance.

Musical Script

A musician was an inpatient, recovering from a car accident. His physical limitations made him very irritable. One of the physical therapists knew hypnosis and gave him the following useful suggestions, after teaching him how to enter trance:

♦ *Whenever you feel frustrated waiting for someone to attend to your needs, you'll close your eyes, go into trance, and hear your impatience as musical notes.*

♦ *You will listen to those harsh notes and gradually replace each one with a gentler note.*

♦ *You will enjoy listening to the new melody.*

♦ *Any time you're waiting for help you can play the new, soothing melody. It will always be available for you, in your mind.*

After hypnosis the musician's response to treatment quickly improved.

Mental Rehearsal

Thomas, a 54-year-old college professor, was in a rehab center after suffering a stroke. He had to learn to use his left arm again and was having trouble with the physical-therapy exercises. The hypnotist in the center taught him to hypnotize himself and then instructed him to watch himself do certain arm exercises. After sufficient mental rehearsal Thomas was able to do what he was supposed to. The mental rehearsals helped with his occupational therapy, too. He practiced, in his mind, washing, shaving, dressing, and then went ahead and successfully did those tasks.

Using Hypnosis in Cancer Treatment

How can a patient with cancer use hypnosis?

◆ To manage pain

◆ To control nausea and vomiting from chemotherapy

◆ To control insomnia

◆ To influence the way in which he or she accepts the disease

◆ To perhaps influence the course of the disease

◆ To encourage an appetite

Reframing, via hypnosis, can make the disease easier to accept. I worked with one patient who needed a mastectomy and easily accepted herself as a one-breasted woman after we did some reframing. She thought of herself as a powerful person who could now swing a golf club easier, with no breast in the way! To this day she's never looked back with regret. Other women, too, have embraced the idea that their disease is being cut out of them and they feel lucky to have the chance to get rid of a diseased body part.

In the Hypnotist's Office

In a medical study at a university hospital, chemotherapy patients were divided into two groups before they got their chemo treatment. One group met with a counselor who hypnotized them, giving specific suggestions that they would experience no nausea and no vomiting. Members of the other group also met with a counselor, but were not hypnotized. Every one of the hypnotized patients went through the chemo with no nausea and no vomiting. The other group had a few who did not have those symptoms, but most did.

Although we know that the mind can influence the body, there is not yet enough evidence to know what the power of the mind can do to help the body fight cancer. Dr. David Spiegel, Professor at Stanford University School of Medicine and renowned hypnosis researcher, worked with women who had breast cancer and randomly assigned some of them to support groups. At the end of a few years he noted that those who participated in the groups, on average, lived a year and a half longer than those who did not attend a group. It is not yet known whether the increased longevity is a result of the social support or of the self-hypnosis that was taught to and practiced by the group participants.

If the group members had been given a pill instead of hypnosis and emotional support, I suspect that pill would have been scientifically tested, analyzed, and then marketed by many pharmaceutical companies. It might be a while before hypnosis is recognized as worthy of intensive study as a possible tool for longevity, but the day is coming.

Throughout the centuries humans have looked toward natural healing remedies, and then away, and then back again. In ancient days, when a child had an earache, Mother said, "Eat this root." Some centuries later, when religion became important, Mother said, "Discard the root. Say this prayer." Soon prayer was called superstition and Mother said, "Drink this potion." Then potions were called snake-oil scams and the command became, "Take this pill." Soon those pills were called ineffective and Mother said, "Here's a miracle. Take this antibiotic." Some mothers, today, are saying, "Antibiotics are overused. They're not natural. Here, take this root."

Hypnosis is one of the many natural healing techniques that doctors and patients alike are now rediscovering.

The Least You Need to Know

- Hypnosis is an important medical tool.

- After an accident or other trauma, you are in a state similar to a hypnotic trance.

- When you are in a trancelike state you are very susceptible to suggestion. The words said to you take on very great importance.

- Hypnosis is useful in harnessing the power of your mind to heal your body.

Chapter 21

Pregnancy and Childbirth

In This Chapter

- So you want to have a baby? Hypnosis can help
- Pregnancy and all that comes with it
- Hypnosis in the delivery room
- Hypnosis to help you at home with your baby

This is the female chapter—full of information about getting pregnant and staying pregnant, giving birth, and taking your newborn home. Hypnosis can help you conceive and then help you get through the next year of your life. Although hypnosis can help with symptoms of PMS (premenstrual syndrome) and menopause, childbirth-related issues are the ones most often brought to the attention of the hypnotist, so that's the emphasis of this chapter.

Pregnancy is not a sickness and childbirth is not, usually, an operating-room procedure. You'll amaze your family and friends by going into a trance, instead of a frenzy, when you begin labor.

Getting Pregnant

This is not your grandmother's pregnancy; this is a new-millennium pregnancy. Test tubes, surrogate mothers, sperm donors, frozen embryos, donor eggs, and high-tech, expensive equipment may be part of your pregnancy saga—if you're lucky.

Focus On This

For every 100 couples trying to get pregnant, 85 to 90 will accomplish that deed within 1 year of trying. Of the 10 to 15 who don't conceive, the majority will have a physical defect that is likely to respond to some medical intervention. And then there are the others. Those are the couples who will benefit from hypnosis.

Hypnoscript

A couple is considered **infertile** if they have not conceived after one year of unrestricted intercourse.

If you've not yet been lucky you're in for a surprise: Hypnosis can be a baby maker for the 20 percent of infertile couples who have no physical cause for their infertility.

You've probably heard all the tales. Aunt Sophie's neighbor got pregnant when she stopped thinking about it, Cousin Harry's boss got pregnant right after she adopted her son, and Gary and his wife announced their good news after an extended cruise/vacation. There are many stories of *infertile* couples who went to a hypnotist and *voilà!* Within a few months they were pregnant. This sounds impressive, but there are just as many stories of couples who didn't go on vacation, didn't adopt, and didn't have hypnosis, and after years of trying (the old-fashioned way) the wife became pregnant.

We may never be able to prove that hypnosis is responsible for certain pregnancies, but there's no harm in going to a hypnotist if you're trying to conceive. It's less expensive than a cruise, and less complicated than adoption.

How Can Hypnosis Help You Get Pregnant?

We know that hypnosis can decrease stress, and there is some speculation that stress can prevent conception. One theory is that when a woman is particularly upset, her hormones are out of kilter and the sperm that enter her body are killed off instantaneously. Another theory is that stress affects the ability of the egg to travel down the fallopian tube. That's based upon the premise that anxiety creates muscular tension, which impedes the ability of the egg to travel through.

A proven fact is that couples who have positive expectations and are confident and optimistic are likely to have more frequent sexual intercourse, and thus more opportunities to conceive.

An experiment about the relationship between hypnosis and conception tried using hypnosis as a contraceptive. Couples who were fertile were instructed to use hypnosis as their only means of birth control. This worked; during the time of the experiment there were no pregnancies. However, no one, certainly not me, dares recommend hypnosis as a contraceptive measure.

When Dr. and Mrs. D. came to my office they had been through several years of infertility and various treatments for it. I was the last resort. I heard from them three months after their visit; they were expecting! Was hypnosis responsible? I'd like to think so, but we'll never know. Here's the script I used after they were each in a deepened hypnotic state:

Remember when you were newlyweds and you really didn't want to have a baby until you graduated? Think about those days. Those days when you were so passionate but so afraid of pregnancy. You can remember those feelings of desire and yearning. Those feelings will return and you'll find that your sexual encounters will be spontaneous and fun ... like they used to be. You'll begin by relaxing each other. From that delightful beginning, everything will happen just like it's supposed to happen.

Take some time now to enjoy yourselves ... and now in your mind's eye, please visualize an egg traveling down a narrow tube. And now the tube is widening .... The egg has plenty of room to pass through ... and the small muscles surrounding the tube are helping in the passage ... visualize these muscles relaxing, creating plenty of space for the egg to pass through ... and soon the egg will be implanted ... and soon it is an embryo ... and it is getting nourished ... and soon it is a fetus ... it will soon become a baby ... and you will soon have a baby. You will soon have a baby.

After you're pregnant, the fun begins.

Congratulations, You're Pregnant

Each three months of your pregnancy is called a trimester, and the first trimester is the one most likely to give you trouble. The trouble comes in the form of morning sickness, the nausea and vomiting that is almost always gone by the end of your third month.

No More Nausea

To help with your nausea, ask your obstetrician if you can take vitamins without iron. The iron in prenatal vitamins bothers some women. Also, increase your carbohydrates—potato, dry toast, rice—and decrease your rich or fatty foods. And, of course, try hypnosis.

Look into My Eyes

Many remedies have been tried for relief of morning sickness. In the 1960s, the drug of choice was thalidomide, which turned out to help the moms but caused catastrophic birth defects in the babies. Be careful about using any antinausea medication.

If you can't hold down food or water you must get help before you become dehydrated or malnourished. Dr. Larry Goldman, a Fort Myers, Florida, gynecologist/ obstetrician, likes to teach his patients how to control their nausea by first teaching them to make themselves more nauseated. After he succeeds he then gives the suggestion *If you can make it worse, then you can make it better.*

Dr. Goldman notes that some women think that nausea is necessary to assure a healthy baby. Although that is not true, when he hypnotizes those moms he suggests that they may retain a small amount of nausea each day, for about 30 seconds.

After Dr. Goldman gives suggestions to eliminate nausea and vomiting he asks his patients to picture themselves eating their favorite foods. He ends his hypnotic suggestions by saying …

Now, at your own rate, finish your meal, and see how there is no sign of nausea or vomiting. You'll become very confident in your ability to eat and digest meals without any significant nausea and no vomiting. You'll know that your unconscious mind will not allow you to vomit, because vomiting deprives both you and your baby of needed nutrition. You'll begin to look forward to eating. You'll enjoy your meals.

During an office visit, without hypnosis, Dr. Goldman will pair a positive suggestion with an important landmark of the pregnancy. For example, prior to the first time that the parents are about to hear the baby's heartbeat, Dr. Goldman will say, *I have found that once we can hear the baby's heartbeat, nausea and vomiting disappear within one week in most of my patients.*

Hypnoscript

The term **waking hypnosis** is sometimes used to describe what occurs when a strong suggestion by a person in authority is absorbed by someone who is not necessarily in a hypnotic trance.

Some practitioners call this kind of conversation *waking hypnosis* because, although there is no formal hypnotic procedure, there is a hypnoticlike response to a suggestion.

I don't like the term "waking hypnosis" because hypnosis implies a mutual relationship, where the recipient of the suggestion has asked for that suggestion. I'd rather call Dr. Goldman's type of influence a strong suggestion. Others call this a "conversational trance."

No More Premature Babies

Hypnosis is also used during pregnancy to prevent premature delivery. Hypnotherapist Naomi Sarna (you met Sarna in Chapter 5 when she was curling up inside numerals) was called to the hospital by Betsy, a five-months-pregnant woman who had begun labor, and was hooked up to a monitor recording the strength and duration of her contractions. Ignoring the noisy environment Sarna quickly induced a trance and then told the patient a story:

The ocean is changeable. There can be storms. The high seas can be rough. And then the storms can pass; and the ocean begins to calm. The water becomes smooth; the waves become flat. And the muscles in your uterus are becoming smooth, and soft, and comfortable, just gently rocking the baby to sleep. You will be aware of the beeper on the monitor. It is slowing more and more. Soon it will stop beeping. The power of your mind can control your body. The power of your mind will benefit your baby.

Betsy had a hypnosis session every day for three days, was declared stable, and went home. She delivered in her ninth month.

No More High Blood Pressure

Hypnosis is used, too, in controlling high blood pressure caused by pregnancy. Hypnosis alone and hypnosis along with prescribed medication have been proven to lower blood pressure and prevent hospitalizations.

If you have high blood pressure during pregnancy, you must go to your obstetrician. Do not use self-hypnosis or go to a hypnotist who is not a physician. Hypnosis can lower your blood pressure, but it will not tell you what's causing the problem. You must know the cause to rule out problems with your kidneys or other organs. It is not safe to simply get rid of the symptoms.

No More Extra Weight

In the last trimester some women are hungry all the time and gain too much weight. Hypnosis is useful for them, too, suggesting they eat vegetables and give up the cookies and cakes.

Childbirth

Nurses, doctors, and dads who've been in the delivery room with a hypnotized mom agree that the effects of hypnosis are astounding. All the scientific studies support their observations, too.

The benefit of being hypnotized is apparent even before the couple reach the hospital. They've both been given the hypnotic suggestion to relax and calmly proceed to the hospital when the time is right. One doctor told me about a clearly unhypnotized dad who called, frantically, didn't identify himself and screamed into the phone:

Man: *Help! Help! My wife is pregnant and her contractions are only two minutes apart.*

Doctor: *Is this her first child?*

Man: *No, this is her husband.*

Hypnotic Preparation

Hypnotic preparation for childbirth decreases anxiety and lessens the need for medication. Emotional and physical recovery is speeded up when medication is limited. Researchers at the University of Wisconsin studied two groups of women in their ninth month, each group consisting of women of similar age, health, and psychological makeup. As you see in the following list, one group was hypnotized, the other group (the control group) was simply put into a state of relaxation.

Hypnosis Group	Relaxation Group
Had a group induction	Had a group lecture
Taught how to deepen their trance	Taught how to relax their muscles
Given suggestions to enjoy childbirth	Instructed on how to distract themselves by staring at something
Given the suggestion that voices in the labor room and delivery room will increase their relaxation	Given directions on how to push the baby out at the right time
Given a suggestion that one of their hands will become numb, and they'll be able to transfer that numbness to any part of their bodies during the delivery	Taught several different breathing techniques to be used during labor
Given an audiotape of their hypnosis sessions	Given an audiotape of their lecture
Told to listen to the tape twice a day	Told to listen to the tape twice a day

During the time of this study all women also attended six childbirth education classes provided by their obstetricians. Every woman in the study was told that the specialized training they received by listening to their tapes would give them greater relaxation, less pain, and a more enjoyable childbirth experience.

The benefits of hypnosis are apparent, as you can see from the results shown in the next list. The mothers who were hypnotized had more positive experiences in every way than the mothers who listened to the lecture. From these results, we can only speculate that moms who have no preparation for childbirth have a difficult time.

Results

Hypnosis Group	Relaxation Group
Shorter labor	Longer labor
Less medication	More medication
Babies had higher *Apgar* scores	Babies had slightly lower *Apgar* scores
Felt less pain	Felt more pain

The women in the control group, when compared to moms who had no preparation at all, might very well have had superior experiences, but the hypnosis group exceeded expectations. Hypnosis taught the women to reduce their awareness of pain, which stopped the typical escalating pain cycle.

Obstetricians who hypnotize their patients develop a unique style. Many rely on hypnotic suggestions that include time distortion, reframing, and dissociation.

Hypnoscript

The index that evaluates the health of a newborn on a scale of 1 to 10 is called the **Apgar score** (named after U.S. physician Virginia Apgar).

Time distortion can help the mom feel as if labor is a short, quick episode. When an obstetrician refers an expectant mom to me and I want to use time distortion, I say, *Every minute in labor will seem like a second, every hour will seem like a minute.*

If I want to reframe labor pains for her I say, *The contractions you'll feel will make you happy. You'll know they are caused by your baby. The milder contractions are telling you that the baby is packing her bags. The stronger contractions are letting you know that she's knocking at the door saying, "Let me out."*

For dissociation I tell the mom: *Other moms may experience pain, but you'll feel only vague discomfort. And the discomfort will seem very far away from you, as if it is occurring in another room.*

Many doctors who hypnotize their patients for delivery do not use the word "pain." Instead they say "pressure," "discomfort," or "signal." Dr. Marc Oster, the psychologist/hypnotist from Illinois whom you met back in Chapter 5 when he was having a root canal, teaches pregnant moms to quickly and easily retreat to a place of comfort in their minds. He concentrates on the phrase "quickly and easily." They practice this for several weeks before delivery, and then during labor and delivery he simply says, "quickly and easily" and they go right to that place.

During hypnotic sessions prior to delivery Dr. Oster pairs contractions with deepening. By the time the patient is in labor it is automatic for her to go into a deeper and deeper trance whenever a contraction occurs. She's been given the posthypnotic suggestion that when a contraction starts she closes her eyes and deepens her trance. When it's over she awakens feeling refreshed.

Dr. Larry Goldman believes that some women expect childbirth to be extremely painful because of tales they've heard from family members, or from television shows or movies that depict torturous labor. He believes that hypnosis empowers the woman to experience labor any way she wishes—if she needs to keep a little pain, he allows it. Dr. Goldman insists that fathers come to class, too. He explains that many people are ignorant about hypnosis and may try to sabotage the childbirth experience that the couple is preparing for. The dads are instructed that they have the role of supporting mom and supporting hypnosis when negative comments about hypnosis come up.

You may be familiar with the Lamaze method that instructs the moms to concentrate on their breathing. This serves the purpose of distracting moms from the pain of contractions. Dr. Goldman, like Dr. Oster, teaches his patients to focus on the contractions and use them to signal the beginning of a deep relaxation state.

In the Hypnotist's Office

Attitude has a lot to do with pain perception and the experience of childbirth in general. Listen to Isadora Duncan, a dancer who achieved worldwide fame at the beginning of the twentieth century: "Childbirth is uncivilized barbarism. It is monstrous torture. It should be stopped. I tremble with indignation when I think of the blindness of men of science who permit such atrocities." Compare her to Golda Meir, prime minister of Israel in the early 1970s: "Men are discriminated against because they can't bear children. Who are these crazy creatures who deem it a misfortune to get pregnant and a disaster to give birth to children? Giving birth is the greatest privilege we women have."

Learning How to Deliver

Dr. Goldman offers his expectant couples a six-session "Hypnosis for Childbirth" class.

In Session 1, the couples learn about hypnosis, experience trance, and watch a video of a hypnotized mom delivering her baby.

In Session 2, the class watches a video about the biology of childbirth. Moms are hypnotized and given this suggestion: *You will look forward to each contraction because each contraction brings you closer to your baby.* The fathers learn how to hypnotize their wives during this class, so that they can practice at home. The moms are hypnotized to pair contractions with relaxation. Dr. Goldman reminds the class that when the heart contracts there is no pain, when other muscles contract there is no pain, and during childbirth when the uterus contracts, there will be no pain. It is a normal physiological process.

In Session 3, a husband and wife who recently delivered come to class to share their experience, answer questions, and show off their baby. Also at this session music is introduced as an induction, the moms are taught a rapid induction method, and couples are taught the basics of self-hypnosis and urged to practice hypnosis at home.

In Session 4, the class takes a tour of the hospital, during which time couples are asked to remember as many physical details of the hospital as possible. Later, these details are incorporated into hypnosis practice sessions at home.

In Session 5, more rapid induction techniques are taught and *glove anesthesia* is taught, which gives the patient the ability, under hypnosis, to numb any part of her body. Couples are taught to rehearse, under hypnosis, labor and delivery, and they are encouraged to practice daily.

In Session 6, couples are prepared for all possible complications and taught that if any complications come their way, it will be easy for them to adapt. During hypnosis, couples are encouraged to look forward to the delivery as a joyful celebration. Dr. Goldman encourages his patients to take medication during delivery if it will help them stay in control. He believes that taking control of her experience is important for every mom.

Hypnoscript

A client instructed to feel numbness in one hand and then given the suggestion that any part of the body touched by that hand will absorb that numbness and feel nothing, is experiencing **glove anesthesia.**

Hypnosis-trained mothers do very well during delivery. According to the mothers and the doctors who treat them, the advantages of using hypnosis during childbirth are …

- Feeling less fear.
- Feeling less pain.
- Experiencing no side effects from medications, for Mom or for baby.

- Feeling in control of the contractions.

- Recovering quickly from delivery.

- Feeling physically and mentally alert, not fatigued, afterward.

- Experiencing a shorter time in labor.

- Staying a shorter time in the hospital.

- Being less at risk for depression after delivery.

The Late Baby

When hypnosis is used on a mom who is beyond her due date and about to have her labor induced, it is another one of those circumstances where we really don't know if hypnosis was the hero. Labor might have begun spontaneously at that time, anyway. But maybe not, and surely it's better to try hypnosis before medication.

Hypnotist Naomi Sarna spent two hours hypnotizing a patient in the hope that labor would begin. Sarna says: "While Mrs. Kirk was in trance I reminded her that she was familiar with opening and closing her body. Ever since she was born she's been opening and closing her fists, her eyes, her mouth. I asked her to visualize those opening and closing movements, one at a time, and then I said, *Now is the time to let your mind wander and become open and relaxed. All the hormones in your body are moving at the proper rate to make your uterus relax and contract. Think of a rose opening—effortlessly, beautifully, comfortably. You know exactly how to begin your contractions. Your hormones will flow at the most useful rate. You are beginning labor.*

Four hours later Mrs. Kirk called from the hospital. She was in labor!

The Least You Need to Know

- Hypnosis can help you get pregnant.

- Hypnosis can help you feel better throughout your pregnancy.

- Moms who learn hypnosis before delivery say that it makes a tremendous difference during childbirth—for the better.

- You'll need to practice going in and out of trance daily. It's a skill that gets better with practice.

Chapter 22

In the Operating Room

In This Chapter

- ◆ What are you thinking?
- ◆ Hypnosis helps you talk to your surgeon
- ◆ Hypnosis helps you listen to your surgeon
- ◆ Getting hypnotized
- ◆ Breezing through your operation, compliments of hypnosis
- ◆ Home sweet home

Once upon a time when you needed surgery, you'd enter the hospital on Monday, relax on Tuesday, have your operation on Wednesday, stay in bed Thursday, benefit from the care of nurses and doctors for another week, and remain in the hospital until you were fully recovered.

Today you can have outpatient gallbladder surgery and outpatient brain surgery! It's urgent that you do all you can to hasten your recovery from surgery. Many, many scientific studies have proved that hypnosis can influence the outcome of surgery.

Your Thoughts Can Affect Your Body

Surgery is a psychologically critical event. Before, during, and after the operation your body will react not only to the physical and chemical interventions, but to the noises and the people in the hospital, the attitudes of everyone you encounter, and your own beliefs, expectations, and thoughts.

Until chemical anesthesia was introduced in 1846, surgery was a brutal experience. It was only in emergencies that a patient would consider an operation. An operation caused so much pain that patients tried to put themselves into a coma or a stupor before their operations began. Sometimes they used alcohol, sometimes cocaine, and sometimes they banged their heads to give themselves a concussion! Franz Mesmer introduced some ideas in the early 1800s that started people thinking about pain control; but his views were not generally accepted. The best surgeons were speedy, in an attempt to limit their patients' agony. As soon as reliable analgesia was developed, it rapidly gained popularity. Anyone who had used hypnosis dropped it in favor of the new anesthetic techniques. It was not until the end of the twentieth century that scientists realized there is a place for both chemistry and hypnosis. In fact, most patients need all the help they can get.

Focus On This

Doctors have published many scientific papers proving that when patients get hypnosis in addition to their ordinary anesthetic, the surgery outcome is more successful. Using hypnosis reduces costs, too. Probably, it's the mysteriousness of hypnosis that has kept it from becoming known as a miracle addition to surgery. Insurance companies and HMOs might lead the fight for acceptance of hypnosis as a routine presurgical process.

Today, half of all surgeries will have you home on the same day as your operation. Short hospital stays are the norm: New mothers must leave the hospital in a day or two; orthopedists do much of their surgery in the ambulatory (outpatient) suite; patients who get a new kidney, who used to stay in the hospital for a month, now go home within one week of their transplant; after a heart attack you might be sent home in a few days—years ago you were hospitalized for a month.

It's very important that you use your mind to enhance your healing; that way when you leave for home you're well on your way to recovery.

Relax Before Surgery

You can be calm before your surgery. You can use hypnosis to give yourself a positive outlook, happy thoughts about your future, and enthusiasm for the experience. Lillian, a dress designer who came to my office the day before her scheduled hospital admission, told me after her operation that I probably went a bit too far in my suggestion to her. I told her, *You will eagerly look forward to your operation. You will think of it as an interesting adventure.*

Lillian said that when she and her husband were leaving for the hospital her husband thought she was nuts when she said, "I'm so excited. I can't wait to get there." When they arrived at the hospital the admitting clerk was taken aback when Lillian said, "Wow, what an exciting experience. I have never had an operation before, so I've missed all this."

Lillian is proof that hypnosis can help you change your ideas about surgery and give you a new and positive attitude.

Relax During Surgery

You can be calm and cooperative during your surgery. Hypnosis can prepare you for the operating room and the recovery room so that you'll have no anxiety, and your body will begin healing promptly. One of the suggestions I gave Lillian was this: *When you awaken from the anesthesia you'll be remarkably comfortable.*

When Lillian opened her eyes, she startled the recovery room nurse who asked her how she was feeling. Lillian groggily mumbled, with tubes protruding from her nose and wires extending from her arm, "Remarkably comfortable." Lillian went on to explain to me, "And the darndest thing is, I meant it. I was perfectly comfortable."

Going Home

Hypnosis can enhance your recovery at home, too. Lillian said that after she was home for a few days she knew she had been "overhypnotized" (her words) when she began to write a thank-you note to the hospital administrator!

Lillian is very hypnotizable, and my suggestions went directly to her unconscious mind. She and I planned all the suggestions together and at the time none of them seemed outlandish. I often use those same words for other presurgical clients. Although Lillian's mind took the suggestions to an extreme, the results were wonderful and she says she'll do it again if she needs surgery in the future.

Words, music, touch, and the general environment can join together to influence the way in which you will or will not feel pain. Chemicals may still be necessary to ease your pain, but your experience will also be affected by these other types of interventions, called *conscious sedation, behavioral anesthesiology,* or *nonpharmacological analgesia.* Words and sentences can be delivered like pills—in prepared, measured dosages.

Hypnoscript _____

When patients are anesthetized without chemicals to put them to sleep, the process is called **conscious sedation, behavioral anesthesiology,** or **nonpharmacological analgesia.**

Communicating with Your Surgeon

Some patients want to know everything about their operations, whereas others want to know nothing. In my experience, those who need lots of information tend to get surgeons who hate to speak, and those who want to be told only that everything will be just fine tend to get surgeons who insist on communicating all possible problems.

There was a time when patients were deliberately kept in the dark. Nowadays, when that does occur it's usually by accident. Many doctors are far too eager to tell a patient everything, even when the patient is not interested or is made worse by the information. How can information make you worse? By giving you too much to worry about.

> ### In the Hypnotist's Office
>
> Patients sometimes complain about lack of communication. Busy nurses and doctors may assume a patient knows about his or her condition, but in fact, no one has taken the time to communicate information to that patient. The head nurse on a surgical floor received a call: "Please tell me the condition of Mr. Stevens in room 405. He was operated on two days ago, and I would like to know how he's doing and when you expect him to be discharged." The nurse checked the patient's chart and replied, "His condition is excellent; if he continues improving at this rate he'll be home the day after tomorrow. Who am I speaking to, please?" "Oh, this is Mr. Stevens in 405. Sorry to bother you, but my doctors don't tell me a thing!"

Your preference for knowing or not knowing medical information about your condition seems to be an inborn trait, consistent with your personality. Do you want to know everything about your surgery, or do you want to know nothing at all?

Everyone is different, and the information you get from your surgeon as well as the suggestions you get from your hypnotist should be adapted to your individual coping style. What's your style? Are you an information seeker or are you a truster? How would you answer these questions?

1. Are you the type who wants to know everything about the surgery?

2. Do you ask the doctor to draw diagrams?

3. Are you online looking for chat rooms of others with your condition?

4. Have you read tons of books about this operation?

If you answered "yes" to these questions you're an information seeker, you cope best by knowing more, and you'll increase your recovery rate if you are given ...

◆ Specific information.

◆ A feeling that your opinion counts.

◆ The opportunity to know exactly what will happen to you from the time you leave your house through the day you leave the hospital.

If you answered "no" to the previous questions 1 through 4, you probably put all your effort into finding the very finest doctors and developing a great trust in them. It's sufficient for you to know that you're in capable hands, you don't need to know exactly what those hands will do. You'll increase your recovery rate if you are given proof that your doctors are excellent and reason to have confidence in your surgeon.

Laura is a "truster" who came to me before her face lift. The fact that it was elective surgery didn't make it any easier for her. Laura was upset because her plastic surgeon gave her a video to watch and pamphlets to read. She was becoming more and more anxious. I gave her the following suggestions:

◆ *When you are given information, you can pay attention to it or you can ignore it.*

◆ *Your body will understand that every time you are offered information, that is a signal it's time to heal.*

Focus On This _____

Dr. Mehmet Oz, cardiac surgeon at Columbia-Presbyterian Hospital in New York City, encourages his patients to be hypnotized before surgery. Says Dr. Oz, "The formal medical use of hypnosis has been scientifically endorsed as a complementary health therapy."

If you're scheduled for surgery, you can expect a visit from the anesthesiologist the night before your operation. If you are admitted to the hospital on the same day as the surgery the anesthesiologist will probably find you early in the morning to have a chat. In tests done at several hospitals it was determined that a five-minute talk with the anesthesiologist prior to surgery boosted recovery rates and made it possible for those patients to be discharged earlier than patients who had the same operation, same surgeon, same anesthesiologist, but no presurgical chat.

We know that words make a difference. In the hospital, right before your surgery, you're in a very suggestible state. The words spoken by the doctor who, literally, has your life in his hands, are powerful words. Those words are strong enough to affect the course of your recovery.

In a progressive hospital you'll be offered a visit with a hypnotist in addition to the anesthesiologist. Hypnotherapist Victoria Hughes, a former member of the Cardiac Complementary Care Center at Columbia-Presbyterian Medical Center in New York City, says that practicing hypnosis in the hospital is challenging because of noisy distractions and intrusions. "But," says Hughes, "it is precisely because the patients can't control anything around them that hypnosis lends itself so beautifully to this situation. Hypnosis empowers them to take control of their inner experiences. This reduces anxiety, promotes a positive mental state, and helps the body recover more efficiently."

Every Word Counts

We know that patients going in for surgery are vulnerable and suggestible. That means that everyone in the operating room, and the personnel who attend to the patient before the operation, too, have an opportunity to add to the patient's positive frame of mind.

For example, when lab technicians are about to take blood they can say, "Watch out, I'm gonna stick you now," or "I'm going to clean your skin with some alcohol and you might be surprised to find that the coolness is already beginning to numb your skin." The aide wheeling the patient from the hospital room to the surgical suite can say, "Good luck," or "Lucky you. I know your surgeon (or nurse, or anesthesiologist) and all her patients do great."

Dr. Elvira Lang

Dr. Lang, who is now Chief of Cardiovascular Interventional Radiology at Harvard Medical School, stunned her colleagues when she was Director of Vascular and Interventional Radiology at The University of Iowa Hospitals. She insisted on teaching everyone who had patient contact—including nonmedical personnel—how to communicate with the patients in a positive, calming, hypnotic manner.

The skeptics changed to admirers when Professor Lang proved that her patients recovered quicker than expected. What was the good doctor's proof? A clinical trial! Remember those clinical trials we talked about in Chapter 19? In the scholarly medical journal, *The Lancet*, Dr. Lang published her study proving that patients hypnotized prior to surgery needed less pain medication, left the operating room sooner, and had more stable vital signs during their operation.

They Do It in Belgium

Dr. Michel Meurisse, eminent Belgian surgeon, noted the successful outcome of 1,400 plastic surgery procedures using hypnosis, and suggested it was time to study the use of hypnosis in thyroid and parathyroid surgeries, as well. And so he did. At a conference of the Royal Belgian Society of Surgery, Dr. Meurisse presented the impressive results of his study of 600 patients undergoing thyroid surgery using hypnosis along with a local anesthetic. Here are the results of one of his studies:

◆ Patients reported surgery was a very pleasant experience.

◆ Patients were in less post-operative pain that nonhypnotized patients.

◆ Patients were discharged from the hospital earlier than usual.

◆ Cost of medical care was reduced.

◆ Patients returned more quickly to professional and social functioning.

Would you take a pill that promised to speed you through surgery? It seems that pill is on the market already. It is hypnosis!

Communicating in the Operating Room

Some anesthetized patients are aware of their surroundings even though they are under anesthesia and cannot feel anything.

How do we know? Patients sometimes recall incidents or words that were spoken while they were on the operating table. To confirm this there was an experiment done many years ago in which 50 patients had their regular anesthetic and then surgery, but 50 other patients had their regular anesthetic but then before surgery, while anesthetized, were told a brief summary of the Robinson Crusoe story by Daniel Defoe. Then they, too, had their operations. Before each of the 100 patients was discharged from the hospital, they were asked several questions including:

1. Do you remember your operation?

2. Do you remember any pain during your operation?

3. Do you remember any stories told during your operation?

4. What does the word "Friday" mean to you?

All patients said "no" to questions 1, 2, and 3. And all 50 patients who went directly from anesthesia to surgery, with no intervening story, answered question 4 by responding: "Friday is the last day of the work week." However, of the 50 patients who heard the Robinson Crusoe story (in that story a significant character is called Friday), 25 patients said: "Friday is the last day of the work week" and the remaining 25 said: "Robinson Crusoe." This established for the skeptics that some patients can hear while anesthetized.

In California, a patient sued her doctors when she had a difficult recovery complicated by an emotional condition. She said, and the jury agreed, that the emotional state was caused by the words that she had heard while under anesthesia. The patient maintained that she recalled her surgeon referring to her body in a derogatory manner during the surgery. She won the lawsuit, but the courts missed the lesson. The lesson should have been that words said in the operating room might be heard by a patient, and can impede or facilitate recovery. Instead, the anesthesiologist was blamed for not keeping the patient in a deep enough state of sedation!

In the Hypnotist's Office

The hypnotic script for clients who want hypnosis prior to surgery should include suggestions to help them ignore any negative or frightening comments that they might hear during their operation. Some of the remarks I hope they'll never hear are: "Someone call the janitor; we're going to need a mop …." Or "Wait a minute, if this is his spleen, then what's that …?" Or "Hand me that … uh … that uh … thingie …." Or "Don't worry. I think it's sharp enough …. Oooooooh, did you ever see that much blood come out of one of those …?" Or "Has anybody seen page 47 of the manual? This doesn't look good."

Because awareness under anesthesia is possible, what happens if one of the nurses or doctors makes an ambiguous statement? The patient may easily misinterpret it. The operating room staff needs to think fast and reframe the comment. If one member of the team says, "That looks nasty," another team member can counter with, "It's easy to fix. I'll make it better right away."

When Dr. Thomas Whalen was in the operating room he heard another surgeon say, during the operation, "She's really oozing a lot. I thought these people weren't supposed to bleed." Dr. Whalen immediately asked the surgeon to pause and then said, directly into the patient's ear, "You can safely direct your blood flow away from the site of the operation. That way the surgeon can work more effectively. At the end of the procedure you can return the blood flow to the site to promote healing." The oozing stopped.

Hypnotic Suggestions

Among the suggestions that I offer to presurgical patients are the following:

◆ *You'll be curious about the operation.*

◆ *It will be easy to fall asleep the night before your surgery.*

◆ *You'll be calm and comfortable before the operation begins, during the operation, and afterward.*

◆ *It will be easy for you to keep your blood away from the surgical site during the operation.*

◆ *You'll be surprised at how quickly your wound will heal.*

◆ *You may be amazed at just how comfortable you'll feel.*

◆ *Discomfort can be a sign that your body is healing. You may not experience discomfort, but if you do, it will be brief and will remind you that your healing has begun.*

◆ *If you hear any comments that sound stupid or negative, you'll disregard them.*

◆ *When you wake up there will be a tube in your throat. It won't bother you at all when you relax the muscles in your throat. When you take deep breaths through the tube you'll be ready to have it removed.*

◆ *You'll notice something or hear something that will catch your attention soon after you come out of the anesthesia. That will be a sign that all went well and you are beginning your recovery.*

Focus On This

Surgeons, like musicians, athletes, and other performers, concentrate so intensely on their work that they often put themselves into a trance. You want your surgeon to be in a trance-like state during your operation. It assures you that your surgeon is concentrating only on you and has shut out the rest of the world. There will be no distractions.

Feel free to take my suggestions to a hypnotist prior to your scheduled surgery. Use all or some of them as your presurgical script, or write your own script (see Chapter 7), or use a presurgical audiotape. (You'll find some in bookstores or for sale over the Internet.)

In the Hypnotist's Office

Marylou came to my office for presurgical hypnosis, and a few weeks after her surgery she reported: "I have some claustrophobic tendencies. When I had cataract surgery the nurse draped my face, cutting out a hole for my eye. And one arm was tethered, the other had IV lines in it. I remember saying to myself, 'Gee, ordinarily I'd be upset, maybe even panicky, with this cloth over my face and my arm held down. How interesting that I'm not concerned.' Later, after the surgery, I recalled that I was given the hypnotic suggestion that I would cope well with any surprises. It was as if my nervousness was replaced by confidence."

More Presurgical Suggestions

I also tell my clients the following:

You will look forward to your surgery because it will make you better. It is a challenge and you are a bright, curious person who enjoys being challenged. When you think about your upcoming operation, it puts you in a good mood. You are confident that you made all the right decisions, all the right choices. And now you can relax and get ready for the challenge, for the adventure, for the new experience. You are hopeful and optimistic. You are thinking pleasant thoughts.

Please visualize yourself the night before your operation. You are relaxed. Notice how calm you are. You are thinking pleasant thoughts. Now please see yourself right before the surgery. How calm you are. And you are cooperative, and you are optimistic. You're in a very good mood. You are curious. You are confident. Very confident. You have excellent coping ability.

Now please visualize yourself during the actual operation. You are in the surgical suite. You see the surgeon, other doctors, nurses, the anesthesiologist. And you see yourself being well cared for. It's easy for you to notice everyone's professionalism, everyone's competence. And as the surgery begins, so your healing begins. You body is already getting prepared to heal. Your vital signs are excellent. Your bleeding is minimal. Your body is responding beautifully. Congratulations, this surgery is a success.

You may wish to add your own suggestions—something about the recovery room, your hospital room, and then your home.

Relief from Anxiety

Some patients need specific suggestions about coping with anxiety. I encourage them to visualize a scene of nature and use that as an image to focus on when they become tense. I then say …

- *It will be easy for you to close your eyes and see your special scene.*

- *As soon as you see that scene you'll feel relaxed and calm.*

- *Concentrating on that scene will make time pass very quickly.*

- *The more you focus upon that scene in your mind, the more safe and secure you will feel.*

Relief from Bad Memories

Some patients need specific suggestions to eradicate the unpleasant memory of a past surgery. They respond well to the following suggestions:

- *This hospital experience is different from past experiences. This one is the easy one.*

- *This operation will be a good experience.*

- *Your mind will enjoy the adventure of surgery.*

In the Hypnotist's Office

Perhaps you've heard of Mary Baker Eddy, the founder of Christian Science. She was an invalid throughout her childhood and adolescence, but as an adult, heard about one of Mesmer's students, Phineas P. Quimby. She asked Quimby to hypnotize her and eventually was cured of all her ailments. Within a few years she began spreading the word that people could be cured by words and needn't take medications. She decided that Quimby was a mediator between herself and God, and thus began the Christian Science religious movement.

You can ask your hypnotist to make you a tape, or buy a ready-made presurgical audiotape, and bring it with you to the hospital. You can play it up until the moment of surgery. If you need it for pain control after your operation, it will be right there for you, too.

Benefits of Hypnosis

Hypnotized patients have no anxiety before their surgery and do a good job following their doctors' instructions. During the surgery, hypnotically prepared patients ...

- Lose less blood than do nonhypnotized patients.

- Have lower heart rates.

- Have lower blood pressure.

- Need less anesthetic.

After the surgery, hypnotically prepared patients have …

- Shorter hospital stays.

- Less pain.

- Decreased need for pain killers; lower usage of narcotics.

- Less anxiety.

- Earlier restoration of bowel and bladder function.

Hospitals and insurance companies benefit, too, because hypnosis results in thousands of dollars of savings, per patient.

> **Look into My Eyes**
>
> With all the evidence showing that hypnosis makes a big difference in patient recovery and in saving money for the hospital, how come hypnosis is not required? Why aren't hypnotists employed by hospitals, surgeons, and insurance companies? How could it be that we still think hypnosis is an exotic, unconventional mode of treatment?

There is a large body of research supporting the notion that hypnosis relieves the stress of surgery and reduces complications from surgery, because when your body is not fearful it is more efficient at healing. In yet another experiment, to again prove the worth of presurgical hypnosis, Dr. Marcia Greenleaf, New York City psychologist and medical hypnotist, and psychologist Dr. Stan Fisher studied 32 heart bypass patients. The patients were divided into three groups. One group was given no intervention. Another group of patients was put into trance and taught to relax. And a third group, called the hypnosis group, was put into a trance and told …

- *You will cooperate during surgery.*

- *You will protect yourself during surgery.*

- *You will let your body know just how to respond before the operation, during the operation, and after the operation.*

- *Your blood pressure will be normal.*

- *During the surgery your blood will stay away from that area, and will return afterward.*

- *You will have rapid return of appetite and thirst.*

Sure enough, it was the patients in the hypnosis group who had the best outcome and were discharged earliest. Of course, patients often don't credit hypnosis with their successful experience. A good hypnotist empowers the patient to feel self-confident, not dependent upon the hypnotist.

It is quite amazing that your bodily functions controlled by your autonomic nervous system—the involuntary physiological responses presumably outside of your conscious control—are affected by your mind. Your mind can control your body.

Hypnotherapist Victoria Hughes says, "I love assisting clients who are facing surgery, because the results are so consistently and predictably good. Everyone gets some benefit from surgical hypnosis. Perhaps they'll get anxiety reduction before their operation, proper blood flow during their operation, and reduced pain and faster healing afterward. Some people get all these benefits."

Home from the Hospital

Hypnosis will also help you when you get home. Go to a hypnotist with a script that is just right for you. Have yourself hypnotized to ...

- Always take your medication on time.

- Stick to your prescribed food or exercise program.

- Continue healing at home.

- Gain your strength back gradually and consistently.

- Talk about your operation only to people who ask to hear about it.

- Remember the good parts of your hospital stay; forget anything else.

- Easily communicate with your doctor whenever necessary.

Hypnosis can help you maintain good health. It can influence your experiences so that you think in a positive way. Like other innovative procedures, it may take decades to be fully accepted, but I predict that within our lifetime we will see presurgical hypnosis recommended and perhaps required.

The Least You Need to Know

◆ Hypnosis is an underutilized technique that does wonders when used prior to surgery.

◆ Influencing a patient's beliefs and attitudes before surgery may influence the course of the surgery.

◆ Hypnosis can create ways of viewing the entire surgical circumstance that will amplify the most favorable outcome.

◆ The benefits of presurgical hypnosis are physical, emotional, and financial.

◆ The astounding results obtained with presurgical hypnosis prove that psychological events can lead to physiological changes.

Chapter 23

Hypnosis and Pain Control

In This Chapter

- ◆ What is pain and what does hypnosis do to it?
- ◆ Hypnosis can take the suffering out of your pain
- ◆ Putting on the magic glove of hypnosis

What ails you? Which body part hurts today? Hypnosis can help. Do you want relief from a migraine headache, a pulled back muscle, a toothache, a heel spur? Hypnosis will block your pain. Since 1958, when the American Medical Association (AMA) declared hypnosis an acceptable treatment, thousands of patients have undergone surgery with no anesthetic other than hypnosis. If it can eliminate the pain of surgery, then surely it'll help your shoulder pain.

Read on and find out how to use hypnosis to stop hurting.

The Mysteries of Hypnosis

Question 1: What's the only means of anesthesia that carries no danger to the patient? Answer: Hypnosis.

Question 2: What's the most underutilized means of anesthesia in America today? Answer: Hypnosis.

Question 3: Can anyone explain why hypnosis is not used more often? Answer: See Question 4.

Question 4: Can anyone explain how hypnosis blocks the feeling of pain? Answer: No, not exactly.

Some excellent hospitals—Stanford University School of Medicine, Beth Israel Medical Center in Boston, University of Texas Southwestern Medical Center in Dallas, Harvard Medical School, University of Iowa Medical Center, and more—regularly use hypnosis to treat patients' pain and anxiety.

But, what about the rest of us? How come we're not routinely offered the option of hypnosis when we go to a doctor or a hospital complaining of pain? How come we're given prescriptions for painkillers, some of which have the side effect of killing our stomach, or, in rare cases, killing us? How come we're not taught self-hypnosis or sent to a hypnotist before the pills are prescribed?

Our medical world is a scientific one. Science is not likely to be thrilled with a method it can't explain. Like most of us, doctors are not comfortable advocating something they don't understand. And that's the trouble with hypnosis—we still don't understand precisely how it works.

What Is Pain, Anyway?

You don't need this book to tell you that when something hurts, that's pain. But, you might be interested in knowing that pain has a purpose. It alerts you to danger. It tells you to look for injury on your body. It makes you pause. It's your brain's way of protecting you.

> **CAUTION**
>
> **Look into My Eyes**
>
> Pain is a warning system. Never, ever use hypnosis or medication to eradicate pain if you don't know why you have that pain. Always know what the pain means to your body before you attempt any kind of pain relief.

Pain begins when something harmful—a disease, a chemical, a cut in your skin, severe heat or cold—carries pain information to your spinal cord. Your spinal cord then sends a pain message up to your brain. Your brain then responds by producing pain. And you feel that pain—most of the time. Sometimes something blocks your brain from reacting to the pain message, and then you do not react to the pain; maybe you don't even feel the pain. How does this happen?

The brain produces *endorphins*, which are chemicals that counter the feeling of pain. Endorphins produce analgesia, which is relief from pain, by blocking the pain pathway in your brain. Some people call endorphins your body's natural painkillers.

What makes your brain release endorphins? Remember Dr. Whipple from Chapter 17? Dr. Whipple's scientific research shows that endorphins are released at the moment of greatest pleasure during sex. People who are very responsive to music—you know the folks I mean, the ones who weep at the opera and get tingles down their spine at a concert—will have their pain blocked during those times. Somehow, our bodies release endorphins in response to great pleasure.

Acupuncture, too, is said to release endorphins. Can words release endorphins? Yes, apparently so, because it's a fact that hypnosis can override pain. There are some theories about how this works. Dr. Helen Crawford at Virginia Polytechnic Institute says, "Hypnosis seems to eliminate or reduce the perception of pain as well as the anxiety that accompanies it. It's as if the brain sends out a message that it does not want to feel the pain; it wants to inhibit it."

Hypnoscript

Endorphins are the category of chemicals produced in your body that eliminate pain. The term "endorphin" is a contraction of the words "endogenous" and "morphine." Endogenous means manufactured by your body, not a drug company, and morphine is a powerful painkiller.

Pain and Suffering

Donald is a sweet young man who has come to my office for hypnosis about once every year or two. When he was in third grade he was having trouble sitting still, in sixth grade he needed hypnosis for help focusing on the ball field, and when he was in middle school we worked on his study habits.

When last he came in, Donald wanted hypnosis before his camp checkup. He's scared to death of injections. I couldn't help but ask:

RT: *Did you go to someone for hypnosis before you had that tattoo put on your arm?*

Donald: *No.*

RT: *Did you have hypnosis before your eyebrow was pierced?*

Donald: *No way.*

RT: *How about before your lip was pierced?*

Donald: *No. Why would I need hypnosis for that? Look, could we get on with this? My doctor's appointment is later on this afternoon.*

Donald is proof that pain does not necessarily have to cause suffering. He had mentally prepared himself for the tattoo and for the body piercings. There was something so positive about those experiences that either he felt no pain or he could easily manage the pain. But, he felt he wouldn't be able to cope with the two-second injection in the doctor's office.

Your report about your pain does not always match up with the degree of damage to your body. Your personal idea about what the experience means to you affects how you perceive that pain. If you are delighted about getting a tattoo you may not feel the pain. Your thoughts—the words you say to yourself—interfere with the transmission of pain.

Even if you've not been tattooed or pierced, you may have had the experience of not feeling the pain someone else may have felt in that same situation. It's been observed that during wartime a soldier with very severe injuries often feels little pain. Why? Because the injury means he's going home—and considered a hero, too. If he'd had that same injury in civilian life as a result of an accident, he'd feel much more pain.

Some people pay no attention to their pain because they're involved in activities that are very important to them. The fact that their activities produce pain is not significant. Charlie is a perfect example. Charlie was sad to be the only one in first grade without a missing tooth. When the dentist said there was a problem and his baby tooth would have to be pulled, Charlie eagerly looked forward to the extraction and experienced no anxiety, no pain. Then there's Jody who didn't complain about her constant nausea and headache, because she was delighted to learn she was pregnant. Her pain was there; the suffering was not.

The feet of marathon runners and ballet dancers would make most of us groan in pain. If these performers do groan, it's after their event, not during it. Same with other athletes. A ballplayer may break a bone in the first quarter of a game and not even notice it until the game is over. Have you ever waited for a ski lift? In subzero weather? Just standing there? Ever wait for a bus under the same weather conditions? When you finally get on the bus you're suffering; when you finally get up on the ski slope you're delighted.

Look into My Eyes

Pain is sometimes necessary, but suffering is always optional. All pain is real, but not all pain is useful. Hurt does not have to lead to harm. You may experience hurt without it harming you.

When suffering is removed, the pain becomes less important, easy to tolerate, and it sometimes even goes away. Our attitude determines whether we suffer. Fortunately, we can use hypnosis for an attitude adjustment.

Using Hypnotic Suggestions to Eliminate Pain

Pain control suggestions come in several varieties. You can be hypnotized to feel diminished pain, no pain at all, or pain in one body part and not another.

Analgesia

I get more success when I give direct suggestions of *analgesia* for pain relief than when I use relaxation suggestions for pain relief. Analgesia suggestions reduce or eliminate the pain, but they permit other sensations to remain. You may have a painful arm, and with analgesia the pain will be very much diminished, but you'll still feel the arm, be aware of it, know that it's in some way bothering you. You'll feel the position it's in, whether it's hot or cold, and maybe some pressure or mild discomfort. It is anesthesia, not analgesia, that takes away all feelings.

When you're hypnotized and really focusing, you have a diminished awareness of your body, anyway, even before you are offered the analgesia suggestions. That gives you a head start; your sensations of pain are already reduced.

The most useful analgesia suggestions are …

- *The pain will diminish.*

- *Before you know it, it will be so vague, so minor, you'll not notice it very much.*

- *You will feel no pain.*

Hypnoscript

Analgesia is the inability to feel pain, and should not be confused with anesthesia, which is the inability to feel *anything*.

Transformation of Pain

Dissociation, that wonderful ability to fully disregard one aspect of yourself or your behavior, helps you move away your pain. Sometimes I suggest that a client distort his or her pain by changing it into something else.

My client Jeff owns a boat and enjoys sailing, so when he needed pain relief after a ski injury I made the following suggestions:

- *Visualize your pain as something you picked up in the ocean.*

- *Now see it clearly, but reduce it in size.*

- *Please make it smaller. Thank you.*

- *Stuff it into a bucket, and take it on your boat with you.*

- *Change it into a paler, lighter color.*

- *When you're ready to get rid of it, toss it out of the bucket, into the ocean.*

- *Watch it as it disappears.*

When Jeff came out of hypnosis he reported that he threw the entire bucket into the water. He watched it sink and then sailed away. Jeff remained pain-free for several days and then the pain returned. When he came in again, we made a tape of the session and that sufficed until he healed.

Phyllis, a mom of two small children, was recovering from a foot operation and the painkillers she was taking made her too groggy to drive. She wanted hypnosis so she could stop her medications. After she was in a trance, I asked her to transform her pain into chocolate milk. She worked hard until she could come up with that image in her mind, but she did. Then I suggested …

- *You don't need all that milk. Pour some into glasses, put some in the fridge, and pour the rest down the drain.*

- *As the milk drips away, so your pain drips away.*

- *Your pain is escaping, just like spilled milk.* (She smiles.)

- *Pour the milk from the glasses down the drain. You'll feel your pain diminish immediately.*

- *Take the remaining milk out of the refrigerator. You may feel some discomfort in your foot now.* (She nods yes.)

- *You can control your pain now. Pour most of this down the drain and most of your pain will be gone.*

- *Decide about the remaining few ounces. When you are ready, please watch yourself get rid of every last drop … of milk … of pain.*

Phyllis said that after she got home and started attending to her kids, it was easy for her to get the chocolate milk image in her mind. Whenever she thought the pain might be returning, she visualized the chocolate milk. By practicing every day she kept the pain away.

Clients do well with the suggestion *The pain is far, far away. It seems to be in the distance. It is barely here. It is barely there. You may wonder who it belongs to.* These are the clients who say, "Well, you didn't take my pain away. I know it's still here. But, funny thing, it doesn't bother me anymore."

Here are some ideas you can try to help ease your pain:

- If you have intense, burning pain, try the suggestion that it will turn into cold, cold snow. (Of course you won't use this suggestion if you are sensitive to cold because of circulatory or other problems.)

- If you have chronic pain, try visualizing the spot as if it is made of wood. Concentrate on it as an inert, wooden object, with no feelings.

- If you have pain in one part of your body, send it to another part. You can tolerate pain more easily in your little finger than you can in your head. And then you can suggest that the pain flow right through your fingertip, out of your body.

Moving the pain away or transforming it works well with audiotapes as well as in person.

Focus On This

Pain is the most frequent symptom seen by primary-care doctors. Even though there is ample proof that words, through hypnosis, can alleviate most pain, that's usually the last pain-relief method tried. The reason? Physicians do not learn about hypnosis in medical school. The solution? Patients will have to educate them just as they educated them about the usefulness of vitamins.

Age Regression

Linda suffers from migraine headaches. During an age regression she went back about six years, to a time of no pain. It immediately took away her headache. She worked on mastering self-hypnosis so that she could always find comfort in regressing to the days before her migraines began.

It is important to practice self-hypnosis at home every day, sometimes twice a day. It is a skill and you'll get better and better at it with practice. See Chapters 6 and 7 for self-hypnosis instructions.

Age Progression

Janice has backaches and sometimes the thought of a limited lifestyle gets her so upset that it accelerates her pain. That's when the cycle of pain and suffering begins and maintains a life of its own.

I asked her to imagine a time in the future when she had no pain. She visualized herself with no pain at her daughter's graduation; at her son's basketball game; at her fiftieth birthday party, dancing; at the wheel of her car, driving; and at her home, waking up.

Try visualizing yourself pain-free in the distant future and then in the not-so-distant future. See yourself clearly participating in activities and having no pain.

In the Hypnotist's Office

Ernest and Josephine Hilgard were scholarly researchers who authored an important textbook on pain and hypnosis, *Hypnosis in the Relief of Pain* (Brunner/Mazel, revised 1994). A primary reference tool, their book includes data from their laboratory at Stanford University. The Hilgards were the first to document the ability of a person to have pain but pay no attention to it. They hypnotized a student who, while in a trance, did not feel any pain, but when asked if he was aware that he had pain, signaled "yes." The pain was still there. He simply had no desire or need to react to it or to experience it. Yet, his "hidden observer" knew it was there all along.

Reframing Your Pain

Another way to deal with pain is to give it a new meaning. Some pain clients benefit when I tell them …

- *When your body starts to heal you'll feel some discomfort. That's good. That's your proof that you are getting better.*

- *Your body is letting you know that it is recovering by sending you messages. You may experience those messages as reminders that your body has feelings. You will enjoy receiving these messages.*

Reframing looks at the pain from a new perspective.

Computer Model

Gerry works as a computer consultant. That's how he got hurt—a customer's printer fell on his foot! When he came for hypnosis to help him get through the day without painkillers, I first checked with his orthopedist to be sure it was okay to eliminate the pain. When the doctor assured me that the diagnosis was unmistakable, and this pain was typical and expected, I proceeded as follows:

- *Now that you're nicely hypnotized, please allow yourself to see, in your mind's eye, a computer. Good. Now see yourself sitting in front of it. Turn it on, and watch the screen as it sets up. Notice that you still have some pain.*

- *Now please shut off your screen; the screen is dark, there is nothing on it. And you have no pain.*

- *Your nerve signals that allow you to feel pain or not to feel pain will be controlled in your mind, by you and your screen.*

- *When you shut off the screen, you shut down the connection between your incoming nerve signals and your brain. You feel no pain.*

- *Enjoy this pain-free state for a while, and then, please, press the button that controls the screen and allow the screen to come on for a few seconds. Then shut it off.*

Focus On This _____

Scientists are not sure how hypnosis works or how it stops pain, but all agree that burn patients respond particularly well to it.

Maybe it's because the patients are in terrible pain and therefore extremely motivated, or because they're traumatized by the event; maybe the pain and trauma encourage regression, and patients want someone to tell them how to feel better. Whatever the mechanism, it works.

- *As you just demonstrated, you can control your pain. Please control your pain for two minutes, now. Shut off the screen and shut off your pain. I'll let you know when the time is up.*

- *Good, now please allow the pain to return, dimly, for 30 seconds and then shut your screen off. I'll tell you when.*

Gerry and I practiced for about 20 minutes. When he was certain that he was the master of his pain, he left the hypnotic state after being given the following final suggestion: *Your screen will remain off. Your pain will remain gone. You have the power to turn on your screen whenever you want, but you prefer to keep it off. You prefer to keep away your pain.*

Glove Anesthesia

This technique gets rave reviews from clients. It's fairly easy to alter feelings in your hand. You'll make your hand numb or tingling or both. Then you'll be told that you can transfer the feelings of that hand to any part of your body that you touch. A numb hand can spread numbness; once you focus on your hand and establish the numbness, it's easily transferred.

Visualization

When you're feeling very happy, silly, or relaxed and comfortable, it's hard to also feel pain. You can diminish your pain by seeing yourself in a place that makes you feel calm, rested, safe, and secure; or having fun, laughing, and being at peace with yourself. But no matter the technique to eradicate pain, I always add the following sentence: *You will feel only the pain that it is absolutely necessary to feel.* It's important for you to feel the pain that is giving you information that you need.

> **CAUTION**
>
> **Look into My Eyes**
>
> Before you accept painkillers for relief of your pain, try hypnosis. In just a few minutes you might experience relief. If you do take painkillers, take hypnosis along with them. Remember, hypnosis has no side effects and no potential for addiction. Sometimes, a posthypnotic suggestion for pain relief can last for years.

The most useful aspect of hypnosis for pain control is that you are no longer the victim of forces beyond your control. Instead, you are in charge of your feelings. You have self-mastery.

Bombardment

Dr. Harold Crasilneck, a well-known hypnosis researcher, has developed the Crasilneck bombardment technique to help patients who are in a lot of pain. It consists of six different hypnotic methods, one after the other: relaxation, dissociation, age regression, glove anesthesia, direct suggestion for anesthesia, and self-hypnosis instruction. For some patients it is the only treatment that works. It's heartening to note that there are health professionals who will not give up on patients who are in terrible pain.

Case Studies

There are recent reports of hypnosis doing wonders for patients suffering from shingles, terminal cancer, fibromyalgia, and bone marrow transplants. Patients suffering from sickle cell disease and chronic lower-back pain also have been studied to see what hypnosis could do for them.

You now know about the power of the mind and the power of words. So many tests and studies prove that hypnosis can make a difference in your health, yet the fields of surgery and anesthesiology continue to ignore the fact that patients respond well to words. Will this soon change?

The Least You Need to Know

- ◆ Hypnosis can usually control your pain.

- ◆ Your attitude has a lot to do with whether you experience pain by itself, or continue on to experience pain with suffering.

- ◆ There are many different approaches to hypnotic relief of pain. If one doesn't work, another probably will.

Chapter 24

Open Wide

In This Chapter

- Hypnosis to the rescue: Fear no more
- Speedy inductions
- Hypnosis in the chair
- Hypnosis for clenching and grinding

Dentists get bad press. Remember Steve Martin as the sadistic dentist in the movie *Little Shop of Horrors?* People talk about going to the dentist as if it were the most painful thing on Earth. It's not, and it's certainly not when it's mixed with hypnosis.

What do you get when you mix hypnosis with dentistry? Trance and dental medication! But seriously, folks ….

Hypnosis and dentistry really do go together. Read about the ways in which you can avoid injections, eliminate nighttime grinding, and actually have fun at the dentist's office.

Scared of the Dentist?

Are you someone who doesn't go to the dentist? Are you afraid? Do you have dental phobia? You're not alone; fear prevents many, many, people from getting proper dental care.

Do you stay away from dentists because you anticipate pain, feel vulnerable, and then are embarrassed by your feelings? Do you think the only way to avoid revealing your embarrassment is to avoid going to the dentist? There is another option for you. You can change your feelings about the dentist and change your experience in the dentist's office. You can do this, of course, using hypnosis.

Hypnosis can rid your mind of its dentist fears, and hypnosis can increase your coping skills so that you'll feel less nervous. Some dental patients use hypnosis so they can avoid chemical anesthesia. They don't like having a numb mouth, or they don't like nitrous oxide (often called sweet air), or they have a medical condition that prohibits them from taking any sedative drugs. Other dental patients request hypnosis in addition to regular anesthetic. They need hypnosis to take away their anxiety and to get them to keep their next appointment.

You may be afraid of the dentist because of tales you've heard. Or you may be fearful because you once had a bad dentist and a bad experience. By now you know the truth—these days, with all the advances in anesthesia, properly performed dentistry is pain free. But, the truth is not helping you. Your mind and body continue to drive you to tears when you attempt to make an appointment with the dentist.

Focus On This

A dentist can work on a hypnotized patient, with hypnosis as the only anesthetic, and accomplish all that would be accomplished with chemical anesthesia. A deeply hypnotized patient will not feel drilling, an extraction, or even a root canal!

Hypnosis is used in dentistry instead of anesthetics or as a tranquilizer in addition to anesthetics. The patient can be hypnotized before the dental appointment, or go to a dentist who also practices hypnosis. Dan's dentist referred him to me because Dan has never made it to an appointment. He means well, he tries, but he just can't get there.

Dan Goes Kayaking

Dan is a handsome man who has a high-profile position and it seems strange that his teeth are discolored and crooked. He's well-dressed, appears affluent, is often in the media, and, he confessed to me, "I try to keep my lips closed as much as possible. I actually have trained myself to speak articulately without showing my teeth."

It's time for Dan to get a grip on this problem. I speak to him for a while, learn about his interests and some of his ideas; but mostly he wants to talk about his fear of dentists. I hypnotize him and then give him the following instructions:

As you drift off into a comfortable place in your mind you'll become aware of an amazing talent that you have. You have the talent of forgetting about one of your arms. Your eyes are closed and you're comfortable and calm. Your body is heavy, your arms are heavy, and one of your arms is just where it's supposed to be … but you don't need to know exactly where that is.

You can be unconcerned ... and you can turn off all feeling in that arm. When you discover the interesting feeling of not feeling, you'll smile. And I'll know ... that you know ... how to have an arm with no feeling .... Maybe it will be a numb arm .... Maybe it will feel like no arm at all .... Maybe it will be a heavy arm that's wandered away .... Maybe it's become a Styrofoam arm, an arm with no feelings because it's made of Styrofoam .... You're a talented man. You can turn off all feeling in that arm.

In your mind, please see your arm sprawled across a table. And watch it. Watch what happens when the arm with no feelings is touched .... Nothing happens .... Watch what happens when that arm is pinched .... Nothing happens. Now watch a heavy book plop right down on top of your arm .... Nothing, again. Now watch an ice cube on your arm. Look at that ... it's melting, but your arm feels absolutely nothing.

You're a talented guy. You have the talent to turn off feeling in one part of your body. Now you can turn off feeling in another part of your body. Let's try your mouth. Please visualize your lips ... your mouth ... your teeth ... your tongue ... and your gums. Your entire mouth area is becoming numb. Watch and see it become more and more heavy ... numb ... unfeeling ... good.

Some people like to go to a dentist and some don't. You don't like it. You don't have to. You just have to send your mouth. And your mouth won't care because you can turn off its feelings.

While you go off to the river to go kayaking, actually see yourself in your kayak, now, please. Good. Now please send your mouth away. Your mouth really needs a lot of work. Please send your mouth to Dr. Mindlin, the dentist you were telling me about.

While your mouth is at Dr. Mindlin's office, please have a good time on the river. Watch yourself in the water. Watch what good control you have. You know how to do the right thing for yourself. You always make the right moves.

While you're in the kayak, your mouth is at Dr. Mindlin's. If you look in another part of your mind you'll see your teeth being examined by the dentist's capable hands. See that? Please watch your mouth while Dr. Mindlin examines your teeth. He's poking and scraping but you feel nothing. Your mouth has no feelings.

It's easy for you to be relaxed and disconnected. You can move your mind away from your body. You can be busy with wonderful pictures in your head ... and your mouth has absolutely no feelings now. In your mind's eye please watch the dentist as he puts instruments in your mouth. You feel nothing. Your mind and body are disconnected.

Whenever you'd like you can close your eyes, imagine your arm lying across a table, and then tell your mouth that it is as unfeeling as that arm .... It is numb. After you have a numb mouth, it'll be easy for you to spend 45 minutes at a time in the dentist's chair.

This dissociation technique worked for Dan. I spoke to his dentist prior to our meeting and was assured that he'd never need to be in the chair longer than a half-hour.

If you suffer from dental phobia, this is a good script to use. Take it with you to a hypnotist or hypnotize yourself (see Chapter 6). To find a dentist in your area who practices hypnosis check the resources in Appendix B at the back of this book.

In the Hypnotist's Office

Have you heard about the guy with the swollen cheek and infected tooth? He asked the dentist: "How much to have this tooth pulled?" The dentist said, "$70." Puzzled by the expense, the patient asked, "What? For only a few minutes work?" The dentist replied, "I can extract it very slowly if you prefer." Just as an excellent dentist is efficient and quick, so an excellent hypnotist can rapidly help you attain a trance state and quickly relieve your anxieties and numb your mouth.

Carolyn Goes Numb

I use dissociation with Carolyn, too, but of a different sort. She is not an adventurous woman and kayaking is not for her. Carolyn has a toothache, but fled the dentist's office in fear before any work could be done. The method I use with Carolyn is one of Dr. Milton Erickson's techniques. It is a confusion technique that will distract Carolyn's attention from the work going on in her mouth. Once she's in trance I tell her the following:

Keep all your fearfulness. Keep all your pain. But, all your pain and fear will be transferred to your right hand. Please walk with your right hand away from you; you don't want to let your pain touch your body. And when you go to the dentist, inform her that she may not touch your right hand. Do not shake hands with the dentist. If anything touches your right hand it will be painful for you. When the dentist begins to work on your teeth you'll feel some discomfort in your right hand, but it won't be bad. Just keep your right hand away from you. And, of course, your mouth will feel nothing.

The techniques that I use for both Dan and Carolyn use dissociation. Remember dissociation? It's the ability to be aware of one part of an experience and totally ignore another part of it. The conscious mind can drift off—to a kayaking trip, perhaps—while the unconscious mind is free to respond any way it would like. The unconscious can easily absorb instructions to forget to feel a feeling.

For Dan and for Carolyn I also said …

◆ *And every minute in the dentist's chair will seem like a second. Ten minutes will pass as if they're ten seconds.* (This is a time-distortion technique.)

◆ *The moment your body is in the dentist's chair you'll feel a deep relaxation and you'll be interested in putting yourself into a trance.* (This is a posthypnotic suggestion pairing one action—sitting in the chair—with a suggestion—going into a trance.)

- ◆ *Every word that I said to you today will stay with you and will come to your mind when you are at the dentist's office.*

- ◆ *In between dental appointments, you'll be comfortable and feel only the discomfort that is necessary.*

- ◆ *You'll surprise yourself by actually looking forward to each dental appointment.*

I do not suggest that patients feel no pain. Instead I say, "Only pain that is necessary." Why would I want a patient to have some pain, if it's possible to eradicate it all? Because pain is an important indicator. It tells us when something is wrong and needs to be attended to. If there's an infection in Carolyn's gum and she doesn't feel it, she'll never get antibiotics to make it go away.

Distraction and suggestion have long been used for pain control in general and dental pain control in particular. In 1905 a Swiss dentist, Camille Redard, was able to keep his patients pain-free. His method? Covering their heads with a transparent blue cloth, he told his patients that gazing at blue light would take away their pain. And so it did!

In the 1960s an engineer from the Massachusetts Institute of Technology and a Boston dentist teamed up to create "white" noise, which they said could suppress dental pain. (Bands of noise containing all audio frequencies are called white noise.) Dentists bought "audio analgesia" contraptions, believing that sound suppressed pain in elaborate physiological ways. The dentists were desperate to alleviate patients' pain.

Distraction and suggestion are not fancy methods, but they do work. Some dentists intuitively try to fill their patients' minds with pleasant sensations by piping in music and providing television monitors and lots of reading material.

Look into My Eyes

Hypnosis is powerful enough to take away feelings of all pain. Do not go to a hypnotist who promises to do that, unless your dentist and doctor agree it's a good idea. You need to feel some pain to pick up the signals your body is sending you. Do not eliminate your pain until you know why it appeared.

Rapid Inductions

Dentists who use hypnosis don't have the luxury of time that I have. I can spend an hour with a patient; dentists must keep their office traffic flowing. Dentists who use hypnosis have mastered the use of very quick inductions. They know how to hypnotize someone in a couple of minutes. And I mean deeply hypnotize, so that extreme dental work can be done.

Dr. Sam Perlman, a dentist in New Rochelle, New York, described to me two quick methods that he uses regularly and speedily.

In the first method, Dr. Perlman instructs the patients, in a slow, soothing voice, to extend their arms out in front of them, with palms facing each other. Dr. Perlman then says, *Watch your arms as they come together at their own rate. Soon your hands will touch each other while you are watching, and you will become very comfortable. Your hands will go into your lap, you'll have a need to close your eyes, and you're more and more comfortable.* Patients are now in a trance, and Dr. Perlman uses a deepening technique if necessary.

In the second method, using a technique developed by Dr. Erickson, Dr. Perlman takes the patient's hand as if for a handshake, presses his index finger on the patient's wrist, and puts his middle finger on the side of the patient's hand with his thumb on the top of the patient's hand. While grasping the patient's hand, Dr. Perlman extends the patient's arm and looks into the patient's eyes, asking, *You're becoming more and more comfortable, aren't you?* When the patient says "yes" (they always do), Dr. Perlman places his left hand above the patient's elbow, bending the arm upward while continuing to extend the patient's arm with his right hand. Dr. Perlman continues eye contact, removing his right hand but keeping his left hand under the patient's arm. The patient's arm will begin levitating, and that's the signal for Dr. Perlman to remove his left hand. The patient is now in trance.

Hypnoscript

When something, someone, or some part of the body, begins to rise up in the air, in apparent defiance of gravity, the action is called **levitation**.

Dr. Perlman's *levitation*/handshake-induction technique sounds more complicated than it is. Try it and see for yourself how it's done. Simply get a consenting person to be the "patient" while you are the hypnotist. See if the person's arm will remain suspended. If yes, then put his or her arm back down and tell the person to return to regular. You've proved that this method works. Should you ever need to hypnotize someone, in an emergency, say, this could be your induction method.

In the Hypnotist's Office

Hypnosis will work for a patient who tends to gag when instruments are placed in his or her mouth, because the gag reflex is significantly diminished during hypnosis. Dr. Perlman once hypnotized a patient for this but didn't mention the term "hypnosis" because he thought it would frighten the patient. He said "deep relaxation" instead. All went well and when re-alerted, the patient was shocked to learn the procedure was completed and he had not gagged. "Wow," the patient said, "this felt like I was hypnotized."

In the Dentist's Chair

Dentists at the Department of Oral Surgery in Stockholm, Sweden, wanted to test the effectiveness of hypnosis during extraction procedures. Seventy clinic patients, all needing to have a wisdom tooth extracted, were given an appointment with the same dentist for several weeks in the future. All patients were then given a test to measure their levels of anxiety. One half of the patients were then sent home and told to report on the day of their appointment. The other 35 were given an audio tape and told to play it once a day until the day of their appointment.

The audio tape was a 20-minute hypnosis tape. It included the following:

 ◆ A relaxation induction

 ◆ Instructions on how to find a safe place to go to in their minds

 ◆ The suggestion: *Your body knows all about bleeding and all about healing. You will enhance what your body knows.*

 ◆ Direct suggestions to alleviate pain

 ◆ Suggestions for dissociation to alleviate pain

 ◆ Two minutes of silence to allow practice for going into a trance, and then soft music to signal awakening

When all 70 patients returned for their dental extraction, they were first given that same test for anxiety. Those who had listened to the hypnosis tape had the same anxiety levels that they had last time, when they were not about to have a tooth extracted. Members of the other group, however, all had high rates of presurgical anxiety. After surgery all patients were followed up the next week to see if there were any differences in their reactions to the surgery or their recoveries. Check the results in the following list.

Patients Hypnotically Prepared	Patients Not Hypnotically Prepared
No anxiety before tooth pulled	High anxiety before tooth pulled
3 percent needed pain medication after surgery	28 percent needed pain medication after surgery
No one had excessive bleeding	Several had excessive bleeding
No one had an infection	Several had infections

Using hypnosis before a dental extraction makes a difference. Why doesn't everybody request (demand) hypnosis?

In the Hypnotist's Office

Dr. Perlman tells the story of one of his patients who was profoundly affected by hypnosis. He told Dr. Perlman that the hypnosis produced the same feeling in him as nitrous oxide analgesia (laughing gas) did. Perlman gave his patient the posthypnotic suggestion that whenever he came into the dental office he'd become very comfortable. At the next visit the patient asked the receptionist, "Are you pumping nitrous oxide through the air conditioning system? I felt it as soon as I walked in."

Children in the Dentist's Chair

Dr. Ted Aspes, a pediatric dentist from Atlanta, Georgia, explains that most children enter a dentist's office with some anxiety and will need sedation, either pharmacologic or nonpharmacologic.

Says Aspes, "We use the 'tell, show, do' method so the children will understand every step of the way. This is a nonpharmacologic calming method. Children, just like their parents, do best when they know what to expect and they encounter no surprises."

When Dr. Aspes is "telling" he is also engaging his patient in a hypnotic experience. "I do most of the talking and once I have the patient's interest I begin to decrease the volume of my voice. The patient must concentrate intently on my words; it's hard to hear what I'm saying. With all that energy going into listening, there's little energy left for feeling discomfort or for worrying."

Dr. Aspes goes on to say, "As my voice gets softer and gentler it's as if I'm singing a lullaby to a baby. The children are relaxed and comfortable, and some even drift off to sleep."

Dr. Aspes' patients are "here" in the dental chair, and "there," absorbed in the task of listening. That is hypnosis! In fact, when the lulled children are monitored there is a significant decrease in their blood pressure and respiration rates. All this, while the dentist is drilling, pulling, and probing!

Try This and Amaze Your Dentist

Dental patients can control their bleeding. When given appropriate suggestions, hypnotized patients can move their blood away from the area the dentist is working on, and then move it back.

How does this work? No one knows. Why does this work? No one knows. Does it work? Yes it does. During extractions and during gum surgery, hypnotized patients, who receive suggestions about controlling their blood flow, will have a 30 percent reduction in blood loss, as compared to nonhypnotized patients.

In my practice, I've found the best suggestions for controlling blood flow to be the following:

- *Please tell your body to provide just the right amount of bleeding.*

- *Your body will know how to stop the blood when your dentist needs a clear area.*

- *Your body will return the blood, at the right time, to the right place.*

- *There will always be sufficient blood to provide nourishment for your tissues.*

These suggestions work, of course, for other types of surgery, too, not just dental surgery (see Chapter 22).

Do You Grind Your Teeth?

Does your bed partner complain that you make noise during the night? Do you awaken with tired jaws, as if you chewed an entire pack of gum all at once? You might have *bruxism*, which is the clenching and grinding of your teeth, usually while you sleep, without your knowing it. Bruxism is a destructive dental problem that can cause facial pain, headaches, and an erosion of your tooth enamel. Five percent of the population has bruxism. Fortunately, it responds well to hypnosis.

At the Oregon Health Science University, School of Dentistry, dentists and scientists studied patients who had bruxism, gave them hypnotic suggestions and a hypnosis audiotape, and then studied them again. There was definite improvement after the patients listened to the hypnosis tape for a few months. The improvement was recorded by instruments that measured the patients' facial muscle activity during sleep.

Hypnoscript
The habit of unconsciously clenching or grinding your teeth, especially in situations of stress or during sleep, is called **bruxism**.

The 10-minute audiotape put the patients into trance and then gave the following suggestions:

- *You'll quickly become aware of muscle tension.*

- *You'll quickly relax those muscles.*

- *Those muscles will relax automatically, even during sleep.*

- *You will not clench or grind your teeth.*

Focus On This

Atlanta children's dentist Dr. Ted Aspes has so many mazes, games, and puzzles in his waiting room that some mothers complain their children want to visit the dentist even when there's no dental problem. Dr. Aspes pairs having an interesting adventure with a trip to the dentist. He says, "We reserve the beginning of each appointment to play with the patient and talk about his or her interests." Pairing a pleasant experience with being in the dentist's office creates a positive association which can easily be reinforced with hypnosis or with soothing, hypnoticlike conversation.

Some dentists give their bruxism patients the hypnotic suggestion to automatically pop their tongue in between their upper and lower teeth. These dentists give their bruxism patients the following suggestions:

- *You'll become aware when you grind in your sleep.*

- *You'll immediately stop, smile to yourself, and feel proud of yourself.*

- *You'll fall right back to sleep.*

When bruxism clients come to me I usually tell them ...

- *Stop grinding your teeth.*

- *You worry too much at night.*

- *Find another way to deal with your worries during the day.*

I then talk to them about possible methods of dealing with anxiety. Bruxism clients, in my experience, are usually a bit nervous and looking for guidance. When I give them firm suggestions—more like orders—they do very well. They don't respond to permissive, indirect suggestions.

Suggestions

I encourage you to add these suggestions to your dental script:

- *You will floss your teeth, brush your teeth, and do whatever your dentist and dental hygienist expect you to do every day.*

- *You will look forward to your dental appointments as opportunities to take good care of your body.*

- *Whenever you have any dental procedure, your healing will begin before you leave the dentist's chair.*

With dental suggestions, as with all hypnotic suggestions, the hypnotist must choose words carefully. While in the hypnotic state, clients are likely to take literally whatever is said to them. One dentist, who prefers to remain anonymous, told me that he inadvertently gave a suggestion to Marilyn, a patient with heightened anxiety, that could have been dangerous. He told her that at her next dental appointment she'd begin to feel hypnotized even before she reached the dental chair. In his mind, he assumed that meant that she'd be feeling trancelike when she was in the waiting room. But, he made a mistake by not explicitly mentioning the waiting room. Marilyn attracted attention in the building's lobby because of her dazed look and she was already in a deep trance coming up in the elevator.

The Least You Need to Know

- Millions of people don't get regular dental care because they are fearful.
- Hypnosis can take away that fear.
- Hypnosis can be used as a dental anesthetic for adults and children.
- Hypnosis can control bleeding during dental procedures.
- If you grind your teeth at night, try hypnosis. It will allow you to stop.

Part 6

Another Side of Hypnosis

Read Part 6 to find out what it's really like to volunteer and to be in the audience at a hypnosis show.

Have you lived in another lifetime? Read about the hypnotists eager to explore your previous incarnations. Also, read about hypnosis in a court of law. Think you'll have a better memory as an eyewitness if you're hypnotized? Think again.

25

Quack Like a Duck

In This Chapter

- ◆ Hypnosis as entertainment
- ◆ Do you want to be the entertainment?
- ◆ Hypnosis for your group
- ◆ Hypnosis in the movies

You've read about hypnotists who are doctors, nurses, and paramedics. But who are the hypnotists you see on television? They're called stage hypnotists, and they are entertainers who use hypnosis as part of their acts. Some of them do magic tricks, too, and many of them refer to themselves as mentalists.

It's important to differentiate between clinical hypnosis, which is fun and can be therapeutic, and stage hypnosis, which is fun for the audience but not necessarily for the subject, and it's not at all therapeutic. I hope I have reassured you throughout this book that clinical hypnosis is safe and can help you. Now we'll be going into a different realm of hypnosis—the realm of practitioners whose only purpose is to entertain their audience.

Gone are the days of stage hypnotists who faked it. Today they use many of the same techniques that I and other clinical hypnotists use. But your experience with a stage hypnotist would be very different from your experience with me.

What if you knew nothing about hypnosis? Would you be skeptical, or would you volunteer to be a subject up on the stage? Read about stage hypnosis and audience members who agree to participate in hypnosis shows. Read about Dr. Svengali and other movies and books that use hypnosis as part of the plot line. How accurately is hypnosis depicted?

Up on the Stage

Do you want to be part of a show for an audience? Is it okay with you to make a spectacle of yourself? Want to have some fun?

Hypnosis is an astounding tool, and audiences are amazed during a hypnosis show. This is public entertainment at its best—no one is bored; everyone is mystified. The audience enjoys watching someone who just a few moments ago was sitting among them, but is now yodeling, quacking like a duck, singing "The Star Spangled Banner," or dancing the hula.

Prime-time hypnosis is not hypnosis to stop biting your nails, or hypnosis to play a better game of golf. Nor is it hypnosis for a speedy recovery from surgery. It is hypnosis as bewitching entertainment, where the hypnotist decides exactly what you'll do, and you have nothing to say about it. In stage hypnosis you give the hypnotist all the power. If it's okay with you to make a public spectacle of yourself—and a lot of us actually like that idea—you'll probably have a good time.

A stage hypnotist can easily get a volunteer to …

- Feel as if a fly is on his nose, and repeatedly swat at it.

- Smell a noxious odor and become nauseated.

- Drink a glass of water and imagine it is very spicy and burns her mouth.

- Feel as if she's stuck to her chair and can't get up.

- Feel as if his arm is made of steel and he can't bend it.

- See a person who's not there.

Focus On This

Sam Clemens, better known as Mark Twain, was fascinated by hypnosis and whenever a traveling hypnosis show came to his town he volunteered as a subject. In those days the entertainers were less than honest, and Sam, as he was then known, signed on as a permanent audience plant. His job was to pretend to be in a trance while following orders to behave foolishly.

Stage hypnotists consistently get good results, and without trickery. During vaudeville days the hypnotist would travel with paid performers who pretended to volunteer and hypnotically "obey the master." The so-called hypnotist did not know hypnotic techniques, so what would happen if an audience assembled and his bogus players did not appear? Not to worry; there was a contingency plan. The hypnotists carried in their pockets a handkerchief soaked in chloroform. If necessary, they'd chant some hocus-pocus gibberish while waving the handkerchief in front of a volunteer's face. When the volunteer became woozy, he or she would be declared hypnotized.

Today's stage hypnotists don't resort to sham. But they do try to select their subjects before the performance begins. Warming up an audience before a show gives hypnotists a chance to spot the high hypnotizables—people who are so deeply hypnotizable and suggestible that they're sure to be entertaining when up on stage.

If you were the hypnotist, how would you know in just a few minutes who in the audience is deeply hypnotizable? You would give all audience members *suggestibility tests* and choose those volunteers who score very well on them. The stage hypnotist's technique of assessing an individual's hypnotizability is not so different from that used by hypnotists in clinical practice, but their purposes are very different.

Hypnoscript _____

A **suggestibility test** is a short relaxation induction followed by a simple suggestion. The greater the response to the suggestion, the more hypnotizable the client or audience volunteer is.

Screening the Audience

If I were a stage hypnotist and had just a couple of minutes in which to determine your suggestibility to hypnosis, I'd give you an induction to relax your body and your mind, and then run through a few direct suggestions. If you respond best to indirect, permissive suggestions—"When you are ready, you might decide to lift your hand off your lap"—I don't want to choose you to be on the stage. I want someone who'll give the audience their money's worth and immediately obey a direct suggestion—"You will lift your hand higher and higher into the air."

Arm Levitation

Here's where I'd tell you, with your eyes closed, to imagine that your arm is becoming lighter and lighter. Your arm is so light that all by itself it is lifting off your lap. Your weightless arm is lifting itself higher and higher into the air and staying there, in defiance of gravity.

If people are not deeply hypnotizable, I'd suggest to them that they're tying a balloon onto their wrist that will lift their arm, and then untie and drift away. So for the purpose of choosing volunteers, I don't want to use the people who need the balloon; they are good, but not superior when it comes to arm levitation. I'd want only the superior responders who are easily hypnotizable and who take direct suggestions, because they make excellent public spectacles.

> **CAUTION**
>
> **Look into My Eyes**
>
> Stage hypnotists need to have charisma. They must attract and keep an audience. When I hypnotize people in a public group, I do not need to charm an audience; I am not an entertainer. Instead, I create a safe, secure environment in which audience members can slowly, at their own rate, explore their talent for hypnotic trance. I do not do entertainment hypnosis.

Eye-Roll Exercise

The only biological indicator of your hypnotizability is how much of the whites of your eyes are visible after you slightly shut your eyelids and then roll your eyes back into your head. People who can be very deeply hypnotized show a lot of the whites of their eyes during this exercise. If I were a stage hypnotist, I'd simply scan the audience and pick out the high hypnotizables by the whites of their eyes.

Eyelid Glue

If I were a stage hypnotist, I'd tell you that your eyelids are so, so heavy that you are unable to keep your eyes open. Then I'd say that your eyelids will shut and remain shut—they are too heavy to open. An interesting suggestion, as part of this script is *the more you try to open your eyes, the more glue you release, the more your eyes remain shut.* (This technique was developed by hypnosis researcher Andre Weitzenhoffer.)

When I saw audience members unable to open their eyes after being asked to try to do so, I'd know they were deeply under. (In case you're worried, the way to have the audience open their eyes is simply to instruct them to open them without using the word "try," or to ask them to come out of hypnosis and come back to regular.)

Embedded Commands

If I were a stage hypnotist speaking to the whole group, I'd modulate my voice and say, after they are in a light trance: *And you will feel tranquil ... your right hand may drop to the side of your chair. You will see a path in front of you ... your left hand may gently curl into a fist. You'll smell the fragrances of the out-of-doors ... you'll take a walk, in your mind ... along that path ... and give yourself a few moments of serenity as you look at the beautiful flowers.*

This is the cue for me to look around the room and note those whose eyes are closed, right hands straight down and left hands in a fistlike shape. Those are the high responders. The thrust of this suggestion is relaxation and walking; the hand placements are secondary. Yet, a good responder will hear and respond to the hand placements, too.

I would have altered my tone when I said those particular words about the hands, and high responders would have reacted to that altered tone. The high responders are the ones I'd invite up on stage.

Focus On This _____

One of the measurement scales researchers use to assess a subject's ability to be hypnotized is the Hypnotic Induction Profile (HIP). In this 10-minute test, the subject quickly enters hypnosis and quickly leaves that state several times. A numerical score is given for each task completed under hypnosis, reflecting the extent to which the subject followed directions while under hypnosis.

Enthusiastic Volunteers

Are you one of those people who has always been interested in hypnosis? Does it seem to call to you? Do you want to try it? People who are drawn to hypnosis usually have some talent for it, and they know intuitively that they should try it. If I were looking for a volunteer who'd be very hypnotizable, I'd take my chances on someone who seems very eager for the experience.

Now you know that when you watch a television show with a hypnotist and audience volunteers, members of the audience are real volunteers, not phony plants. But usually they've been selected because they are likely to go along with the program. They've already proven that they can do one or more of the following, or similar, exercises:

- Levitate their arms with ease
- Show lots of the whites of their eyes during an eye-roll exercise
- Show enthusiasm about volunteering
- Keep their eyes tightly shut during an eye-closure suggestion
- Follow along with embedded suggestions

Audience members who respond quickly and easily are the ones I would want up on the stage with me.

Watch Out! I Was a Stage Volunteer

Is it dangerous to recruit audience volunteers? Many academic hypnotists think so. They believe that hypnosis should never be used as entertainment and are horrified that people permit themselves to be hypnotized in a nontherapeutic environment. There's always the possibility that someone who is hypnotized may have a rare, unexpected reaction. If that reaction occurred in the office of a health professional, he or she would do something about it. If that reaction occurs on stage, there's nothing to do about it, because the show must go on.

Here are the stories of volunteers who've participated in stage hypnosis.

Gladys Sings a Song

Gladys, today an active and talented older woman, was a child vocalist known as Baby Peggy. She told me:

I performed in vaudeville and in films at Paramount Studios during the 1920s and 1930s, and in the later decades I performed in the Catskill Mountains. There were acts—trapeze artists, jugglers, hypnotists, dancers. I never thought the hypnosis was true. It looked to me like the audience members were making believe. I didn't know anything about it, but I chose not to believe in it.

But then, years later, a peculiar thing happened to me. I was at a social gathering at the home of a fellow teacher, and one of the guests was doing a group hypnosis experiment. I agreed to participate, and the next thing I knew the oddest thing occurred. The guest said the word "okay" and I immediately stood up and started to sing, "No More Hooky," a song that was in a film I was in when I was a girl. I didn't sing that song in the film, but here I was singing, giggling, and amazed at what I was doing. Maybe there is something to this hypnosis.

Look into My Eyes

Hypnosis is not dangerous or risky; however, the hypnotist may be. The stage hypnotist is more interested in providing a good show than in protecting you. In the entertainment milieu, the hypnotist is not likely to assess your psychological suitability for a proposed stunt. Not all entertainers know how to help audience volunteers who may become frightened by the proceedings.

Gladys probably was given the suggestion that she'd not remember what was told to her while she was hypnotized at the social gathering, so she surprised herself when she stood up to perform. The song she chose to sing was associated in her mind with hypnosis from her entertainment days when she performed on the same stage as hypnotists.

Ellen Is Puzzled

According to Ellen:

I was in the audience at a hotel nightclub when I was requested to go up on the stage and be one of the participants in a hypnosis show. I thought I was being cooperative and wanted to follow directions, but the hypnotist abruptly told me to return to the audience. I felt like a failure and was embarrassed. I kept wondering what I did wrong. This was more than 30 years ago and when I think about it now it still upsets me. I would like to know why he wanted me to leave, especially since I did not volunteer in the first place.

When you volunteer for stage hypnosis you serve at the discretion of the hypnotist. Ellen may not have been meeting the hypnotist's expectations for entertaining the audience and thus was abruptly terminated. A volunteer is not necessarily treated with respect.

Stuie Crawls, Hops, and Whistles

Stuie's story went like this:

I volunteered at an Atlantic City hypnosis show because I always wanted to be hypnotized, and I thought this would be a good chance. The guy spoke so fast that I don't think I heard what he said. But before I knew it I couldn't walk. I could only crawl. I saw myself crawling around the stage, and I heard the audience laughing, but I didn't feel like it was me crawling around. I thought I was still sitting in the chair. Before I knew it I was getting up and hopping around the stage, and then the next minute I was back in my seat in the audience. But that's not all. I didn't really feel back to myself, and then the hypnotist clapped his hands and I stood up and started whistling. I don't know why. When I stopped whistling I sat down, and it took me until the end of the show to get my bearings back. I don't think I would volunteer again, but I would go to a hypnotist because now I know I can go under.

Stuie made a fool of himself, but was psychologically intact so that by the end of the show he was back to himself. My concern is for the person who is not as psychologically stable as Stuie. Remember, stage hypnosis is not clinical hypnosis. The nightclub performer is not a trained mental health professional who carefully chooses words and writes a script to help you have a better life. The stage hypnotist is interested in the audience and not necessarily in you.

Lois Reacts to a Pinch

Lois had this to say:

I was coaxed to go on stage and I remember closing my eyes and being told to relax. I followed the hypnotist's commands and I couldn't open my eyes. The hypnotist was doing interesting things on stage. I heard them, but I couldn't open my eyes to see them. I felt that I could see with my brain. Before I left the stage the hypnotist told me that if I saw him snap his fingers I'd think that the guy next to me had pinched me, and I'd react to that pinch. I thought that whole idea was silly, but I went along with it. Then I was told I could open my eyes, and I was sent back to my seat. In a few minutes, suddenly, with no warning, I found myself pushing the guy next to me and saying "cut it out."

In the Hypnotist's Office

I recently watched the *Rosie O'Donnell Show* where a hypnotist put Ms. O'Donnell and two guests "under his spell." In a dramatic, authoritative way he commanded them to taste some foods, describing the foods as tasting different from the way they actually taste. Some foods were plain, some spicy, others sweet. Each hypnotized guest experienced the suggested, not the actual, tastes of the food. The hypnotist stood behind the guests while they tasted and frequently patted their shoulders in what appeared to be a gesture of encouragement. Probably, though, during the preshow warm-up they were hypnotized and given the suggestion that whenever he touched their shoulders they would go more deeply into trance and comply more with the suggestions.

Lois volunteered to go up on stage, and then agreed to follow the hypnotist's commands. Note that the hypnotist never re-alerted her; when she left the stage she was still in a trance. She thought the suggestion given to her was silly, but consented to continue the hypnosis, anyway. If Lois were the type who found it repugnant to make a public fuss or to call attention to herself, she would not have volunteered in the first place. Her actions, though surprising to her, presumably were not against her value system. When you are in a hypnotist's office you know, in advance, what you will be told. If you think something is silly and don't want to follow through with it, you simply open your eyes and come back to normal. All clinical hypnotists take you out of trance; not all stage hypnotists do.

The Dangers of Stage Hypnosis

As an advocate of clinical hypnosis, I am concerned that stage hypnotists give the wrong impression. People whose only exposure to hypnosis is through an entertainment hypnotist may believe that all hypnosis is coercive. They may never realize the great benefits that hypnosis has to offer. Also, I suspect that some volunteers do suffer afterward—perhaps they don't suffer terribly; but their experiences may not be entirely pleasant. They can experience some discomfort or confusion that might last for a few hours or a few days, particularly if the hypnotist is harsh.

Some of the dangers that exist in stage hypnosis result from techniques clinical hypnotists do not use:

- You have no say in choosing the suggestion. Gladys would not have chosen to sing a children's song in front of her colleagues.

- You may not know that you've been given a posthypnotic suggestion. Stuie did not like the idea of standing up and whistling.

- If you know you were given a posthypnotic suggestion you may want to eradicate it. Lois did not want to create a fuss, yet she yelled at her seat mate.

- There is no opportunity for a postsession debriefing. Ellen is still perplexed about her experience, after all these years.

- There is no opportunity for a presession interview to learn what suggestions might not be good for you.

Focus On This

The most renowned hypnotists agree that clinical hypnosis poses no danger. Dr. David Spiegel, professor at Stanford University School of Medicine says, "Physicians often worry that hypnosis involves risks to patients. Actually, the phenomenon is not dangerous and has fewer side effects than even the most benign medications." This is true for clinical hypnosis. Stage hypnosis, though, can leave the volunteer somewhat disoriented.

A Lawsuit

Paul McKenna is a stage hypnotist in the United Kingdom who was sued by Christopher Gates, a man who volunteered to go on stage and was hypnotized for over two hours. During that time he danced like a ballerina, conducted an orchestra, acted as if he were a bus conductor, and acted as if he were a million-dollar lottery winner.

After the hypnosis, Mr. Gates's personality changed and he began evidencing some strange behaviors. Four doctors diagnosed him as suffering from an acute schizophrenic episode. He sued Paul McKenna for bringing on his mental illness. The courts ruled against Mr. Gates, saying that it was coincidental timing. They said that there is no evidence that hypnosis could cause mental illness in a mentally healthy person, and thousands are hypnotized every year with no ill effect. Statistically, it is more common to come down with a mental illness than to be harmed by hypnosis.

I wonder about this case. Yes, hypnosis is safe. But what about the hypnotist? If a person is in fragile mental health, anything can trigger a breakdown of defenses. Does a stage hypnotist screen volunteers to rule out precarious mental health? Of course not.

Does a clinical hypnotist evaluate a client's mental health? Yes, of course. Hypnosis is safe, but the hypnotist must know when not to use it.

In the Hypnotist's Office

I often travel throughout the United States speaking about hypnosis. Sometimes I speak to groups of physicians or other medical professionals; other times I speak to social groups and clubs. When I start my hypnosis lecture to any large group I ask, at the very beginning before I begin my actual speech, if anyone would like to be hypnotized. Usually one or two hands go up. Then I go ahead and talk, explaining hypnosis, giving examples, and answering questions. About 45 minutes later I again ask who would like to be hypnotized. Usually everyone volunteers! This proves that people need to feel they can trust the hypnotist, and they need to know what to expect. When those two criteria are met, hypnosis is welcomed.

Hypnotizing a Group

I'm not an entertainer; I'm an educator. I don't do *Oprah*, but I do talk about and demonstrate hypnosis in public forums. You can often find me lecturing to …

- Physicians and nurses at hospitals.

- Guests at health spas (I'm a regular workshop leader and lecturer at Rancho La Puerta in Mexico).

- Salespersons at their national meetings.

- Clergymen at their annual retreats.

- Psychotherapists at community mental-health centers.

- Annual trade association meetings.

When I speak to these groups, I have a mission. My mission is different from the stage hypnotist's mission. Although it would be lovely if my audience were entertained and amazed, my primary goal is to educate.

I explain and inform and try to promote a positive attitude toward hypnosis. The hardest part of the event, for me, is not the part about hypnotizing a large group—I can do that with ease—it's getting everyone to agree on one or two suggestions. For every 50 people who want the suggestion to be "to eat less," there's one who is underweight and can't tolerate eating less. For every 50 people who want the suggestion to be "to drink more water," there's a person with a bladder problem who can't tolerate drinking more water. Of course, the suggestions for a group cannot be individualized. The suggestions a group will agree upon most regularly are:

- *You will easily remember the names of people you're introduced to.*

- *You will exercise on a regular basis.*

- *You'll be on time for work and for all appointments.*

It's easy to hypnotize a room full of people because the interest in the experience seems to be contagious. It becomes the norm to be hypnotized, and nobody wants to be left out.

Focus On This _____

When I hypnotize large groups and ask for mutually acceptable suggestions for the script, people come up with a variety of possibilities. If I distribute paper and pencil and ask for written requests, the two most popular suggestions people will not say aloud, are: They need help talking to authority figures, and they need help falling asleep at night.

The differences between stage hypnosis and hypnosis at a public lecture are shown in the following list.

Stage Hypnosis	Public Lecture
Mission is to entertain	Mission is to educate
Hope is to amaze audience	Hope is to inform audience
Shows that hypnotist can control the subject	Shows that the subject is in charge of his own hypnosis
No secrets of the process are revealed	Explains the hypnotic process
Authoritative approach	Encourages audience questions
Encourages use of hypnosis for fun	Encourages use of hypnosis for personal improvement
Volunteers expect to be controlled	Volunteers expect to be helped
Hypnosis is presented as a magic spell	Hypnosis is presented as a natural state
Audience is somewhat in awe, maybe fearful	Audience is relaxed
Volunteers may be embarrassed or humiliated	Volunteers are respected
Hypnotist needs to be a good entertainer	Hypnotist needs to be a good hypnotherapist

When I participate in corporate employee health programs and conduct a group hypnosis for smoking cessation, the results are just as good as when I do individual quit-smoking sessions. That's not true for weight-loss programs, though. The group suggestions are often too general, and dieters usually get better results with individual sessions.

Are They Faking?

Do the hypnotized subjects up on the stage seem too good to be true? Are they faking it? Probably not. It's so easy for a good hypnotist to deeply hypnotize a good subject that there's no reason for fakery.

Michael C. Anthony

An excellent stage hypnotist who regularly performs around the world at hotels, convention centers, corporate events, and resorts is Michael C. Anthony. His show is popular at college campuses, too. He hypnotizes his audience rapidly and professionally.

Katie was in the audience when Michael C. Anthony performed as part of the NYU orientation. Here's her account of that evening:

My skeptical side didn't want to believe in this. I thought the whole thing was some large prank or joke. When Mr. Anthony called for volunteers, kids raced up. At the beginning I wasn't sure if they were on the level and I figured they were faking it. But, as the show continued I began to realize that hypnosis was actually taking place. The people up on that stage had absolutely no inhibitions. They were oblivious to everything around them due to the hypnosis.

Throughout the show there were times I was hysterically laughing because some of the bits were so, so funny. The greatest and funniest part of the show for me was when the hypnotist told someone to slow dance with a broom. Before you knew it, the guy up on the stage was passionately stroking the broom and had a sly smile on his face. He was actually whispering to the broomstick. Overall, this show was an amazing experience. I left the auditorium in awe of hypnosis.

Michael C. Anthony, like many stage hypnotists, is an excellent hypnotist. He knew exactly which volunteers might not make good subjects and asked them to return to their seats. Then he let the remaining volunteers know what he expected from them and they immediately complied. In his gentle, professional tone, he remained in total control of both the folks up on stage and those in the audience.

From watching Michael C. Anthony's performance I learned that in my office I shouldn't become alarmed or concerned if there's loud noise outside while I'm hypnotizing a client. His volunteers remained deeply hypnotized in the midst of chaos. One of the bits that he performed was to instruct his volunteers to each carry out a particular action, simultaneously. So one person was singing, another chasing a canary, and a third trying to flirt with the guy seated next to her. Each was so well engaged in their scene and concentrating so deeply that they were not bothered by their neighbor's actions.

Trance Logic

In 1959, Dr. Martin T. Orne, one of the twentieth century's great scholarly hypnotists, did an experiment to, once and for all, settle the debate about pretending to be hypnotized. His experiment identified a certain trait found only in hypnotized people: People who are hypnotized respond to illogical situations in a different way from those who are not hypnotized.

Dr. Orne arranged for a good hypnotist to hypnotize several subjects. The hypnotist did not know that half of those people were told not to allow themselves to be hypnotized, and instead to pretend to be hypnotized. Their goal was to fool the hypnotist. They accomplished this by pretending to follow along but actually engaging their minds in other endeavors. They had been carefully instructed in how to resist hypnosis. Remember, if you have no motivation to be hypnotized, it's very hard to hypnotize you.

The suggestion given to each subject was that he or she would see Jack, one of their colleagues, sitting in a chair. But in reality, Jack wasn't there and the chair was empty. The subjects who were faking all said they saw Jack in the chair. When Jack appeared in person, the pretenders said they didn't see Jack or that he was someone else. They insisted that Jack was sitting in the empty chair. The truly hypnotized subjects saw Jack in the chair and then were very surprised to see him also standing in front of them. They seemed puzzled and couldn't understand why there'd be two of him. They accepted the ridiculous possibility that there could be two Jacks!

Accepting an illogical possibility while in a trance is called *trance logic.* The pretenders in Dr. Orne's experiment gave themselves away because they tried to be rational about seeing Jack. They came up with rational reasons and responded in a conventionally logical way. The hypnotized group used trance logic and mixed their real perception—Jack standing in the room—with the hallucination suggested by the hypnotist—Jack sitting in the chair. They did not attempt to be logical; they were using trance logic.

Hypnoscript

Trance logic refers to the ability of a hypnotized person to accept a suggestion even though it is impossible and illogical.

Hypnosis on the Big Screen

It's no wonder that you might be skeptical about hypnosis. From John Barrymore to Bugs Bunny to Jodie Foster, hypnosis on the screen often depicts an innocent young thing put under the spell of a powerful, demonic hypnotist. In 1931, actor John Barrymore starred in the movie *Svengali*. It's the story of Svengali's obsession with a young girl named Trilby. The only way Svengali can get Trilby into his life is by constantly hypnotizing her and stealing her away from her true love. Svengali's eyes glow when he casts his spell; he is depicted as diabolical and exerting total control over the sweet Trilby.

Between stage hypnotists and movie hypnotists, it's quite amazing that anyone dares to go into a hypnotist's office! Please understand that your experience with hypnosis will be interesting and helpful to you; you will *not* go to Svengali.

The Least You Need to Know

- Stage hypnosis is entertainment. It is done for the good of the audience, not for the good of the volunteer up on stage.

- Volunteers are usually people who are extremely hypnotizable. What you see is the truth; they really do respond so fully.

- The danger of volunteering is that you have no input into what you'll be asked to do.

- When you're hypnotized you tend to use trance logic, which is no logic at all; you tend to accept illogical situations as the truth.

Chapter 26

You Once *Were* a Duck

In This Chapter

- ◆ Were you here before?
- ◆ Hypnosis to help remember
- ◆ Remembering more
- ◆ Too crazy to be true
- ◆ In a court of law

Some hypnotists insist hypnosis can transport you back to a previous life— a life that you once lived in another body. There are other hypnotists who think that's a crazy idea. What do you think? Do you have a good memory? Can you remember everything that's ever happened to you? Can you remember things that never happened to you? Perhaps you can.

How Many Lives Have You Lived?

Back in the 1950s, *The Quest for Bridey Murphy*, a most unusual book, became a phenomenal bestseller. The author, Morey Bernstein, was a businessman who had an interest in hypnosis and hypnotized Virginia Tighe, later given the pseudonym Ruth Simmons, a soft-spoken young mother, to recall and revisit first her childhood, and then her previous lives.

According to Bernstein, after Tighe was hypnotized to gain access to a past life, she began speaking with an Irish brogue and danced a jig, giving details of a previous life as a lass named Bridey Murphy in nineteenth-century Ireland. Although later investigators failed to find any record of a Bridey Murphy in Ireland, or any historical accounts of the incidents she described, the public continued to be fascinated by the idea of hypnosis and the possibility of a past life. When it was discovered that Tighe had been recounting tales told to her by her long-forgotten Irish nanny, it made no difference. People who never before thought about hypnosis or reincarnation, and people who never before bought books, climbed on the Bridey Murphy bandwagon.

Hypnoscript

The theory of **reincarnation** maintains that after we die our soul is born into another body where it continues to live until that body dies. The cycle is repeated over and over. **Past-life regression (PLR)** therapy uses age regression to help a client reach a memory of him- or herself that may have occurred eons ago.

Focus On This

The Search for Bridey Murphy was published in January, 1956, by Doubleday & Co. of Garden City, New York. By March of the same year, 200,000 copies were sold. It was on the *New York Times* bestseller list for 26 weeks, and was eventually translated into 30 languages and sold in 36 countries.

Hypnotists who believe in *reincarnation* and in past lives guide their clients backward in time. This process is called *past-life regression (PLR)* therapy. Clients have been known to come up with incredible tales of themselves having different personalities, different appearances, and sometimes being a member of the opposite sex—or even an animal.

Hypnotists who endorse PLR believe that each life you live offers an opportunity to learn an important spiritual lesson. They say that your conscious mind doesn't remember a previous lifetime, so hypnosis is necessary to facilitate the learning of that lesson. They also believe that your experiences from a past life can cause trouble for you in this life, and by examining your past life under hypnosis, your current problems will be relieved.

Elizabeth Nahum, a hypnotherapist who does past-life regressions with her clients, uses their reports as metaphors to help her clients with problems of daily living. Nahum believes that each memory produced is a clue to what the person needs to learn in this lifetime. Nahum says her goal is to "free up emotional energy by resolving psychological issues. Past-life regression therapy is a process, not a cure."

Believers in reincarnation consider it a religious conviction, having nothing to do with a cure for an emotional problem. But you don't have to be a follower of an Eastern religion to believe in reincarnation and past lives. Dr. Brian Weiss, a well-educated and well-qualified physician in Miami, Florida, leads the parade in advocating past-life regression, and his books about the subject sell very well. Dr. Weiss's first book,

Many Lives, Many Masters, has sold more than 1 million copies (!), and he is said to have a client waiting list of 2,000.

In one of his books, Weiss writes about regressing a chronic migraine sufferer who finds out that centuries ago he was a soldier. He saw himself being walked off a cliff while someone was sticking a spike in the back of his neck. Soon after this regression, according to Weiss, the patient's migraines disappeared.

When an authoritative source, such as a physician, believes in past lives it reinforces the belief system of some who are in doubt. Weiss believes that we all have intuitive wisdom and past lives. He is not alone. Polls reveal that 27 percent of adults in the United States believe in reincarnation.

And then there are the nonbelievers. Nonbelievers say that past-life regression is appealing because both the therapist and the patient never have to worry about being proved wrong. Facts are impossible to verify when all the players have been dead for centuries.

Dr. Melvin Sabshin of the American Psychiatric Association (APA) has stated, "The APA believes that past-life regression is pure quackery. There is no accepted scientific evidence to support the existence of past lives, let alone the validity of past-life regression therapy."

As for me, well, I have a hard enough time remembering events from this lifetime; dredging up memories from a former life is out of the question.

> **CAUTION** **Look into My Eyes**
>
> PLR therapists say that clients can usually find the origin of a present-day phobia in a past life. Apparently, once the phobia is understood as coming from a former life, the client ceases to have it. Unfortunately, while there are plenty of past-life stories, there's no way to substantiate them.

Age Regression

Remember age regression from Chapter 4? It's the hypnotic process whereby the client is instructed to go back in time and visualize a past experience.

I've hypnotized clients suffering from pain to go back in time to when they were pain free. I've age regressed clients back to their childhood to relive a troublesome relationship to help them understand their behavior in a current relationship.

Age regression can help you re-experience a traumatic situation without having the negative outcome. The hypnosis can provide a safety net. In your mind, under hypnosis, you can visualize the traumatic scene of years ago as if it had a new and different ending. This time it is an ending that you can control; an ending that has a favorable outcome. During age regression you can relive a memory as if it is happening now or as if you are a bystander watching it happen. You can control your response to the situation with the help of your hypnotist.

Dr. Melvin Gravitz, forensic hypnotist and professor of psychology, reports the case of a 22-year-old depressed woman whose symptoms of social discomfort began during her adolescence. Gravitz age regressed her to the time that her difficulties first appeared, and she then remembered a particular argument that she had many years ago with her mother. During the argument the patient wished that her mother was dead. Shortly thereafter, her mother did die.

While hypnotized, the patient figured out she had been blaming herself for her mother's death. She was weeping, agitated, and still hypnotized, when Gravitz intervened by playing the role of the mother. He spoke to the patient as if they were in the middle of a fight and then explained that it was normal for mothers and teenage daughters to argue, and arguments don't kill people. Gravitz spoke to the girl in the role of the mother, explaining that she wished her to have a happy life. The "mother" then clarified that her death was caused by heart disease, not her daughter's thoughts. Gravitz then gave the posthypnotic suggestion that all useful and good information heard during this session would be remembered.

This was a successful age regression, conducted by a skilled, trained, licensed, and very experienced psychologist. This was not a past-life regression.

Remembering Too Much

What happens if you use hypnosis to trigger your memory? Will hypnosis help you if you want to remember past incidents, not from another life, but perhaps from your childhood or maybe from last year? Yes and no. Yes, under hypnosis you will produce more memories than if you tried to remember without hypnosis. But, no, those memories might not be all that accurate.

 Focus On This

Hypnotically recalled memories are not any more accurate than nonhypnotically recalled memories. When you are hypnotized and asked to remember something, you may recall a distortion of the actual memory, and you will recall it with certainty. Hypnosis increases your confidence for stating both correct and incorrect information.

Unfortunately, 30 percent of present-day psychotherapists use hypnosis in an effort to help their patients recall the past. They erroneously believe that hypnosis will reveal the truth about the past. Hypnosis, alas, is not a truth serum. Memory, alas, is not an exact tape recorder. And, more unfortunately, hypnosis *is* a confidence builder. This means that when hypnotized you remember an incident that might or might not have actually occurred, and hypnosis will make you feel confident that your memory is correct and that it did occur.

Contrary to popular belief, your memories are not stored in a recording compartment in your brain waiting for you to press the play button. Memory is an entanglement of actual events and your perception of the events. Your perception, everything you are experiencing with your senses, determines precisely how you admit the experience into your memory.

Hypnoscript

The process of putting your experience into your memory is called **encoding**. Keeping your encoded memory available over time is called **storage**. Recovering your information from storage is called **retrieval**.

When an event occurs and you put it into your memory, that process is called *encoding*. *Storage* is the process by which you keep the memory, and *retrieval* is the process of getting it back from storage.

Can You Create Memories?

Sometimes we are certain that a situation has occurred, we're sure we remember it, but actually it never happened at all. The fact is, we all are capable of innocently creating memories of events that never took place.

Try this experiment:

- Think of a family member who is younger than you and who is in good emotional condition—a strong, psychologically healthy person.

- Make up a story about this person. The story should take place on a lake, in a car, in school, or in a store. You should be in the story, along with the younger person, and it should have taken place years ago.

- Jot down at least five things that could have happened if the story were true.

- Tell your story to that family member.

Here are three sample stories:

Story 1: Leah said to her younger brother, Joey, that she recalls that many years ago when they were in high school they (1) went ice skating on the lake. While they were skating (2) a girl fell on her head on the ice. Leah quickly (3) left the ice, (4) removed her skates, and (5) ran to a phone to summon help. (6) Joey waited on the road to direct the paramedics when they arrived. (7) He felt like a hero.

Story 2: Peter reminded his younger cousin, Evan, that one year on the way to the (1) annual family Thanksgiving dinner, Peter's family's (2) station wagon had a flat tire. Evan's family had already arrived at Grandpa's house and they were (3) impatiently waiting for Peter's family. When they finally got there, (4) Peter bragged that he was the only one in his family who knew how to change the tire. (5) Evan looked up to his older cousin.

Story 3: Charles told his brother Zachary that he remembers when they were in elementary school, one day (1) the mother who was driving carpool forgot to pick them up. Her child got sick during school and was sent home. She neglected to inform their mom that she wouldn't be coming back to school at three o'clock. (2) Charles and Zack waited a while and then (3) Zack started to cry. (4) Charles comforted him by giving him some leftover snacks from his lunch box. Finally, (5) a fifth-grade teacher, leaving for the day, spotted the boys and escorted them back into the building where (6) they called their mom. (7) Zack cried when he finally saw his mom.

> **CAUTION**
>
> **Look into My Eyes**
>
> If you're asked to remember an incident and you can't, ask for proof that it did happen and that you were there. Look for a photo of the supposed event, or find other people to corroborate the story. Don't immediately assume that you simply lost your memory of the occurrence. It's possible that your initial response was correct; you were not involved in that incident.

When telling your story, talk to the person about your made-up memory as if it is real. Mention the incident casually and then talk about each of the numbered items. Ask a question. Charles might ask Zack if he remembers the snack he gave him or if he remembers which teacher rescued them. Peter might ask Evan if he remembers what the station wagon looked like or if he remembers which foods Grandpa permitted them to eat while they were waiting for everyone to assemble. Leah could ask Joey to describe the injuries sustained by the injured girl. Talk about different aspects of the imagined incident. Talk about the feelings that the other person expressed.

Because you are older, you're a credible authority, and your story is more likely to be believed. After you speak about the incident a few times over several hours or days, you'll notice something interesting. Details of the memory will begin to surface, even though there is no real memory. When you begin a conversation about the made-up event, the other person will contribute to the conversation, providing new and original "memories." The other person will continue to embellish the memory as long as you continue to chat about it. Congratulations! You've implanted a false memory. Now please apologize and explain that you were doing an experiment to prove that you can implant a memory—without hypnosis.

In many laboratory studies it has been proved that false memories are easily created, particularly in children, who naturally have good imaginations. It's easy to do this simply by asking kids to repeatedly think about fictional events. In one experiment the children were initially asked if they ever went to the hospital emergency room and they truthfully answer "no." They were then told to think about the ER, and it was described for them. They were told about nurses and doctors and an ambulance ride, and then they were encouraged to think about what it would be like. A short time later, when the same children were again asked if they had ever been to the hospital emergency room, 30 percent of them say "yes."

Adults, too, can easily be misled, particularly if …

- They are encouraged to visualize the scene.

- They are discouraged from asking questions about their experience.

- They are highly hypnotizable to begin with.

These false memories are not implanted using hypnosis. This is a regular waking state with no induction.

I Saw It, I Know I Saw It

If you can create a memory of something that doesn't exist, imagine what you can do with a memory of something that really did happen. When you innocently add to an actual memory, that new story you create replaces the earlier memory in your brain. The next time you look for information about that event you'll retrieve the new, not-quite-accurate memory.

When you try to remember something, you want to remember the whole story. Sometimes you can't, and that's when you entangle good guesses with a true memory. The result is a *confabulated memory*. The next time you attempt to recall a scene you'll get the one with the new ideas in it. This is not a lie; it is now your true memory.

Dr. Elizabeth Loftus, a leading expert on memory, describes our ability to remember, as follows: "Think of your mind as a bowl filled with clear water. Now imagine each memory as a teaspoon of milk stirred into the water. Every adult mind holds thousands of these murky memories. Who among us would dare to disentangle the water from the milk?"

Hypnoscript

When you fill in the gaps of a memory by fabricating some details you are confabulating. The new scene and the old scene merge to create a new, **confabulated memory.**

Look into My Eyes

The more information and details a person has about an event—the sight of it, the sounds, the feelings—the more likely that person will believe that they actually experienced that event, even if they did not.

After the Fact

Memories fade with time. Details are lost over time; accuracy diminishes. As your memories weaken, they become vulnerable to post-event information. Post-event information includes …

◆ Statements heard about the event.

◆ Ideas and impressions about the event.

◆ Opinions about the event.

Do you remember your high school graduation? If I tell you in an authoritative way that I know it rained during your graduation, you might add that to your memory. If I tell you I heard that the class valedictorian gave a very emotional speech, you might begin to remember that, too. Then, when I say I love graduation ceremonies because I enjoy seeing the many generations celebrating together, you might conjure up a vision of grandparents and babies joining your family. These bits of information are presented after the graduation. They are post-event interferences with your memory and they change your memory.

Some people incorporate such interferences as memories more readily than do other people. But it is possible for anybody to absorb post-event information. You never know if your mind will reject or accept a story. It depends upon the presentation and your particular mindset of that moment.

Do you remember when the *Challenger* space shuttle exploded? The morning after that explosion in 1986, a psychologist asked 40 students to write one paragraph describing where they were and what they were doing when they heard the news of the disaster. Two and a half years later the same students were contacted and asked the same question. When their answers were compared with their earlier answers, not one was 100 percent accurate, and 15 of them were totally off the mark.

Focus On This

When you are convinced that a memory is true, that certain events did happen, you will be able to pass a polygraph (lie detector) test. The polygraph machine measures your conviction about whether or not something is true. It cannot measure the accuracy of your memory.

Many of the original memories simply faded with time and were replaced with confabulated memories. One student, stunned when shown his original paper, said, "This is my handwriting, but I'm still sure things happened as I just said they did."

Recovering Hidden Memories

Some psychotherapists and hypnotherapists hypnotize their patients to recover past memories. Some excellent therapists do a good job of this. Many, though, contaminate their patients' memories. Memories fabricated during hypnosis are false memories, or *pseudomemories*. During therapy with a psychotherapist who is trying to dig up hidden memories, patients who come up with impossibly fantastic tales suffer from false memory syndrome.

It's easy for me to contaminate your memory. I can begin before you're hypnotized. I can suggest ...

- *You'll feel better when you remember that terrible thing your brother did to you.*

- *You'll be healed when you uncover your buried memory about your mother.*

- *Play back that VCR in your brain and stop at the part where your are frightened by your father.*

- *You'll feel much better if you get this off your chest.*

- *Don't you trust me enough to tell me about that incident with your teacher?*

- *Please think back to the first time you were abused.*

If you're interested in complying with my instructions and want to please me and also get rid of your symptoms, of course your "memories" will reflect what I've suggested.

Hypnoscript

Pseudomemories, or false memories, are memories created by suggestion while under hypnosis. If you have had such memories created in your mind, you suffer from false memory syndrome.

Look into My Eyes

Be sure you know your hypnotist's agenda. You can easily be misled and have false memories implanted. If you're a nice person who likes to please others, and your hypnotist expects you to produce memories of a traumatic childhood, you just might come up with those memories. When you articulate them and they're reinforced, you will believe them; they will become your true lies.

Are There Any Dangers in Hypnosis?

I think hypnosis is safe and is a wonderful tool. I think it should be used much more than it is. I recommend hypnosis to eliminate bad habits and to encourage good habits. I insist upon hypnosis before surgery, and recommend it before a visit to the dentist and before taking a test. I know that hypnosis can help you at work and at play.

But there is one area where I caution you: Watch out for hypnotists who want to recover your hidden memories. This is an area that I stay away from and don't recommend to my clients. Some very skilled psychotherapists can do an age regression and cure a present-day problem. But there are many hypnotists who are not skilled and are searching for hidden memories. Those therapists can implant false memories. Be very careful and read Appendix B, where I tell you how to locate a good hypnotist.

When the Unbelievable Is Believed

In 1692, Americans were convinced that witches were doing black magic. During the Salem witch trial in Massachusetts, neighbor accused neighbor, fear was rampant, and innocent people were hanged. Think this could never happen in modern day America? Think again.

A wave of conspiracy theories and satanic-cult theories swept through America in the 1980s and early 1990s. In prime time, movie stars talked about their suddenly re-membered years of sexual abuse. It became all the rage to reveal a past abuse, and in some hospital settings, where therapists held daily sessions with their patients, supposed crimes of torture and mass murder were uncovered.

Focus On This

Pamela Freyd is the director of the False Memory Syndrome Foundation, which she and her husband helped start after their daughter accused him of abuse. Says Freyd, "The thing that strikes me as strange with recovered memories of childhood abuse is this: We're asked to believe that the proof that it happened is that someone forgot it."

A book by Ellen Bass and Laura David, *The Courage to Heal*, told readers that almost every symptom of distress could be caused by repressed memories of childhood sexual abuse. The authors insisted that if you are unable to remember any explicit incident, but have a vague feeling something did occur, then it is probably true. The book encourages readers to use processes similar to self-hypnosis to produce images of abuse. As you now know, those images, produced when you are in a suggestible trancelike state, will soon become encoded in your memory, and then be regarded as true.

In 1991, a Houston woman checked into a private psychiatric hospital for a two-week evaluation. Two years later, at a cost to her insurance company of $1.1 million, she emerged. During her so-called treatment she was convinced that she abused her children, poisoned her husband, was from a family of cannibals and killers, and participated in satanic rituals. Now that you know how easily false memories can be implanted, you can understand how this true horror story came to be.

Pamela Burgess, a Chicago woman, claimed that from 1986 to 1992 she was convinced by doctors that she was part of a satanic cult, had abused her two sons, and had cannibalized people. Hypnosis was one of the techniques used to recover these "memories." Ms. Burgess won the largest settlement ever given in a false memory lawsuit.

Can you really bury so many absurd, crazy memories? Can you live in a family, in a community, and be a cannibal? Can you be part of a ritualistic cult and then hide that information from everyone you know and from yourself, too? Some therapists think so, and they think the way to uncover what they call the truth is to hunt for (recover) your buried memories. They like to hunt with hypnosis, even though it's been proven that although you can access your memory with hypnosis, the memories you get are not necessarily accurate.

Hypnosis researcher Campbell Perry warns therapists: "Any memory that might turn up in age regression might be a fact, a lie, a confabulation, or a pseudomemory caused accidentally by inappropriate suggestions by the hypnotist. Most of the time, even an expert can't distinguish between these."

The Ingram Family

In September, 1988, 22-year-old Ericka Ingram attended a religious retreat that addressed issues of sexual abuse. It was run by young volunteers from her fundamentalist church. During and after the retreat Ericka accused her father, Paul Ingram, of raping her continuously since she was five years old. Julie, Ericka's younger sister, was at the same retreat and she came away with an even more incredible accusation. Not only had her father raped her, but the friends in his weekly poker game, all police officers, also raped her in her bed while her father watched. (The girls slept in a bunk bed, but Ericka presumably slept through all this.)

Within a few months, the sisters expanded their accusations. They had been tortured, watched 258 babies being killed, and were scarred from fire—all at the hands of their dad and his buddies. When the girls' bodies were examined, there were no scars. Their backyard was dug up in search of evidence of even one baby murdered, no less hundreds, but no bodies were found. Yet, Paul Ingram was accused, convicted, and sent to prison.

What Really Happened?

When Ingram was accused he was horrified, but then he said he was guilty! He confessed to years of satanic ritual abuse, of killing babies, and of raping and torturing his daughters. You'll figure out how it happened because you know about suggestibility and hypnosis. Here are some clues to help you understand Paul Ingram's confession and conviction:

- Ingram is a member of a fundamentalist, charismatic sect that believes that Satan is literally here on Earth and has the power to possess people, making them do things they're unaware of.

- The court-appointed psychologist believed that he could get at the truth (repressed memories) by first relaxing Ingram.

- At one point during the interrogation, Ingram visualized his daughter tied up with a gag in her mouth, asking for help.

- He saw a camera taking pictures of the orgy. No one was holding the camera and there was no tripod.

- He saw himself raping his daughter while she was in a position that made that impossible.

- He saw himself participating in a group rape and engaging in satanic rituals.

In the Hypnotist's Office

During his interrogation, Paul Ingram, chairman of the local Republican party and chief civil deputy of the sheriff's department, hard-working and happily married church-going family man, confessed to bizarre, inconceivable acts. The town's God-fearing citizens, frightened of evil, thought Ingram had fallen under the spell of the devil. They believed he was part of a baby-killing satanic cult, and he soon believed that, too. Eventually, born-again, religious Paul Ingram admitted to being a high priest in a satanic cult, a man who cannibalized children, murdered infants, and raped his own daughters! He confessed to these crimes, was believed by the legal community, and served 14 years of a 20-year sentence. Paul Ingram was released April 8, 2003.

How Could This Happen?

What happened to Paul Ingram happened because the entire legal community was ignorant about hypnosis and memory, and was scared to death of the devil. This happened because the people interrogating him inadvertently put him into trance and then gave him suggestions about the supposed incidents.

Probably Paul Ingram and his daughters are all highly hypnotizable, highly suggestible, and they all easily created false memories. When the girls heard two full days of incest and sexual abuse stories, they had trouble separating truth from fantasy and they confabulated memories. When Paul Ingram heard days of accusations from detectives while he was in a trancelike state, he created pseudomemories.

Ingram could not believe that his daughters would make up such stories, so the only logical conclusion for him was that their tales were true. Initially, he couldn't remember any incidents at all, but he kept trying.

Ingram followed the advice of the psychologist and tried hard to recall the events. The detectives, the psychologist, and his pastor talked with him daily trying to get him to remember. They tried to stimulate his memory by feeding him bits of information. To access Ingram's hidden memories, they suggested that he pray, relax, make his mind a blank, and visualize images of events they mentioned. Ingram was probably born highly suggestible, and so he didn't need a formal hypnotic induction to enter the trance state. All he had to do was follow the suggestions of the people who were trying to help him recall, and this was enough of a ritual to put him in trance.

The relaxation techniques that the psychologist thought would uncover repressed memories instead made Ingram vulnerable to suggestions, which he then believed to be true. During his sessions with the interrogators Ingram would enter a trancelike state of deep concentration, trying to focus on their suggested images. Eventually, he saw them all, and then some. When they'd finish their daily session, Ingram usually remarked as he opened his eyes, "It's almost like I'm making this up, but I'm not."

> **Look into My Eyes**
>
> During the height of the recovered-memory craze, the television personality Roseanne, appearing on the *Oprah Winfrey Show*, said, "If someone asks if you were sexually abused as a child the only possible answers are, 'yes,' and 'I don't know.'" Probably Roseanne truly believed that all children experienced sexual abuse. It was several years before mental-health professionals began to assert that some memories were false.

> **Focus On This**
>
> Parents accused of abusing their adult children are fighting back. Those who insist they are innocent are confronting their children's therapists and demanding an explanation. Of course there are guilty parents, but there are also plenty of guilty, albeit well-meaning, therapists, too.

Ingram was essentially in a hypnosislike trance state and then was asked suggestive questions, pressured to remember, told he had hidden memories that he'd soon access, and encouraged to visualize the events. After he confessed, Ingram was even more confident that he was guilty. His pseudomemories, induced in the hypnotic state, were confident memories. He was now sure that he was guilty as charged.

Remember trance logic? That's the ability of the hypnotized person to accept as possible a situation that is impossible. Ingram does that when he believes his gagged daughter is speaking, when he sees a camera with no photographer, and when he says he raped his daughter, when there's no access to her body. Believing that he could and did participate in a group rape and a satanic ritual is also a form of trance logic.

Interestingly, after he confessed and the detectives, pastor, and psychologist stopped coming by each day, Ingram felt less certain about his guilt. But it was too late. He was imprisoned, the rest of the family broke apart, and the taxpayers paid three quarters of a million dollars for this investigation of a highly suggestible man, father to two highly suggestible daughters.

Suggestions of abuse can be true, of course, but there is no reliable method for differentiating between a confabulation, a pseudomemory, and a real memory.

Hypnosis and the Law

If you are being hypnotized in a courtroom in order to remember a crime, who should hypnotize you? A police officer? A social worker? An attorney? States are struggling to pass laws on the use of *forensic hypnosis*. In 1987, the state of Texas passed legislation allowing peace officers to hypnotize witnesses; however the peace officers must be trained and pass a certifying exam in the use of hypnosis as an investigative tool.

Hypnoscript

Hypnosis used as part of legal and investigative proceedings is called **forensic hypnosis**. During hypnosis some people are able to remember many long-forgotten details of an event. This memory of detail is called **hypermnesia**.

Other states think hypnosis should never be used. They believe that memories retrieved via hypnosis should be discounted in courtrooms because hypnosis, done poorly, gets contaminated results. Yet, even though *hypermnesia*, or enhanced recall, is not necessarily a byproduct of hypnosis, we do know that hypnosis done well, by competent, experienced professionals, might refresh a witness's memory.

Some forensic hypnotists have been known to encourage witnesses to guess. As you already know, when people guess and fill in the gaps of their memories, they change the underlying memory. A professional who is well-trained in hypnotic technique will not create pseudomemories and will not suggest conclusions during the interrogation.

It's easy to ask a suggestive question, and it's done all the time without hypnosis. Think of the different responses you might get from an eyewitness, depending upon the question you ask:

- How fast was the bus going when it smashed into the green car?

- How fast was the bus going when it sideswiped the green car?

- How fast was the bus going when it caused the accident?

- How fast was the bus going when it hit the car?

A professional who is well-trained in forensic hypnosis can do the job better, and with fewer complications, than an untrained person who might unwittingly implant false memories. Courts should be concerned with the qualifications of the forensic hypnotist and the hypnotic techniques used.

Parting Words

Hypnosis is wonderful—it's effective, and less costly, and quicker than most other methods of solving problems. Have fun with it.

Dr. Larry Dossey, physician and best-selling author, has written that "When the history of our medical age is written, the explorers of hypnosis will, I believe, occupy a high place. If so, the honor will be fitting; for what territory is worth greater attention than our own mind and its potential to heal?"

And you, dear reader, are now one of the explorers of hypnosis. May you use it to change your life in all the ways you wish, and to appreciate who you are in all the ways you are unique. May you prosper with hypnosis.

The Least You Need to Know

- Memories recovered under hypnosis are not necessarily accurate.

- Hypnosis makes you feel confident that your memory is accurate.

- You can change your memories, and the new memories become as real to you as true memories.

- Highly suggestible people can easily, unwittingly, create false memories.

- Hypnosis is a safe and marvelously useful procedure, but hypnotists who are looking for memories of abuse may implant those memories during questioning.

- In a court of law, hypnotists should be specifically qualified in interrogation techniques.

Hypnosis Resources

Books and Journals

The following books range in content from fun to scholarly. Some are newly published and some are old classics.

Alman, Brian. *Keep it Off*. New York: Dutton Books, 2004.

Boyne, G. *Transforming Therapy: A New Approach to Hypnotherapy.* Glendale, CA: Westwood Publishing, 1989.

Crabtree, A. *From Mesmer to Freud: Magnetic Sleep and the Roots of Psychological Healing*. New Haven, CT: Yale University Press, 1993.

Crasilneck, H. B., and J. A. Hall. *Clinical Hypnosis: Principles and Applications*, 2nd ed. Orlando, FL: Grune & Stratton, 1985.

Elman, Dave. *Hypnotherapy* (originally, *Findings in Hypnosis*). Glendale, CA: Westwood Publishing, 1964.

Erickson, M. H. *The Collected Papers of Milton H. Erickson on Hypnosis.* E. Rossi, ed. 4 vols. New York: Irvington Publishers, 1980.

Fisher, Stanley. *Discovering the Power of Self-Hypnosis*. New York: Newmarket Press, 2002.

Hammond, C. D. *Handbook of Hypnotic Suggestions and Metaphors*. New York: W.W. Norton, 1990.

Hilgard, E. R., and J. R. Hilgard. *Hypnosis in the Relief of Pain*. Rev. ed. New York: Brunner/Mazel, 1994.

Hunter, M. E. *Creative Scripts for Hypnotherapy*. New York: Brunner/Mazel, 1994.

Liggett, Donald. *Sports Hypnosis*. Champaign, IL: Human Kinetics Publishers, 2000.

Loftus, E., and K. Ketcham. *The Myth of Repressed Memory: False Memories and Allegations of Sexual Abuse*. New York: St. Martin's Press, 1994.

Lynn, S. J., I. Kirsch, and J. W. Rhue. *Handbook of Clinical Hypnosis*. Washington, D.C.: American Psychiatric Association, 1994.

McGill, Ormond. *The New Encyclopedia of Stage Hypnotism*. Glendale, CA: Westwood Publishing, 1996.

Moore-Ede, M., and S. LeVert. *The Complete Idiot's Guide to Getting a Good Night's Sleep*. New York: Alpha Books, 1998.

Olness, K., and D. P. Kohen. 1996. *Hypnosis and Hypnotherapy with Children*, 3rd ed. New York: The Guilford Press, 1998.

Pattie, F. B. *Mesmer and Animal Magnetism: A Chapter in the History of Medicine*. New York: Edmonston, 1994.

Schafer, D. W. *Relieving Pain: A Basic Hypnotherapeutic Approach*. Northvale, NJ: Jason Aronson, 1996.

Spiegel, H., and D. Spiegel. *Trance and Treatment: Clinical Uses of Hypnosis*. Washington, D.C.: American Psychiatric Press, 1978.

Streeter, Michael. *Hypnosis*. New York: Barron's Educational Series, Inc., 2004.

Temes, R. *Medical Hypnosis: An Introduction and Clinical Guide*. New York: W. B. Saunders, 1999.

Yapko, M. D. *Suggestions of Abuse*. New York: Simon & Schuster, 1994.

———. *Essentials of Hypnosis*. New York: Brunner/Mazel, 1995.

———. *Treating Depression with Hypnosis*. New York: Brunner/Routledge, 2001.

Zahoure, R. *Clinical Hypnosis and Therapeutic Suggestion in Patient's Care*. New York: Brunner/Mazel, 1993.

In addition to the preceding books, I recommend two major scholarly journals, available at libraries:

American Journal of Clinical Hypnosis

and

The International Journal of Clinical and Experimental Hypnosis

Hypnosis on the Web

If you drop the word "hypnosis" or "hypnotherapy" into an Internet search engine, you'll be busy for weeks reading about hypnotists, hypnotherapists, stage hypnotists, hypnosis training schools, hypnosis theories, histories, stories, and on and on and on.

The major academic hypnosis organizations on the web are as follows:

American Society of Clinical Hypnosis
www.asch.net
Excellent information.

American Psychological Association
www.apa.org/divisions/div30
You'll find this site useful if you are a psychologist.

Australian Society of Hypnosis
www.ozhypnosis.com.au
Check out the Australian "information for the General Community" page.

British Society of Medical and Dental Hypnosis
www.bsmdh.org
Interesting Frequently Asked Questions (FAQs) on this site.

International Society of Hypnosis
www.ish.unimelb.edu.au
Here you can read about hypnotists all over the world.

Milton H. Erickson Foundation
www.erickson-foundation.org
Click on "Institutes" to find an Ericksonian hypnotist anywhere in the world.

UCLA Scientific Hypnosis Database

www.hypnosis-research.org

This is a scholarly database. Use it to research particular situations.

There are many other websites to check out. Some are good, some are interesting, most are informative. Here are some web addresses to get you started:

www.apmha.com

www.bobberkowitz.com

www.deeptrancenow.com

www.drlarry.com

www.hypnosisinmedia.com

www.hypnosisonline.com

www.hypnosistoday.com

www.infinityinst.com

www.jacobbimblich.com

www.ngh.net

www.ont-hypnosis-centre.com

www.reeseresolution.com

www.royhunter.com

www.selfhypnosis.com

www.tranceformation.com

www.triroc.com/sunnen

My website is www.drroberta.com. Please visit to find out about hypnosis-by-phone and to ask me any questions. I look forward to being useful to you.

B

Locating a Good Hypnotist

Hypnosis is not a licensed profession in most states, therefore in those states anyone, even your dog, may legally claim to be a hypnotist. How do you know if the person you choose from the Yellow Pages is well trained and experienced? Here's what to do to locate a trustworthy hypnotist:

- ◆ Ask your friends and your doctor. Word-of-mouth is a good way to get a reliable referral.

- ◆ Ask your potential hypnotist if he or she is a member of either ASCH (American Society of Clinical Hypnosis) or SCEH (Society for Experimental and Clinical Hypnosis). Members of both organizations have thorough training and good credentials.

- ◆ Choose a hypnotist who also is a licensed physician, nurse, psychologist, social worker, or mental-health counselor.

Here are some warning signals that may indicate a hypnotist to watch out for:

- ◆ A hypnotist who insists you had a past trauma that you are not remembering

- ◆ A hypnotist who thinks your problem is deep-rooted and requires weeks, months, or even years of treatment

- ◆ A hypnotist who thinks you have a need to keep your symptom, even though you think you want to get rid of it

- A hypnotist who is not a medical doctor but wants to treat your medical condition without speaking to your physician

- A hypnotist who does not interview you and doesn't want your input into your script

Don't let me scare you. Armed with information from this book, you probably know as much about hypnosis as most hypnotists. You will choose wisely.

If you are lucky enough to live in or near a city listed here, feel free to contact one of my colleagues. Their specialties range from executive coaching to pediatric asthma, from terminal illness to smoking cessation, from eyewitness testimony to childbirth, and plenty more. If they don't treat your particular condition, they probably know someone in town who does.

Anbar, Dr. Ran. Syracuse, New York. 877-464-6323

Berkowitz, Dr. Bob. New York, New York. 212-988-8008

Bimblich, Jacob. Brooklyn, New York. 718-338-8198

Deutsch, Dr. Larry. Ottawa, Ontario, Canada. 613-526-3745

Ewin, Dr. Dabney. New Orleans, Louisiana. 504-561-1051

Giles, Rev. C. Scot. Wheaton, Illinois. 630-668-1141

Gravitz, Dr. Mel. Washington, D.C. 202-331-9722

Gurgevich, Dr. Steven. Tucson, Arizona. 520- 886-1700

Gustafson, Paul. Burlington, Massachusetts. 888-290-3972

Hall, Dr. Howard. Cleveland, Ohio. 216-844-7700

Harte, Richard. New York, New York. 212-490-0721

Hogan, Kevin. Eagan, Minnesota. 612-616-0732

Larkin, Dorothy. New Rochelle, New York. 914-576-5213

Ledochowski, Igor. London, England. 07970-710-726

Olness, Dr. Karen. Cleveland, Ohio. 216-368-4368

Oster, Dr. Marc. Highland Park, Illinois. 847-604-1593

Perlman, Dr. Sam. New Rochelle, New York. 914-636-6363

Reese, Bob. Roanoke, Virginia. 540-989-4485

Roth, Melissa J. Birmingham, Alabama. 205-933-5705

Sarna, Naomi. New York, New York. 212-727-7967

Sunnen, Dr. Gerard. New York, New York. 212-679-0679

Temes, Dr. Roberta. I can be reached at 718-646-5537.

Glossary

affect bridge   The connection (or bridge) you make when your hypnotist helps you connect a feeling you have now to the incident that provoked the feeling for the first time.

age progression   The hypnotically produced process of seeing yourself in the future.

age regression   The hypnotically produced process of seeing yourself as you were in the past.

analgesia   The inability to feel pain even though you are fully conscious.

anesthesia   The inability to feel anything at all.

autohypnosis   The process of getting yourself into the hypnotic state without a hypnotist.

autonomic nervous system   Controls your unconscious bodily functions such as your heartbeat, blood pressure, and digestion.

behavioral anesthesiology   Also called conscious sedation or nonpharmacological analgesia, this is the condition of anesthesia caused without chemicals that put you to sleep.

bruxism   The habit of unconsciously grinding your teeth.

catalepsy   The inhibition of all voluntary movements because of intense focus on an alternative reality.

Chevreul's Pendulum   An exercise in which a person attempts to move a handheld pendulum by focusing his mind rather than by moving his arm.

clinical   Any process that pertains to the direct treatment and/or observation of patients.

clinical hypnosis   The process that transpires when a hypnotist speaks to a client while that client is in an altered state of consciousness.

clinical trial   An investigation that searches for a new treatment for a specific disease by evaluating the effect of that new treatment on volunteer patients.

confabulating   When you fill in the gaps of your memory by guessing or fabricating some details, you are confabulating.

confusion technique   A bombardment of bewildering terms and instructions presented by a hypnotist to facilitate a resistant client's trance state.

conscious sedation   *See* behavioral anesthesiology.

deepening   The process of using words to intensify the hypnotic experience.

dermatologist   A medical doctor who specializes in treating disorders of the skin.

dissociation   Paying attention to one part of what you're experiencing and ignoring the rest of the experience.

embedded suggestions   Emphasized words or phrases purposely inserted into a regular conversation or hypnotic induction.

encoding   The process of putting your experience into your memory. This happens automatically, all day long, without any effort on your part.

endorphins   The category of chemicals that your body produces to eliminate pain.

false memory syndrome   The condition you suffer from if false memories were created by suggestion while you were hypnotized.

forensic hypnosis   Hypnosis used as part of legal and investigative proceedings.

glove anesthesia   A hypnotic pain-control technique. You are given the suggestion that your hand is numb and that numbness is transferred to any part of your body that your hand touches.

habit   A pattern of behavior acquired through frequent repetition.

hetero-hypnosis   The process by which you are hypnotized by another person.

hidden observer   A term coined to describe the part of your personality that maintains an objective grasp on reality while you are engrossed in a hypnotic experience.

hypermnesia   The enhanced recall of detailed information from past events while under hypnosis.

hypnotherapy   Psychotherapy that uses hypnosis as part of its treatment.

Hypnotic Induction Profile (HIP)   An established hypnotic susceptibility scale that formally tests your responsiveness to hypnosis.

ideomotor movements   Subtle muscle movements that occur in response to a thought or feeling; they are automatic responses that you do not control.

imagery   The term for the pictures in your mind that represent specific objects or events and the feelings that you associate with those pictures.

indirect suggestion   Hints that prompt you to think about a particular situation and about a subtly suggested course of action.

induction   The process that a hypnotist uses to guide you from your ordinary state of consciousness into the trance state.

levitation   The rising up into the air of something, someone, or some part of the body in apparent defiance of gravity.

metaphor   An implied comparison between two unlike things that surprisingly do have something in common.

neutral hypnosis   The state you are in after an induction is given, but before suggestions are offered.

nonpharmacological analgesia   *See* behavioral anesthesiology.

pacing   A technique during which the hypnotist recognizes and matches your speech patterns and some of your movements and behaviors.

past-life regression (PLR)   A process used by hypnotists who believe in reincarnation and past lives to guide their clients backward in time to their previous lives.

pendulum   A pendulum is a weight suspended in such a way that it is free to swing.

phobia   A persistent illogical fear.

posthypnotic amnesia   The inability of a person to remember what was said during a hypnotic session.

posthypnotic suggestions   Suggestions told to you while you're in trance to influence your future behavior.

pseudomemories   False memories created by suggestion while you are in a hypnotic state.

re-alerting   An imprecise term referring to the process of coming out of the hypnotic trance; also called "reawakening" and "returning to regular."

reframing   Looking at a situation from a new viewpoint.

script   The suggestions the hypnotist says to you while you are hypnotized.

sleep hygiene   All your habits of daily living that promote good sleep.

sports psychology   The study of the psychological and mental factors that influence performance, and the application of that knowledge to real-life situations.

suggestibility test   A test consisting of a short relaxation induction followed by a simple suggestion, used to gauge your receptivity to hypnosis.

trance   A state of heightened mental alertness, diminished physical movement, and susceptibility to suggestion.

trance logic   Refers to the ability of the hypnotized person to accept a suggestion even though the suggestion is impossible and illogical.

trichotillomania   The irresistible urge to pull out your own hair.

waking hypnosis   A strong suggestion given by a person in authority and absorbed by another person who is not necessarily in a hypnotic trance.

Hypnosis Through the Ages

In ancient days, healing temples were established based upon the philosophy that expectation, motivation, and belief are important components in trying to change a condition.

Centuries later, individual practitioners throughout the world began to recognize, practice, and write about the effect of deep concentration and focus (hypnosis) on medical conditions.

The most prominent of such innovators are listed in this appendix. Investigate these hypnotists of distinction to learn about their unique accomplishments.

In the Eighteenth Century

Father Johann Gassner (1727–1779)

Franz Anton Mesmer (1734–1815)

The Marquis de Puysegur (1751–1825)

The Marquis de Lafayette (1757–1834)

In the Nineteenth Century

Abbe Jose de Faria (1756–1819)

John Elliotson (1791–1868)

James Braid (1795–1860)

James Esdaille (1808–1860)

Ambroise-August Liebeault (1823–1904)

Jean-Martin Charcot (1825–1893)

Hippolyte Bernheim (1840–1921)

In the Twentieth Century

Joseph Breuer (1842–1925)

Morton Prince (1854–1929)

Emile Coue (1857–1926)

Pierre Janet (1859–1947)

Clark L. Hull (1884–1952)

Ernest R. Hilgard (1904–2001)

Josephine Hilgard (1906–1989)

Milton H. Erickson (1910–1980)

Martin T. Orne (1927–2000)

In the Twenty-First Century

Theodore X. Barber; Boston, Massachusetts

David Spiegel; Palo Alto, California

Herbert Spiegel; New York, New York

John G. Watkins; Missoula, Montana

Index

B

C

I

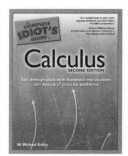